HISTORIC TOWNS
OF TEXAS

- HOUSTON
- TEXANA
- HELENA
- EGYPT
- EAST COLUMBIA
- WEST COLUMBIA
- MATAGORDA

By Joe Tom Davis
Photos by J. C. Hoke

EAKIN PRESS ◆ Fort Worth, Texas
www.EakinPress.com

This book is dedicated in memory of
a much-admired friend and expert in Texas lore,
Mrs. Ruby Baty of Wharton, Texas

Contents

Acknowledgments

I could not have written this book without the assistance of three colleagues and friends at Wharton County Junior College. I am especially indebted to Mrs. Patsy L. Norton, director of the J. M. Hodges Learning Center, and two members of her able staff. Much of my reading and research was done in the Hodges Learning Center, where an extensive collection of Texas history titles has been acquired since 1964 through the generosity of the Raymond Dickson Foundation and proceeds from the book, *The History of Wharton County*, by Annie Lee Williams. This book was written in collaboration with Assistant Director J. C. Hoke, who is also an outstanding photographer. Mr. Hoke accompanied me on five trips and provided all of the on-site photos in this book along with numerous photographic reproductions. The quality of his work has truly enhanced my writing. A special "thank you" is also due Mrs. Cynthia Huddleston, circulation technician, for promptly obtaining reference materials through interlibrary loans.

Special praise is due the personnel of the Karnes County Museum for giving Mr. Hoke and me access to essential documents and photos pertaining to Old Helena. We spent a delightful afternoon inspecting the historic structures on or adjacent to the old courthouse square.

I also appreciate the assistance of William Farquhar, the retired general manager of the Lavaca-Navidad River Authority, who made me aware of two rare photos of the Texana area and provided two studies of Texana by the Texas Archaeological Survey. I am grateful to Luther Hamilton and David Seligman of Edna for granting permission to photograph their historic houses. Laddie Matusek of Edna provided me with valuable information about another Texana building, the old Westhoff Mercantile store.

Several residents of East and West Columbia were especially helpful. Mrs. Laurie Kincannon, Texas history teacher at West Columbia

Junior High School, gave me a personal tour of the historical sites. Judge Thurman Gupton allowed me to borrow the unpublished manuscript "Historical Narrative: Varner, Patton, Hogg Plantation" (1979) by Katherine Smith and Katherine Grier. Mrs. Beth Griggs gave permission to reproduce photos from the book *A Window To The Past: A Pictorial History of Brazoria County, Texas* (1986). Special thanks is due the personnel of the Varner-Hogg State Historical Park. Park Ranger Jeff Hutchinson gave me a tour of the grounds in the summer of 1989. Curator Winnie Trippet and Park Ranger #3 Roger Shelton also provided valuable individual assistance in the summer of 1990.

At East Columbia Mrs. Bonnie Maynard graciously showed the interior of the Weems House. Mrs. T. M. Smith, Jr., allowed us to photograph the Aldridge-Smith House and to reproduce her personal photos of T. M. Smith and the steamboats *Alice Blair* and *Hiawatha.*

Matagorda residents were equally hospitable. J. C. and Babe Stanley gave me access to the unpublished manuscript "History of the 'Old House'," the home of S. Rhoades Fisher, which the Stanleys purchased in October 1987. Doug and Geraldyne Havard invited us into their home and gave permission to reproduce the photo of Matagorda in 1860. Mrs. Ruby Baty of Wharton contributed a fascinating commentary and tour of old Matagorda and the historic cemetery. Mr. Jack Brannon of Bay City provided an old photograph of "Tadmor."

I am very thankful to Mrs. Anita Northington and Mrs. Mary Louise Dobson of Egypt, who graciously allowed us to photograph the Egypt Plantation big house and the Green Duncan home, respectively.

The staff of the Houston Metropolitan Research Center at the Houston Public Library provided much-needed expertise in locating photographs of city founders and builders.

I am indebted to Anita Northington and Mrs. Eve Bartlett for allowing me access to the family files in the Northington-Heard Museum at Egypt and the Wharton County Historical Museum at Wharton, respectively.

A special thank you is due my very talented niece-by-marriage, Mrs. Penny Grissom Bonnot, who designed the attractive book cover. Mrs. Bonnot is an art teacher at Bonham Junior High School at Temple, Texas.

Introduction

This is the first volume in a series of books about historic towns of Texas. Volume I covers two capitals of the Republic, the first major seaport, an important steamboat terminal, an outlaw haven, a significant crossroads settlement, and the ghost of intended Houston. Only one of them survives as a major city today, but they were all important in their glory days.

Town histories tend to focus on institutions rather than individuals. This book, however, is about much more than general stores, hotels, banks, and churches. An emphasis is placed on the achievements and exploits of the town founders, builders, and prominent later residents.

Both East and West Columbia were founded by Josiah H. Bell, the deputy for Austin's first colony. First known as Marion or Bell's Landing in 1824, East Columbia became a bustling shipping point and major steamboat center. The boardinghouse of Ammon Underwood, a wealthy merchant, planter and cotton factor, still stands today. Both Dr. Anson Jones and Carry Nation lived in East Columbia for a time. During the Civil War the Dance pistol factory was located there. Today East Columbia is a tiny residential settlement with more state historical markers than streets. Its shady Main Street is graced by three grand homes built in the 1830s.

Two miles to the west is a town first known as Columbia. Founded by Josiah Bell in 1826, it became a hotbed of revolutionary sentiment and was the capital of the Republic of Texas for a time. Stephen F. Austin died at Columbia, and General Santa Anna was held prisoner there for six weeks. A few miles away is Orozimbo plantation, which has a fascinating history of its own. A two-story brick mansion built at Columbia in 1835 evolved into the Varner-Hogg State Historical Park. An oil discovery made West Columbia a boom town in

1918. Today this small town is best known for Columbia Lakes, an adjacent planned community and resort center.

Egypt is the oldest town in Wharton County. Its biblical name was inspired by a fertile location and severe drought in 1827. The town's founder, John C. Clark, and his slave mistress were later parties to a famous Texas Supreme Court decision. Four of Egypt's first settlers played key roles in the political, military, economic, and religious history of early Texas. This crossroads town was on one of the first mail routes in Texas and was a focal point for the Methodist missionary effort during the era of the Republic. Today visitors can tour a symbol of Egypt's early importance, a plantation "big house" built by a town founder in the 1840s.

Matagorda was founded by Elias Wightman in 1829 and soon became the major seaport and one of the largest towns in Texas. Five notables of the revolutionary period are buried there, and two of their homes still stand today. By the 1850s Matagorda was renowned as a cultural, social, educational, and resort center. The town could also boast of the oldest Episcopal church in Texas and the finest hotel of its time. During the Civil War many men of Matagorda died in a tragic naval incident. The last reminder of Matagorda's glory days — status as the county seat — was lost to the new town of Bay City in 1894. Ironically, this once-famed seaport is now landlocked due to the deltation of the Colorado River.

Houston is a monument to optimism. Located fifty miles from the Gulf of Mexico, it was *not* the first choice of the Allen brothers as a site for their dream inland seaport. Their 1836 promise that seagoing vessels could sail there without obstacle did not become a reality until the ship channel opened in 1914. Another early promotional problem — the oppressive heat and humidity — was overcome a century later as Houston became the most air-conditioned city in the world. This capital city began as a money-making scheme, and that business image persists to this day. Tourists still shun a place more identified with oil, petrochemicals, and space than with pleasure. Gleaming skyscrapers symbolize this fourth-largest city in the United States, not preserved historical sites. Precious little is left of old Houston, but a handful of philanthropists have transformed a raw country town into a twentieth-century educational, medical, and cultural center.

The old towns of Texana and Helena were both put under curses which came to pass; one is underwater today while the other is forlorn and forgotten. Texana, the ghost of intended Houston, was the first town in present Jackson County and an important military post during the Texas Revolution. Nearby was Camp Independence, the headquarters of the postwar Republic of Texas army and the scene of the most famous duel in Texas history. Texana was the first choice of the Allen brothers in fulfilling their dream: the creation of an inland, deepwater seaport. After being rebuffed by a local landowner, they chose a site on Buffalo Bayou and founded the city of Houston. In the 1850s Texana became a thriving port and the home of the prominent Brackenridge family. After the complacent city fathers refused to pay a bonus for building the railroad through their town in 1881, the line was built six miles to the north, marking the birth of Edna and the death of Texana. Today the old town site is partially covered by the waters of Lake Texana.

Helena, the self-proclaimed "Toughest Town on Earth," was a haven for outlaws, rustlers, and gunfighters after the Civil War. Before trailing their Longhorn herds north to Kansas, many a rowdy drover "raised hell" in the town's saloons, where whiskey could be bought by the keg. A favorite spectator sport involved betting on the outcome of the infamous "Helena Duel" in which the loser was literally slashed to death. In such a violent setting, it is ironic that a random killing spelled the town's doom. When a drunk's stray bullet killed the son of Karnes County's richest rancher, the man vowed "to kill the town that killed his son." After he gave a free right-of-way on the condition that the railroad bypass Helena, the once-prosperous "Bad Man's Paradise" became little more than a ghost town, a forgotten intersection in the road known today by only the most avid history buff.

Writing this book has been a fascinating learning experience for me. I have discovered that these seven towns hold some of the best kept secrets in Texas history. I trust that the reader will share my new-found appreciation of these town founders and builders. Of course, I take full responsibility for any errors made in telling of their achievements.

I

East and West Columbia: Plantations, Politics, and Steamboats

Josiah H. Bell, the founder of both Marion (now East Columbia) and Columbia (now West Columbia), was Stephen F. Austin's deputy and trusted friend. Columbia, located on the prairie end of his league of land, was a hotbed of revolutionary sentiment, the capital of the Republic of Texas, and the place where Austin died. Today, just outside town, an 1830s mansion has become the centerpiece of a state park. Nearby is the storied Orozimbo plantation, where General Santa Anna was held prisoner.

Marion (or Bell's Landing), located two miles away on the banks of the Brazos River, was the major shipping point for Austin's colony, an important railroad and steamboat terminal, and the site of a famous gun factory during the Civil War. Two prominent merchants, Ammon Underwood and John Adriance, amassed fortunes there. A pioneer settler, Dr. Mason Locke Weems II, was the son of George Washington's first and most popular biographer. Dr. Anson Jones, the last president of the Republic of Texas, lived at East Columbia for a time, as did Carry A. Nation, the notorious saloon-wrecker of the 1890s.

Josiah Hughes Bell, a native of South Carolina, was born on August 22, 1791. As a young man he moved to Missouri Territory and was elected justice of the peace of Breton Township in 1813. After selling his farm five years later, Josiah married Mary Eveline McKenzie of Kentucky, and the couple settled at Natchitoches, Louisiana. It was there that Bell happened to see Stephen F. Austin, a personal friend and former business associate in Arkansas Territory.

In July 1821, Austin had gone to San Antonio and was accepted by Governor Antonio Martinez as heir to his deceased father's Spanish land grant. After exploring the lower reaches of the Colorado and Brazos rivers, Stephen Austin described it as "the most favored region I had ever seen" and decided to request that area for his colony. Writing to Governor Martinez from Natchitoches in October 1821, he outlined his desired colonial boundaries as running from the San Jacinto River to the Lavaca River, an area estimated at 18,000 square miles and eleven million acres. Since some fifty families had already agreed to move to his grant in November and December, Austin informed the governor that he was appointing Josiah Bell to act as his deputy and temporary justice of the peace *(sindico)*. On October 6, 1821, Austin issued a permit to Bell authorizing a land grant of 640 acres for himself, 320 acres for his wife, 160 acres for each child, and 80 acres for each slave.

Bell had only six and one-quarter cents in his pocket when he and Mary and their two slaves, Moses and Rachel, settled on the Brazos River near old Washington in early January 1822. Two months later, Governor Martinez informed Austin that the Mexican revolution had upset his father's contract with the Spanish government and suggested that Stephen journey to Mexico City to obtain confirmation of the grant. When Austin departed San Antonio on March 13, 1822, he appointed Josiah Bell to carry on for him and assume direction of incoming colonists. In November 1822, the new governor of Mexican Texas, José Felix Trespalacios, ordered the election of an *alcalde* and a military commandant for both the Brazos and Colorado settlements. Bell was elected as *alcalde* on the Brazos, and Andrew Robinson was chosen to command the militia.

After the Mexican Congress approved his land grant in April 1823, Austin returned to Texas in August to find that some of Bell's preliminary land allotments had brought discord. A tract on the Colorado that Austin had chosen for himself was occupied; another Austin reserve on the lower Brazos was taken by Bell and Martin Varner, both of whom wanted to move from their original settlement in present Washington County down the Brazos to present Brazoria County. On December 4, 1823, the gracious Austin conceded the disputed land in a letter to Bell:

> I thought all parties were satisfied relative to the land below when you left here. There will be no cause for dissatisfaction . . . I am not difficult to please . . . I have heard since you are dissatisfied that I should take a quarter of a league there and have made reflections that

if it had not been for you the whole settlement would have b[roken]
etc. I will never suffer any man to lay me under an obligation without more than an equivalent and shall therefore not take an inch at
that place if I have to drink river water. You can therefore remove as
soon as you please with the assurance that no one shall interfere with
you . . .

On March 31, 1824, Austin appointed Bell as lieutenant of the
militia on the lower Brazos; he was to command "on the Brazos and
Oyster Creek from the Fort and on the Bernard from the Mound to the
sea shore." Austin's reliance on Josiah Bell is apparent in one of his letters:

I rely greatly on your prudence and judgment in preserving harmony
. . . [Those not worthy] must be ordered off . . . Examine Red
River emigrants very closely and take care no bad men get in — let
us have no black sheep in our flock. Should a man of notorious bad
character come in, I . . . authorize you to whip him not exceeding
fifty lashes and seize sufficient of his property to pay a guard to conduct him beyond the Trinity River. One example of this kind is
wanting badly and after that we shall not be troubled . . .

In January 1824, Bell made camp on Bell's Creek, two miles
from its entrance into the Bernard River. Later that year he built a
"landing" of log-lined docks and timbered steps on the Brazos River
just below Varner's Creek. This cluster of docks, sheds, and freight
warehouses was called Bell's Landing by the colonists, but Josiah Bell
referred to the budding river port and supply depot as Marion. Located
some thirty-five miles from Velasco and the mouth of the Brazos, Marion became the head of navigation and the most important shipping
point in Austin's colony. Schooners from New Orleans could make the
trip from Velasco in several days if the wind was right and soon could
dock at Marion with supplies for the settlements above.

On August 7, 1824, Bell's land grant of one and a half leagues,
including three miles of river front, was officially recorded after being
surveyed by Horatio Chriesman. By Christmas, Bell moved his family
into a "good dwelling house" where James Hall Bell was born on January 2, 1825.[1] This structure was located at the intersection of Austin

1. James entered St. Joseph's College at Bardstown, Kentucky, in 1837, but returned to Texas upon the death of his father. After attending Centre College at Danville,
Kentucky, between 1839 and 1842, young Bell served with the Somervell Expedition in
repelling a Mexican invasion of Texas, then returned with General Somervell when he retreated to Texas. James studied law with William H. Jack, attended Harvard University

and Front streets and faced the Brazos River. Noah Smithwick, a blacksmith and gunsmith from Tennessee, who first visited Texas in the summer of 1827, was probably describing the Bell abode when he told of visiting a simple pole cabin where all the family was dressed in buckskin. According to Smithwick, they sat on stools around a crude clapboard table and ate on wooden plates with forks and spoons made of split cane stalks. Although he never saw this family again, Smithwick was told that they later prospered.

Sometime in 1826, "Old Squire Bell" (as he was called by the colonists) cut a two-mile-long road from Bell's Landing through the timber to the prairie end of his league, where he founded a new town called Columbia. This road, Brazos Avenue, was very rough and was usually covered with mud and slush. Bell laid out his new town with a public plaza and twenty square blocks of eight lots each in the business section. He also set aside "garden plots" — outlots of one acre each — along Brazos Avenue between the two towns. In October 1837, Bell sold this intervening area to Walter C. White, who divided it into town lots as the Columbia Town Tract.

In 1827 Josiah Bell moved to a fine plantation home south of Columbia. Nestled in a beautiful grove of live oaks, this double-log house had six rooms, a detached kitchen, and an office in the yard. The place was bordered by a split-rail fence and was surrounded by fields, orchards, stock lots, a blacksmith shop, and slave quarters to the west. Itinerant preachers were frequent guests, and Sam Houston later used the office in the Bell yard.

In 1829 Bell built an English school on the prairie one mile west of Columbia. Thomas J. Pilgrim, who taught there and in the Columbia area between 1831 and 1836, said that Bell's place was a "welcome home to every stranger, where the hungry are fed, the naked clad, the sick nursed."

Squire Bell's neighbor, Martin Varner, was born in 1787 in Page

---

from 1845 to 1847, then went into a law partnership with Robert J. Townes at Brazoria.

He and brother Thaddeus produced 120 hogsheads of sugar in 1852, ranking them twenty-second in Brazoria County. While living in Columbia in 1857, Judge Hall persuaded J. M. Kuykendall to write an invaluable series of recollections of various pioneers of the 1820s. These were later published in "Reminiscences of Early Texans," *Southwestern Historical Quarterly*, 6 (1902–1903): 236–253.

After four years as a district judge, James served as an associate justice of the Texas Supreme Court from August 1858 until August 1864. Judge Hall was secretary of state for a year under Reconstruction Governor A. J. Hamilton and later engaged in mining operations in Mexico. He died in Austin on March 13, 1892.

County, Virginia, but moved to Missouri at an early age. While fur trading on the Texas side of the Red River in December 1816, Varner was seriously wounded when attacked by Osage Indians near the mouth of Choctaw Bayou. Sometime before 1821 he married Betsy Inglish, whose father was an early Red River settler. In 1821 the couple moved south to join Austin's colony and first settled in present Washington County some two and a half miles west of Robinson's ferry (later Independence). When another Red River pioneer, Daniel Shipman, visited the Varners in early April of 1822, he described their home as a primitive log cabin with a dirt floor. Since Martin had no bread, Daniel shared some of his cornmeal and they enjoyed a mush supper. After finding the weather too dry to produce a corn crop, Shipman returned to North Texas that summer.

In late February of 1823, Varner was visited by Horatio Chriesman, whose wife had recently died. After staying with his host a month while recovering from an illness, Chriesman struck a deal with Varner: Martin would furnish the provisions while Horatio would work the corn crop. It was Chriesman who surveyed Josiah Bell's first league of land a few miles below the La Bahia Road on October 10, 1823. Chriesman later told a story to illustrate Varner's prowess as a hunter. It seems that James Whiteside, a neighbor living along the Navasota River, had to return to the United States on business, leaving his wife and two sons alone. Soon they were left with nothing to eat but lettuce. Upon hearing of their plight, Varner shot a large buck and sent it to the destitute family.

After voting in a colonial election in April 1824, Varner visited Ohio the next month. On July 8, 1824, he received a league of land in present Brazoria County on the banks of Varner Creek, a tributary of the Brazos River. There he built a two-room log house near the creek bank for his wife, daughter, and two servants. He later named his only son Stephen F., in honor of his friend, the empresario. Varner raised sugar cane and used the molasses to produce the first rum distillery in Texas on his plantation. In July 1829, he and partner Israel Waters sent a sample bottle of rum to Austin, who wished them success and noted that theirs were the first "ardent spirits" of any kind ever made in the colony.

Noah Smithwick visited Varner sometime before 1834 and later told two stories about his host. When Varner held a dancing party at his home "near Columbia," the fiddler was still absent when the guests arrived. When the group asked one of Varner's slaves to sing and play dancing music, he performed on the clevis, a U-shaped piece of iron with holes in the ends through which a pin is run to attach a whipple-tree to a wagon tongue. Varner's other slaves scraped a cotton hoe with a case knife, and everyone had a good time dancing to the "music."

According to Smithwick, Varner told the next story on himself. It seems that Varner purchased a barrel of wheat flour, and his wife baked some heavy, hard biscuits from this rare luxury. Since young Stephen Varner had never sampled a biscuit, he quickly helped himself and took another one outside to eat. He soon returned for another, prompting his curious father to follow him, only to discover that the boy had "punched holes through the center (of each biscuit), inserted an axle, and triumphantly displayed a miniature Mexican cart."

A strange, fascinating tale surrounds the death of Angeline Caldwell Kerr, an early traveler in the Columbia area. Angeline, her husband James, and their three small children came to Texas from St. Genevieve County, Missouri, in the spring of 1825. James Kerr, a friend of Austin, had agreed to be the surveyor general of Green DeWitt's colony. As the family traveled into the interior of Texas, the frail, worn-out Angeline died of the "fever" on June 7, 1825, in a temporary camp on the San Bernard four miles west of Columbia. Since her husband James was out surveying at the time, Angeline's body was sealed in a hollowed-out oak log for burial, and the funeral services were read by Mrs. Mary E. Bell. Within weeks little Ison and John James Kerr also died en route to San Felipe, leaving their father with only three-year-old Mary Margaret.[2] In 1853 this only surviving child had her mother's body reinterred in the church cemetery at West Columbia. When the log was split open to transfer the corpse to a pine box, the onlookers were shocked to find the body in a perfect state of preservation. When the air reached it, however, the body turned to dust before their amazed eyes. Today one can still see the door-sized flat tombstone of Angeline Caldwell Kerr, the oldest one in the cemetery (dating back to 1825).

---

2. In August 1825, James Kerr laid out the colony capital town of Gonzales. Two years later, he settled at Old Station on the Lavaca River in present Jackson County. When John Henry Brown was twelve his father died at Columbia, so the lad lived with Kerr for a time on the Lavaca.

In September 1833, James Kerr married Sarah Grace Fulton, the foster daughter of John J. Linn of Victoria. The couple later had three boys and a girl. Kerr was a practicing physician in his twilight years and died at the age of sixty on December 23, 1850. Kerr County was created and named for him on January 26, 1856. Today there is a state marker on FM 822, eight miles north of Edna, and the Kerr family cemetery is in a pasture behind it.

One of the earliest settlers in the Columbia area was Dr. James A. E. Phelps. A practicing physician from Mississippi, Dr. Phelps was in the original company of Austin colonists sent to Texas on the *Lively,* a schooner from New Orleans which anchored off the mouth of the Brazos on December 23, 1821. Phelps received title to one league and two labors of land in present Brazoria County on August 16, 1824. His Orozimbo plantation was located on the west bank of the Brazos twelve miles northwest of Columbia. Named for an Indian chief, this cotton plantation featured a fine, two-story, wooden "big house" with twin columns framing the front porch. The census of 1826 showed James as having a wife, two sons, two daughters, one servant, and fifteen slaves. Delayed by the settling of family affairs back in Mississippi, Dr. Phelps did not actually establish residence at Orozimbo until March 1830.

William C. and Catherine Jane Carson were among the first of Austin's "Old 300" colonists to arrive in the area. After traveling overland from Louisiana by wagon with their three children, the Carsons received title to a league of land on the San Bernard River on May 15, 1827. The invalid husband had hoped the climate would improve his health, but he died only three months after their arrival. Catherine then moved her family to Bell's Landing, where she operated a boardinghouse and became a friend of Ammon Underwood.

Henry Smith, who would later serve as provisional governor of Texas during the Revolution, arrived at Bell's Landing in March 1827. The next year Thomas J. Pilgrim, a licensed Baptist preacher and schoolteacher, stayed with the Bell family at Columbia while walking from Matagorda to San Felipe, where he opened an academy and the second Sunday school in Texas before being forced to suspend his activities in 1829. That year John R. Harris of Harrisburg opened a store with 130 customers at Bell's Landing. Beginning in October 1829, Josiah Bell advertised the sale of lots in Marion in the *Texas Gazette* at San Felipe, but his real estate promotion met with little success. When Mrs. Mary Austin Holley visited in December 1831, she described the town as having "two or three cabins, a country store, and one frame house painted white." On a second trip in 1835, Mrs. Holley noted that a large warehouse had been built by Walter C. White. When William Fairfax Gray visited in 1837, he observed that Marion had only eight or ten houses, mostly shanties, and described Hall's Tavern as "a perfect shell, dirty and crowded, surrounded by mud."

Henry S. Brown, a famed Indian fighter, settled at Columbia in

1832. Fighting under the command of John T. Austin, the mayor of Brazoria, Brown led one of two forty-seven-man companies in the first bloodshed between Texas and Mexico, the Battle of Velasco. Among those in Captain Brown's company were John G. Robinson and his son Joel, who had settled on the Bernard three miles from Columbia in 1831.[3] William J. Russell used his schooner, the *Brazoria,* and its two cannons in the attack. After eleven hours of fighting, two-thirds of Col. Domingo de Ugartechea's men were dead and wounded, and the Mexicans had exhausted their ammunition. On June 26, 1832, Ugartechea surrendered Fort Velasco to Captain Austin. Soon thereafter, Brown served as second to William T. Austin in his duel with John A. Wharton. Henry Brown died at Columbia on July 26, 1834, and was buried there; a surviving son, John Henry, later achieved fame as a Texas historian.

In April 1833, Asiatic cholera was brought to the mouth of the Brazos by a family from New Orleans, where an epidemic was then raging. Brazoria, which had been laid out in 1828 by John Austin, was in the middle of a swamp, and the Brazos River overflowed its banks there in May 1833. As the water receded, cholera spread in the town and took entire families. This dread disease decimated the country from Velasco to Columbia and destroyed all the planted crops before the water disappeared in late June. As a result of this disaster, the seat of government for the municipality was moved from sickly, unhealthy Brazoria to the higher ground of Columbia in the summer of 1834.

Like his friend, Empresario Austin, Josiah Bell initially favored a conservative, conciliatory policy in dealing with Mexican authorities. Whenever discontent among the colonists became serious, Austin would draft a forceful, instructive note to Bell, who could be trusted to circulate its calming effects among his neighbors on the lower Brazos. Bell was critical of those taking part in the Anahuac Insurrection of June 1832, and signed a call for a convention to meet at San Felipe on July 7. He joined others in urging such a gathering to repay the generosity of the Mexican government by inducing "our deluded and unfortunate fellow citizens to return to their homes." While Austin was imprisoned for ten months in Mexico City, the Matagorda *ayuntamiento*

---

3. In 1833, the Robinson family settled on Cummings Creek near the La Bahia Crossing in present Fayette County. During the Texas Revolution, Joel W. Robinson joined Company F, led by Capt. William Jones Elliot Heard at Gonzales. Joel was in the six-man party that captured General Santa Anna the morning after the Battle of San Jacinto.

(governing council) sent attorneys Peter Grayson and Spencer Jack. Their legal efforts resulted in Austin being released on bail on Christmas Day of 1834. Among the colonists paying the cost of their trip was Josiah Bell.

As the land around Columbia became more settled and crowded, the restless Martin Varner decided to relocate. On April 4, 1834, he sold his plantation to Columbus R. Patton for $13,000. After sending his family north to the Red River area, Varner joined the Texas army on April 19, 1836, and was assigned to guard baggage and tend the sick at Harrisburg during the Battle of San Jacinto. In July he rejoined his family and resettled in northeast Texas in Red River County near old Fort Lyday in 1837. The county census of 1840 showed Varner as owning forty-five cattle and one horse, and having 1,280 acres under survey. The next year he located his two land grants for service in the Texas army and became the first white settler in newly created Wood County. After settling four miles south of present Hainesville in Redland Community, Varner was murdered in 1843.[4]

When Varner sold his Columbia land, the deed was executed in the name of family agent Columbus R. Patton, the third oldest of seven sons. Columbus and an older brother, William Hester, first arrived in Brazoria County in February 1832. Their father, John D. Patton, had sent them from Christian County, Kentucky, to find and buy land for a sugar plantation. In 1835 the Pattons built a two-story brick mansion, using some of the fourteen-inch-thick log walls in Varner's old cabin as the nucleus of the first floor. The slave-made pink bricks came from the clay of the Brazos riverbed. The mansion had high ceilings and large windows, which in every room provided cross-ventilation. The large central hall joined the front and back doors with a par-

---

4. Martin, his son Stephen, and a slave were building fences when a Mexican named Gonzales rode up. A former employee or employer of Varner, Gonzales engaged him in a heated argument before starting to mount his horse. At that instant he wheeled, shot Martin in the back, and killed his son. In grabbing the Mexican, the slave was knifed and severely wounded but managed to drag his assailant to the mortally wounded Varner, who killed his enemy.

Martin died several days later, but his wife saved the slave's life by sewing up his stomach with thread and needle from her sewing kit. He and Mrs. Varner then buried the three victims, with Gonzales being put to rest in an unmarked grave removed from the other two men. When Betsy Varner died eight years later, she was buried next to her husband and son.

Local legend has it that Gonzales was a rich man who had buried $10,000 in gold somewhere in Wood County. Since the location was supposedly engraved on a medal he wore around his neck, the treasure site has never been found.

lor on one side and a bedroom on the other. An upstairs central hall also served as a breezeway and was flanked on both sides by large bedrooms with windows on three walls. The furnishings were valued at $195 and included twelve chairs, three folding leaf tables, one "sopha," two settees, and one sideboard. The main entrance of the Greek Revival style home faced tree-shaded Varner Creek, the plantation link to the outside world. Small cedar barges were loaded with sacks of raw sugar from a delta sloping to the twenty-five-foot-deep creek, then floated down the stream to Bell's Landing and the Brazos River.

When John D. Patton died in August 1840, he was buried in the brick-walled family cemetery 200 yards north of the mansion on a bluff overlooking Varner Creek. His wife, Margaretta (Annie) Hester Patton, was also buried there in September 1843, as was their eldest son, St. Clair, who died in December 1849.

On March 1, 1835, Dr. James A. E. Phelps helped organize the first Masonic Lodge in Texas. Meeting secretly under an oak tree at the John Austin place near Brazoria, Phelps and Masonic friends Anson Jones, John A. Wharton, Asa Brigham, Alexander Russell, J. P. Caldwell, and Warren D. C. Hall agreed to apply to the Grand Lodge of Louisiana for a dispensation to form and open the Holland Lodge, named in honor of John Henry Holland, the Most Worshipful Grand Master of Louisiana. After the dispensation arrived, Holland Lodge No. 36 of Brazoria held its first session on December 27, 1835, meeting in the room used for a courthouse. Worshipful Master Anson Jones presided in the chair, and Dr. Phelps was elected treasurer.

In 1834 and 1835, Columbia had a track on which match horse races were run for purses up to $1,000. During this time Josiah Bell was the proprietor of the Columbia Jockey Club. Although the town was occupied by the Mexican army just before the Battle of San Jacinto, the Jockey Club sponsored racing seasons just before and following the invasion. In November 1836, P. R. Splane of Columbia made a public wager of $10,000 or less on one of his horses against any competition. In the midst of all this gambling, the second oldest Bible Society in Texas was organized at Columbia in 1835.

This sporting town was also a hotbed of revolutionary sentiment. On June 28, 1835, Warren D. C. Hall chaired a citizens' meeting at Columbia which recommended organizing a militia, appointing a committee of public safety and correspondence, and asking the political chief to take steps for the calling of a public council that would provide Texas with a provisional government. This public meeting was followed by similar gatherings at Mina, Lavaca, and Gonzales. When a convention was held at San Felipe on July 14, 1835, the Columbia delegation — John A. Wharton, Sterling McNeel, James F. Perry, Josiah Bell, and James Knight — led an unsuccessful effort to call a general consultation of all Texians. Four days later, the Safety Committee of Columbia — William H. Jack, John G. McNeel, John A. Wharton, and Warren D. C. Hall — announced that all men ages eighteen to fifty should meet on July 19 at Columbia, Brazoria, and D. H. Milburn's plantation to organize three militia companies and elect officers.

After Gen. Martín Perfecto de Cos, the new military commandant for Texas, ordered the arrest of Lorenzo de Zavala, William Barret Travis, and five other dissidents, William H. Wharton presided over a protest meeting at Columbia on August 15, 1835. This group of citizens declared that no individual would be turned over to the military authorities and that a general consultation of all Texas citizens was "indispensable." Five days later, a committee chaired by Branch T. Archer met at Velasco and appealed for each jurisdiction to elect five delegates for a general consultation to be held on October 15 at Washington-on-the-Brazos.

After Stephen F. Austin was released from eighteen months' confinement in Mexico City, a banquet and ball honoring his homecoming was held in Mrs. Jane Long's hotel at Brazoria on September 8, 1835. Endorsing the Columbia call for a general consultation, Austin sent out six personal warnings about the crisis, then led a group of 100 volunteers to the Gonzales front, where he was chosen commander-in-chief of the Texas army on October 11, 1835. Four volunteer companies were organized in Brazoria County for the expedition against General Cos, including an artillery company from Columbia led by Warren D. C. Hall. On October 6, Josiah Bell wrote Austin and told him that the coastal area was in a defenseless state, "barer of men than any other part of the Country and entirely destitute of arms." Bell feared that the women would be exposed to a slave uprising, an Indian attack, or a seaborne invasion.

Among those responding to the call to arms was Ammon Underwood, who left Columbia on October 4 to join the Texas army. Born in Dracut, Massachusetts, on February 13, 1810, Underwood migrated to Texas from Lowell, Massachusetts, in April 1834. According to his journal, he came "to satisfy a wild and roving notion." For several months Ammon was a clerk and bookkeeper for various business firms before starting his own mercantile business at Marion. That operation stayed in the family for eighty-nine years.

The journal he kept between 1835 and 1838 offers some fascinating personal observations about the Texas Revolution. Here are some of Ammon's diary entries for 1835:

June 9 — "The political state of this country is in such an unsettled condition that I am at an entire loss what to do . . ."
August 15 — ". . . Their proceedings (the Columbia meeting) were conducted with much intreague and deception knowing that a majority of the people were opposed to that measure (general consultation) for many pertinent reasons . . ."
September 22 — "The wary cry is raised. The soard is gerded on, the war horse prepared and ready to be mounted. Much unanimity of feeling prevails at present. The volunteer list was opened in this place (Columbia) yesterday and nearly all the young folks have subscribed as volunteers to meet Gen. Cos who is reported to have arrived at Copano with four hundred armed troops."

After taking part in the successful siege and assault on San Antonio, Underwood left San Felipe on Christmas Day 1835. He was back home in time to enjoy a ball at the spacious Columbia hotel built by Josiah Bell in 1832 and managed by Fitchett and Gill. In April 1836, Ammon was named acting post commissary at Columbia.

On December 25, 1835, at Columbia, the municipality of Brazoria held a well-attended meeting presided over by Josiah Bell. In his "Private Memoirs," Dr. Anson Jones of Brazoria commented on his role at the meeting:

. . . I drew up, offered, and advocated, as chairman of the committee, resolutions in favor of a "Declaration of Independence from Mexico" and calling a Convention of the people of Texas on the first Monday in March, 1836, to make the Declaration, and to frame a Constitution . . . .

Fearing to trust the vote, I proposed . . . the resolutions be signed by those who approved them, and go to the country as the expression of the individuals whose names should be appended . . . We succeeded in getting about twenty or thirty names from among those who were present; but . . . nearly everybody signed before they were published . . .

The people of the country were at first startled by the boldness

of the Columbia Resolutions, but . . . by the 2nd of March following, there were but few in the country who did not acquiesce in the
propriety of the course proposed in those resolutions.

Another resolution fixed the basis for representation in said convention.

The provisional state government adopted these resolutions of the
Columbia meeting and made a call for the convention accordingly.
When the convention met at Washington-on-the-Brazos, there was a
unanimous vote for independence on March 2, 1836.

A few days later, a Paul Revere ride was made from Columbia.
When a courier arrived there with news of the Mexican siege of the
Alamo, Guy M. Bryan, a nephew of Austin who had been attending
Mr. Pilgrim's school there, was dispatched with a warning letter to
Brazoria. Guy then dashed on to Peach Point, where he obtained a
fresh horse and arrived at Velasco with the Alamo news during the night.

On March 19, 1836, doctors James Phelps and Anson Jones set
out to join the Texas army, and both were attached to the medical staff
as hospital surgeons. Dr. Jones served as a surgeon at San Jacinto and
Dr. Phelps was left behind at Harrisburg to attend to the sick. The day
after the historic battle, Phelps set up a hospital for wounded Mexicans
in the home of the interim vice-president, Lorenzo de Zavala. Capt.
William H. Patton, a veteran of the Battle of Velasco and the Siege of
Bexar, led Fourth Company (from Columbia), Second Regiment in the
Battle of San Jacinto, and also served as Gen. Sam Houston's aide-de-camp.

After receiving news of the fall of the Alamo, General Houston
retreated eastward from Gonzales on March 13, 1836. His controversial decision to abandon the heavily-populated area between the Colorado and Brazos rivers triggered a panic civilian flight known as the
"Runaway Scrape." All residents of Columbia and Marion were taken
down the Brazos by steamboat to Galveston. Widow Catherine Carson
and daughter Rachel stayed behind in hopes of hearing from her two
sons in the Texas army. Finally, the two brave women fled to Damon's
Mound and then Richmond before camping twelve miles from the
Trinity River in Montgomery County. Mrs. Carson actually heard the
cannon firing at San Jacinto on April 21, but thought it was thunder.

At Bailey's Prairie, east of Columbia, John and Ann Raney
Thomas were reluctant to abandon the Brit Bailey property they had
recently purchased for $9,000. At the last minute the couple decided
to take only one change of clothes each so as not to overload their
wagon. Ann, however, managed to sneak aboard a little trunk containing her set of fine china from England. Leaving it beside the road later

was her greatest disappointment. The Raneys eventually crossed the Sabine in a party of one hundred. Disillusioned by the turn of events, John took a huge loss when he sold all of his Brazoria County land and property to Edwin Waller for $2,000 at Liberty.

On April 21, 1836, Gen. Jose Urrea reached deserted Columbia but did not damage the town. He rushed on to Brazoria the next day. Urrea found the residents cooperative but did destroy the Masonic Lodge there, including records, books, and jewels. Luckily, Anson Jones had secured the charter from the lodge room and was carrying it in his saddlebags during the Battle of San Jacinto.[5]

John Adriance, a Columbia merchant and newcomer, served with Jacob Eberly's volunteer company detailed to guard the Brazos crossing during the Runaway Scrape. Adriance was born in Troy, New York, on November 10, 1818, and worked in a textile company before coming to Texas in October 1835. After the Battle of San Jacinto, he and Judge George B. McKinstry of Columbia were among the volunteer guards who escorted prisoner Santa Anna on the steamboat *Laura* from Galveston to Velasco, arriving there on May 10, 1836. For the next three years, Adriance and C. Beardslee were partners in a mercantile business at Columbia.

After hearing news of the San Jacinto victory, Ammon Underwood loaned a horse to Columbus R. Patton on April 22, 1836, then hurried back to Marion, where he was the first to arrive on May 2. The steamboat *Yellowstone* arrived with the women and children on the eleventh; the *Laura* docked the next day with W. C. White and Colonel Knight on board. By then Ammon noted in his journal that he "had got things pretty well righted." He soon formed a business partnership with John P. Coles and David H. Milburn, and also served as postmaster from 1836 until 1845.

A Columbia resident, Maj. William H. Patton, was placed in charge of guarding Santa Anna and his entourage and took them to Velasco on June 7, 1836. That day the prisoners were visited by Bartolome Pages, a Mexican who managed to converse privately with Santa Anna and told him that with sufficient funds, he would travel to New Orleans and arrange for their escape. Santa Anna then gave Pages a letter addressed to Don Francisco Pizarro Martinez, the Mexican consul at New Orleans, who was instructed to finance the escape attempt.

On June 15, the *Laura* carried the Mexican prisoners upriver to

5. The original charter became the property of Holland Lodge No. 1 at Houston. The other original documents are now with St. John's Lodge No. 5 at West Columbia.

Bell's Landing, where they were transferred to the Patton plantation outside Columbia the next day. For the next six weeks, Santa Anna, Col. Juan Almonte, Secretary Ramon Caro, and aide-de-camp Gabriel Nunez stayed in the "Race House," a wooden structure on the plantation grounds.

Shortly after their arrival, a drunk Texian staggered unchallenged past the guards to the Race House, where he asked Colonels Almonte and Nunez if he could view their leader, who was in bed at the time. When his request was ignored, the drunk fired a wild shot through a small window into Santa Anna's room. The would-be assassin was later punished by Major Patton.

During this period a beautiful Spanish lady who lived near Brazoria came to visit Santa Anna, bringing some small edibles and two bottles of fine wine for her fallen hero. While conversing in Spanish with the general, she dropped a glove at his feet. The suspicious Major Patton picked it up and found a scribbled note in one of the fingers. When the indignant *señorita* demanded its return, Patton asked Virgil Phelps to translate the note. Its contents revealed that the marked bottle of wine was poisoned, and that the other one was drugged and intended for the guards; there were even horses in the nearby woods for Santa Anna's escape! In the mass confusion that followed, the stymied Mexican leader managed to gulp down some of the poisoned wine. His captor, Major Patton, quickly drove the general to Dr. Phelps's Orozimbo plantation, where the good doctor used a stomach pump to save his life.

In midsummer a rumor spread that Commander-in-chief Thomas J. Rusk had ordered Santa Anna to be tried by court-martial and executed. The rumor started in June, when members of the Texas army were detailed to bury the bones of Fannin's men at Goliad, then returned to Victoria and vowed to make Santa Anna pay for the Goliad Massacre. Many of these soldiers were undisciplined, bored, three-month volunteers who had arrived in Texas after the Battle of San Jacinto. When the execution rumor reached Sam Houston at San Augustine, he wrote an angry letter to General Rusk denouncing the scheme, and the plot was foiled.

On July 30, 1836, the four Mexican prisoners were moved for their own safety to remote Orozimbo plantation, located twelve miles northwest of Columbia. In his diary Colonel Nunez recorded the transfer as follows:

. . . We arrived at half past three. The doctor's home is beautiful. It has an orchard with various fruits, flowers, etc., besides the cotton plantation. Here one can enjoy greater comfort.

Shortly after Santa Anna's arrival at Orozimbo, an abortive attempt was made to free him. The plot involved drugging his guards with a sleeping potion, then having the prisoners steal away to the nearby woods, where a rescue party was hiding with extra mounts. The night of the planned escape was rainy and very dark. Just as planned, the guards fell into a drugged sleep, and the men crept toward the house where the alerted prisoners awaited. Suddenly, some dogs began to bark, lamplights came on in the darkened house, and the would-be rescuers fled into the night. Neither Dr. Phelps nor his neighbors owned any dogs, however, and none could be found when a search for them was made.

Several weeks after the incident, a reticent traveler came by Orozimbo and told Dr. Phelps about three dogs belonging to a neighbor of his. It seems that the friend had left his dogs when he went off to fight in the Texas army. After he was executed by order of Santa Anna in the Goliad Massacre, the dogs apparently sensed the death of their beloved master, refused to eat, and ran off. The traveler surmised that those lost, vengeful dogs — either in flesh and blood or phantom form — had scared off Santa Anna's rescuers. People laughed at his tale, but there have been reported sightings of ghost dogs near Orozimbo ever since.[6]

On August 16, 1836, Bartolome Pages arrived at Bell's Landing on the small, armed schooner *Passiac,* which he had purchased with 5,000 pesos obtained from the Mexican consul at New Orleans. Pages immediately went to Orozimbo, where he was seated in the parlor next to Secretary Ramon Caro. Whispering in Spanish, Pages informed Caro that he could not attempt a rescue because his hand-picked crew

---

6. The most recent sighting came in 1974, when a couple was en route to visit the old Orozimbo plantation site. The day was growing dark and it was starting to rain when they suddenly saw three dogs sitting perfectly still under a tree by the side of the road. To the husband these dogs, with their wild, strange eyes, resembled wolves. His wife, however, remembered the legend of the Hawaiian ghost dog when she noticed the skinned-looking white leader standing between the other two.

When the couple returned later, the dogs were still standing motionless under that same scrubby oak tree. Even when a whitetail deer suddenly bolted across the road, the dogs would not give chase or even bark. This unnatural response convinced the woman that these were truly the ghost dogs of Orozimbo, and she vowed never to return to that foreboding place again.

had been detained by New Orleans authorities. He also told Caro that Orozimbo was simply too far from the coast for a successful escape. After telling Caro that he would send the prisoners supplies from the *Passiac,* Pages was dragged from his chair by a guard, rebuked for not speaking in English, and ordered to leave. Caro then relayed the conversation to Santa Anna, who became enraged and swore not to pay any of the expenses incurred by Pages in New Orleans.

Major Patton was absent during this visit. Upon discovering that Bartolome's passport instructed Mexican naval vessels to aid him on his "secret mission of the highest importance," Patton arrested him, co-conspirator Caro, and the *Passiac* crew. All were later released except Pages, who was placed in irons as a spy.

As a result of this escape conspiracy, Santa Anna and Juan Almonte had a heavy ball and chain attached to their legs for fifty-two days at Orozimbo. During this time the despondent Santa Anna overdosed on opium three times. Shortly before his presidential inauguration on October 22, Sam Houston brought a large basket of food to Santa Anna and apologized for his confinement in irons.

Tradition has it that an angry Texas soldier tried to shoot the Mexican leader at Orozimbo but held his fire when Mrs. Phelps threw her arms around the intended victim. It should be noted that both of Santa Anna's captors, Major Patton and Dr. Phelps, were fellow Masons.[7]

Stephen F. Austin arrived in Velasco on June 27, 1836, after serving as one of three commissioners seeking aid in the United States. He was soon entertained in the handsome Columbia home of his old

---

7. In late December 1842, Col. William S. Fisher and 308 volunteers attacked Mier, Mexico, after defying an order by Gen. Alexander Somervell to return to Texas. After a bloody two-day battle, the Texians surrendered and were marched to Salado, where the drawing of seventeen black beans and the "Lottery of Death" took place. Orlando Phelps was among the twenty men from Brazoria County who took part in the Mier Expedition.

When Santa Anna learned that Orlando was the son of Dr. James A. Phelps, the man who had saved his life near Columbia, he had the prisoner brought to the presidential palace. Young Phelps was treated by Santa Anna's personal physician, given good clothes and $500 in gold, and ship passage to Texas. One hundred and four other Mier prisoners were finally released on September 16, 1843.

For years Santa Anna continued to send fine bedspreads and other presents to the Phelps family at Orozimbo. In April 1845, Dr. Phelps was appointed to a Brazoria committee charged with preparing an address in favor of annexation. He died in 1847 and was buried on the plantation. His grave was marked by the Texas Centennial Commission in 1936. The old Orozimbo property is now the Black Ranch.

friend, Josiah Bell, who urged Austin to be a candidate for president of the Republic of Texas.

On July 23, ad interim President David G. Burnet issued a proclamation calling for presidential and congressional elections on the first Monday in September. He also called for the new Congress to convene at Columbia on the first Monday in October. Burnet did not refer to the town as the capital of Texas, only that Congress would meet there. There were two reasons for naming Columbia: it had the most adequate housing accommodations *and* a newspaper. Gail and Thomas H. Borden had recently located *The Telegraph and Texas Register* there and published their first Columbia issue on August 2, 1836. Obviously, the government would need a printer for its voluminous proceedings. John W. Wade, who worked as a compositor on the *Telegraph,* had been detailed to help man the "Twin Sisters" during the Battle of San Jacinto.

In the September presidential election, Sam Houston won an overwhelming victory, receiving 5,119 votes to 743 for Henry Smith (who tried to withdraw from the race) and 587 votes for Austin. A major factor in Austin's poor showing was the unfounded, persistent rumor that he was implicated in the past land frauds and speculations involving his personal secretary, Samuel May Williams.

On September 16, Columbia businessmen pledged that ten buildings with nineteen rooms for offices would be made available, along with all chairs and tables necessary for both houses of Congress. A local committee was appointed on September 27 to prepare buildings for Congress. The whole expense of housing fell upon private citizens; Congress made no effort to rent buildings. Housing facilities were so scarce that President Houston stayed with Josiah Bell and used his small outbuilding as an office. Some government officials roomed at Mr. Bell's hotel, Polley's Rooming House, or at the boardinghouse run by Rachel Carson and Ammon Underwood at Bell's Landing. While Columbia was the capital, a bed space sold for fifty cents. Those wanting privacy had to pay for all the bed spaces in the room. Little wonder that some congressmen chose to sleep in bedrolls under the trees and take their meals at the Bell Hotel.

On Monday, October 3, 1836, the First Congress of the Republic of Texas met at Columbia. Ira Ingram was elected speaker of the House of Representatives, and Richard Ellis was chosen as president pro tem of the Senate. Francis R. Lubbock, a recent arrival from New Orleans, said that the crowded, bustling town

. . . presented a wild and romantic appearance . . . There was something in it new and attractive, the fine old live oaks, other majestic trees of the forest, the woods near the town filled with bear, Mexican lions, deer, turkey, and game of every kind.

It made my thoughts fly quick and fast when my mind took in the facts: This is the capital of a republic, with the heads of departments, the Congress in session, and hosts of people in the town — President, judges, representatives, senators, captains, colonels, generals, men of mark, men that would attract attention and respect in any country.

Among the Texian heroes Lubbock saw in Columbia were Sam Houston, Mirabeau B. Lamar, Henry Smith, Stephen F. Austin, James Collinsworth, William H. and John A. Wharton, Anson Jones, Edward Burleson, Mosely Baker, David G. Burnet, Jesse Grimes, Sterling C. Robertson, Albert Clinton Horton, Alexander Somervell, Richard Ellis, Thomas J. Rusk, Ira Ingram, and Albert Sidney Johnston. Unfortunately, Columbia was also teeming with discharged army volunteers anxious to sell their bounty-land scrips for a few nights of gambling and wenching.

Two buildings housed the Texas Congress. One was a large, two-story house of five rooms, divided by a wide hall and stairway into two large rooms on both floors, along with an ell. Located on the south side of Brazos Avenue, the house was built by Capt. Henry S. Brown in 1832. After he died there in July 1834, the house was used as the storehouse of W. C. White and Company. The House of Representatives remained in this larger capitol building, which was torn down in 1888. It was located along present State Highway 35, just across from the old Bruno's Drug Store on Main Street of West Columbia. The State of Texas placed a historical marker at the site on April 21, 1932.

The Texas Senate met in a smaller structure, a one-story building built by Leman Kelsey about 1833. Located on the north side of Brazos Avenue, it contained a large central room and a shed room in the back, where Secretary of State Austin had an office. To combat the winter cold, the doorkeeper of the Senate was sent to Brazoria for a heating stove. This dilapidated structure was destroyed by the Galveston storm on September 8, 1900, and a historical marker was placed on the site on April 21, 1932. A replica of the Kelsey building was constructed nearby in 1977 and dedicated by Governor Dolph Briscoe on April 21 of that year.

Up the street from the two buildings stood the old "Capitol

Oak," a huge live oak with a triple trunk. According to local tradition, the Texas Declaration of Independence was first read publicly under its limbs. In an interview with the *Galveston News*, Joseph P. Underwood recalled that three oak trees grew close together, had a common root system, and were known as Austin's, Houston's, and Lamar's trees. They were blown down in the 1900 storm.

At 4:00 P.M. on October 22, 1836, Sam Houston and Vice-president Mirabeau B. Lamar were inaugurated in the hall of the House of Representatives. Once Houston finished his inaugural address, he paused a few seconds, then dramatically removed the sword he wore at San Jacinto and presented it to Speaker Ingram with these words:

> I have worn it with some humble pretensions in defense of my country; and, should the danger of my countrymen again call for my services, I expect to resume it and respond to their calls if needful, with my blood and my life.

For the key post of secretary of state, the president named Stephen F. Austin, who initially declined the offer because his health was "gone" and due to a pressing need to close his land office business. Houston refused to accept Austin's decision, however, and Congress overwhelmingly approved the appointment. Other cabinet choices were Henry Smith as secretary of the treasury, Thomas J. Rusk as secretary of war, S. Rhoads Fisher as secretary of the navy, J. Pinckney Henderson as attorney general, and Robert Barr as postmaster general. William H. Wharton was appointed as minister to the United States.

The Texas constitution provided that both houses of Congress would select the members of the judicial branch. James Collinsworth was chosen as chief justice of the supreme court; the four district judges and associate justices were Shelby Corzine, Benjamin C. Franklin, Robert M. Williamson, and James W. Robinson.

In one of his first acts as president, Houston asked Congress for permission to free Santa Anna and send him to Washington, D.C. It was hoped that the Mexican general could convince officials there that Mexico would recognize the independence of Texas and thus hasten annexation of Texas to the United States. After much wrangling between the two houses, a resolution finally passed making Houston responsible for the disposition of Santa Anna. On November 25, 1836, Santa Anna and Juan Almonte were released and sent to Washington escorted by Col. George Hockley, Col. Barnard Bee, and Maj. William H. Patton. When he was released, Santa Anna gave his silver spurs and pearl-handled dirk to his first jailer, Major Patton.

The First Congress meeting at Columbia passed some notable legislation. One such act was the Boundary Statute, passed on December 19, 1836. This controversial law defined the southwestern boundary of the Republic of Texas as the Rio Grande from its mouth to its source, then due north to the 42nd parallel. Such a claim split the old province of New Mexico and included Santa Fe, Taos, and Albuquerque. It was thought that the millions of acres of public land lying between San Antonio and Santa Fe would serve as a magnet to draw people to Texas and to pay off the Texas debt. The Republic had a valid claim to only the *lower* reaches of the Rio Grande, which had been accepted by both Cos and Santa Anna in their surrender terms. The preposterous Texas claim to the *upper* reaches of the Rio Grande was motivated by land greed and geographic ignorance and would lead to a bitter ten-year dispute ultimately settled by force in the Mexican War. The shape and size of Texas today can be traced to this boundary act passed at Columbia.

The First Congress also passed a series of acts converting the old Mexican municipalities into county units. By the end of 1836, the twelve functioning municipalities of 1835 had been divided into the twenty-two original counties of Texas. One of them, Brazoria County, was created by an act of Congress on December 20, 1836, and was completely organized on February 20, 1837. A portion of the county was lost to Fort Bend County in 1837, and the eastern part was transferred to Galveston County in 1838.

With regard to finance, Congress on November 18, 1836, authorized President Houston to issue up to $5 million in Republic of Texas bonds. Sold in denominations of $1,000, they bore interest of ten percent and matured in thirty years. To redeem these bonds, Congress pledged all the revenue from the sale of the Republic's public domain.

The Customs Act, passed in December 1836, set a tax on imported goods ranging from one percent on breadstuffs to fifty percent on silks. Customshouses were erected at the principal ports of entry. Customs revenue was the only real money the Republic received, since the tariff had to be paid in specie rather than the government's own worthless paper money. The tariff proved to be the most productive tax, providing from fifty to eighty percent of government revenue each year.

The First Congress also ratified the Texas constitution, created a judiciary, appointed committees, and provided for an army and navy, protection from the Indians, a postal system, and a land office.

On November 7, 1836, President Houston sent a message to both houses of Congress in which he noted, "The present position of our government is one of greatest inconvenience and absolute embarrassment." After complaining of no rooms for the committees of Congress, or offices for the chief departments of the executive branch, the president suggested that business could not profitably proceed unless Congress adjourned to some point with better accommodations.

Columbia citizens failed to provide the promised buildings and furnishings for the government. It was said that Josiah Bell did not want to provide adequate space, fearing that the resultant crowding would keep his hogs from running loose. In any event, both the House and Senate appointed committees to recommend a new site for the capital on November 2. The Senate committee favored San Jacinto (Groce's Retreat) while the House group wanted Nacogdoches. Finally, the two houses met in joint session on November 30 to decide the matter. Fifteen towns entered the competition, and on the fourth ballot, Houston defeated Washington by a vote of 21 to 14. On December 15, 1836, President Houston signed an act making this new town going up on Buffalo Bayou the capital of Texas effective the first day of April 1837, until the end of the congressional session of 1840.

When the First Congress adjourned on December 22, 1836, Columbia was, for practical purposes, no longer the seat of government. However, there was one final act to perform: the burial of Stephen F. Austin. His state department office and living quarters had been the small, unheated shed room in the Senate building. After working long hours into the night, his severe cold became pneumonia. On Christmas Eve, Austin left the office with a severe chill and burning fever. He was moved into the clapboard home of Judge George B. McKinstry the next day, but his condition was hopeless by the morning of December 27. As his brother-in-law, James F. Perry, and stepson Austin Bryan stood by, Stephen F. Austin raised himself from a floor pallet in front of the fire, then whispered in delirium, "Texas recognized. Archer told me so. Did you see it in the papers?" Those were his last audible words, and the forty-three-year-old Austin died at half past noon.

In announcing his death, President Houston said, "The father of Texas is no more. The first pioneer of the wilderness has departed . . ." He ordered all civil and military officers of the Republic to wear crepe on their right arms for thirty days. Austin's body lay in state for two days at Columbia. On December 29, a long funeral cortege led by

Houston accompanied the body along the two-mile road to Bell's Landing. There the steamboat *Yellowstone* carried Austin's remains downriver to Brazoria, then overland to Peach Point plantation, the home of Austin's brother-in-law, James F. Perry. Burial was in the Gulf Prairie cemetery with final graveside military honors rendered by a detachment of the First Regiment, Texas Infantry, led by Capt. Martin K. Snell. After Austin was eulogized by James H. Bell, Sam Houston picked up a symbolic handful of the rich Peach Point soil and sprinkled it over the coffin as the final prayer ended.[8]

Josiah Bell died at his plantation on May 17, 1838, leaving an estate valued at $140,000. Two years later his widow tore down the original house and built a new home on the site her husband had reserved for it. Eighteen years to the day after Josiah's death, Mrs. Bell was thrown from her carriage and died from the injuries on May 30, 1856. Her gravesite and headstone can be seen today in the cemetery at West Columbia. (The owners of the old Bell plantation in 1991 were the sons of Judge R. B. Loggins.)

In 1838 Ammon Underwood purchased a two-story log house built by colonist Thomas W. Nibbs in 1835. Ammon and Mrs. Catherine Carson then started a joint business venture by enlarging the original log structure into a boardinghouse. In January 1839, Ammon married Catherine's daughter Rachel in the Underwood house. In April 1842, Catherine Carson married Gail Borden, Sr., a widower and the father of the inventor of condensed milk, and they also moved into the boardinghouse. A wide lawn separated the big white plastered house and the river, and an orchard grew on one side. Since the house faced the Brazos, the double galleries spanning the front offered an ideal place to watch steamboats.

Underwood also had a successful mercantile business at Marion. It was housed in a large brick building close to the Brazos; his own wharves and loading docks were at the water's edge. He also

---

8. Austin considered Peach Point his only real home in Texas. His only sister, Emily Margaret, lived there with her husband, James F. Perry. A bedroom and study in the Perry home were reserved for Stephen's use. He rested at Peach Point until 1910, when his body was reinterred in the State Cemetery; an empty tomb still marks his original burial place.

Today only the Austin bedroom and study of the original large Perry home are preserved; the rest of the plantation house was destroyed by the 1909 storm. The tiny, two-room white structure contains a variety of memorabilia and serves as a private Perry family museum to Austin's memory. Stephen Samuel Perry, Jr., the present owner of Peach Point, is a fifth-generation direct descendant of the original 1832 settler.

owned two working plantations and was a cotton factor, making him a very wealthy man by the time of the Civil War.

After the capital moved to Houston in April 1837, Columbia rapidly declined. By 1842 this little village claimed only two stores and a hundred residents and was known as West Columbia. Soon after Josiah Bell's death in 1838, the port town of Marion adopted a new name, East Columbia, for a time. A busy Front Street running along the Brazos attested to its growth, and a number of fine, large houses were built along shady Main Street. Soon the bustling river town dropped the "East" and claimed the name of Columbia. (It was not until 1924 that the U.S. postal service officially listed the town as East Columbia, late Columbia.)

During this period, organized religion gained a foothold in the Columbia area. In October 1836, the First Texas Congress ruled that the Senate building would be cleared for public preaching every Sunday. For the next decade the various Columbia churches held services there. When the government moved to Houston, the local Presbyterian church purchased the old capitol building where the House of Representatives had held its sessions. On June 13, 1840, the Bethel Presbyterian Church of Columbia — the third oldest such congregation in Texas — was organized by Rev. William Y. Allen with ten members. After land for a church and cemetery around it was donated by the widow of Josiah Bell in 1851, the church building was completed in February 1852.[9]

The Texas Mission District was formed in 1838 with six Methodist circuit ministers assigned to it. That December Jesse Hord was assigned 150 miles of coastline on the Houston circuit, including all of Brazoria County. Reverend Hord held his first services at Columbia in March 1839. His assistant, Rev. Isaac L. G. Strickland, was ill much of the time but managed to organize a society of six members at Columbia before dying in Mrs. Bell's home in July 1839. The Methodist church in Columbia was officially organized with five charter members on March 7, 1840, and a substantial brick church was built in 1855.

In October 1844, Rev. George Washington Freeman of Missis-

---

9. This house of worship was destroyed in the 1900 storm. Bethel Presbyterian Church was moved to East Columbia in 1882, and a new building was erected there. When it was demolished by the hurricane of 1932, the Presbyterians purchased the vacant Armstrong Memorial Methodist Church built in 1840. Bethel Hall and classrooms were added in the 1950s. Today the historic Bethel Presbyterian Church, located at the corner of Main and Duval streets, serves both East and West Columbia.

sippi was elected Episcopal missionary bishop of Arkansas, Indian Territory, and Texas. In 1847 he organized St. Luke's parish at Columbia and St. John's at Brazoria. These parishes became two of the six charter members when the Diocese of Texas held its primary convention in 1849. For half a century, layman John Adriance conducted Episcopal services at Columbia, and Bishop Gregg appointed him as lay reader for both St. Luke's and St. John's.

Dr. Anson Jones, the last president of the Republic of Texas, practiced medicine in the Columbia area. After being appointed minister to the United States in June 1838, Jones was elected to fill out the Senate term of William H. Wharton, who accidentally killed himself in March 1839. Anson served as president pro tem of the Senate during the Fifth Congress, then returned to his old medical circuit — the plantations between Brazoria and Columbia — in April 1841. While Mrs. Jones stayed in the home of Mrs. Josiah Bell, Anson visited his former patients and purchased medical supplies for a new office, Shierburn's store building in Columbia, which he rented for twelve dollars a month. By the fall he had established a practice and taken lodgings for his family at Ammon Underwood's boardinghouse.

After being appointed secretary of state by President Houston, Dr. Jones took office in January 1842. While the president commuted between Houston and Galveston, Jones returned to Columbia for three weeks that April. There he busied himself seeing patients, posting books, and making out statements. In June he took another leave of absence and renewed his medical practice at Columbia. It was not until November 1842 that he returned to his government post at Washington. Dr. Jones left his wife Mary and son Sam at Dr. Phelps' plantation and his medical practice in charge of Dr. D. C. Gilmore.

Morgan R. Smith, a native of New York City, went into the mercantile business with Thomas J. Pilgrim at Columbia in 1838. When Pilgrim moved to Gonzales the next year, Smith and John Adriance established the mercantile firm of Smith and Adriance. The partners sold family and plantation supplies in exchange for cotton, and they extended credit to settlements west of the Trinity River. The firm used caravan trains to transport commodities to and from Matamoros, then shipped these goods to Cuba, New Orleans, and European ports. Smith carried stock of $500,000, and Adriance had daily cash receipts totaling as much as $5,000 in addition to credit sales.

In 1842 the partners introduced the use of "cotton floaters" to transport cotton bales on the Brazos. These gum-elastic floating bags were made of stout linen sheeting folds. Fifty of these floaters could carry 100 bales of cotton on six inches of water.

From 1841 until 1847, the two merchants and financiers were also joint owners of Waldeck plantation, one of the largest sugar plantations in Texas. Waldeck was located on the old Lake Road near West Columbia and joined the Patton place on the north. It was named for Count Joseph Boos Waldeck, who came to Texas in 1842 representing some German nobles (the Adelsverein) wanting to invest in Texas land. The count visited the plantation as the guest of Smith, but did not purchase it.

In 1842, Morgan Smith began to accept security other than cotton, thus adding slaves, work animals, acreage, and equipment to Waldeck. After dissolving his partnership with Adriance in 1845, Morgan purchased John's interest in the Waldeck property two years later. In 1849 Smith installed the latest equipment at Waldeck. His sugar mill, the finest in Texas, was a huge, brick, castle-like structure with a double set of sugar kettles. The $50,000 refinery produced white cut loaf sugar and cubes. A nearby ravine was made into an immense cement reservoir holding water for the sugar mill and refinery. Plantation slave cabins, barns, cribs, and a church were all made of brick. Smith's total investment in Waldeck plantation was $114,000, with an annual sugar crop worth $70,000. In 1852 he was the second greatest sugar producer in Brazoria County with 520 hogsheads, or 521,000 pounds.

In 1853 Smith married Elizabeth B. Brower in Brooklyn, New York, and brought his bride home to a fine brick mansion surrounded by a park containing $25,000 worth of statuary. When the Civil War erupted, Morgan sold Waldeck to Col. Hamilton Bass at a loss and moved to Boston, Massachusetts, where he later committed suicide. (In 1926 the old Waldeck plantation was purchased for its oil potential by the Texas Company and leased for grazing cattle.)

In the early 1840s, John Adriance promoted a plan to make Columbia the eastern terminal of a railroad running to the Pacific coast by way of San Antonio. After buying up all the land between Josiah Bell's two original towns, Adriance sent Horace Cone to France to obtain a multimillion-dollar loan for the project. The plan collapsed, however, when Cone suddenly died after returning to Texas. Adriance's dream became a reality years later when the Southern Pacific railroad built such a line west from Harrisburg.

Columbia (formerly Marion) became the home of a newspaper on

October 20, 1842, when Samuel J. Durnett published the first issue of *The Planter's Gazette,* a weekly paper devoted to covering the county's agricultural interests. The yearly cash price for the paper was five dollars in advance (later reduced to four dollars) and the credit price was seven dollars due at the end of the year. On June 17, 1843, Durnett changed the paper's name to *The Planter* and began to devote extensive space to the steamboat traffic on the lower and middle Brazos River.

On December 2, 1843, *The Planter* reported the sinking of the sidewheeler *Mustang,* the first steamboat to ascend the Brazos to Washington twelve months earlier. Overloaded with cotton, the *Mustang* sank when her uncaulked seams burst at Jones Wharf a few miles above San Felipe. A week later *The Planter* reported that the steamer *Lady Byron* had departed for Washington with 900 barrels of freight. Between 1842 and 1852, the sister ships *Brazos* and *Washington* brought down 1,200 bales of cotton from old Washington to Velasco.

Due to the threat of renewed hostility with Mexico, *The Planter* announced the organization of the Columbia Minute Men on August 23, 1844. Men were to sign up at the newspaper office or the Smith and Adriance store. When the volunteers paraded for drill on September 14, James C. Wilson was elected captain and James H. Bell the first lieutenant. Two of the more prominent minutemen were John Adriance and Ammon Underwood.

In October 1844, John Adriance was elected mayor of West Columbia. The next month Dr. Anson Jones, a former boarder with Ammon Underwood, took office as president of the Republic of Texas. In August and September of 1845, *The Planter* advertised the opening of the fall term for two schools, the Columbia Institute and the Columbia Female Seminary. In August of that year, a meeting was held by the Association of Columbia for the Preservation of Temperance. The meeting was presided over by President J. Wilson Copes; among the new members were Ammon Underwood and John Adriance.

When the Mexican War began in April 1846, Brazoria County provided a mounted volunteer company led by Capt. S. L. Ballowe and Lt. William Reese. After being given a gala send-off and silk flag by the ladies of Columbia, the unit aided Col. William Childs in taking Independence Hill during the successful Monterrey campaign.

Two of the most historic homes gracing East Columbia's Main Street were built during this period. In 1837, Dr. Mason Locke

Weems II brought his wife and son to Texas. [10] When their ship attempted to dock at Matagorda, it was fired on by local residents who mistook the vessel for one of Jean Lafitte's marauding pirate ships. Dr. Weems managed to retrieve one of the cannon balls, and it is still in the family's possession today.

The Weems family first settled near present New Gulf, then built a house in East Columbia about 1839. This "Doctors' House" was still standing in 1991 and contained several of the original fireplaces. The house was home to three generations of doctors, and the ground floor was used as one of the first hospitals in the area. (The last family member to live there was Mrs. Weems Craig. The house then stood vacant for twelve years before her daughter, Frances Ann Freeman, sold the place, not including the original furnishings, to Everett and Bonnie Maynard of Katy, Texas, in 1988.)

Nearby is a house known today as the Aldridge-Smith house. It was built between 1837 and 1841 by William Aldridge, a prosperous planter and landowner. In 1853 the entire Dance family moved to Bra-

---

10. His father, "Parson" Weems, won fame and fortune as George Washington's first — and most popular — biographer. Mason Locke Weems was born on October 11, 1759, in Anne Arundel County, Maryland. As a young man he traveled to England to train in an Anglican seminary. In 1784, Reverend Weems was appointed rector of All Hallows Church near his Maryland home. He served two other Episcopal parishes before leaving the ministry in 1794.

For the rest of his life, Parson Weems was a book peddler and author. He was first employed as the southern agent for Mathew Carey, a prominent Philadelphia publisher who founded the firm of Carey and Lea in 1785. His Jersey wagon loaded with books, the parson preached and vended his wares at court days all over the rural South.

Reverend Weems wrote a little book titled *The Life and Memorable Actions of George Washington* in 1800, shortly after the general's death. When he wrote the fifth edition in 1806, Mason added the famous legend of the cherry tree along with other "new and valuable anecdotes" about Washington's youth. In this edition, Weems tells the reader of little George cutting down a beautiful cherry tree with his new hatchet. When his father demanded the name of the culprit the next morning, the six-year-old lad bravely cried out, "I can't tell a lie, Pa; you know I can't tell a lie. I did cut it with my hatchet."

In his book Parson Weems also exalted Washington's other private virtues —veneration of God and religion, patriotism, magnanimity, industry, temperance and sobriety, and justice — and thus created the image of America's first national hero. Mason's pen transformed the country's first president into a pure republican, a moral example and demigod in the public mind. The Weems life of Washington has gone through eighty-two editions, the last appearing in 1927.

Parson Weems also wrote biographies of Benjamin Franklin, William Penn, and Francis Marion; they, too, are really moral tracts. The bookseller-author died in 1825 at "Bel Air," his substantial home in Dumfries, Virginia.

zoria County from Green County, Alabama, and purchased 450 acres in the Cedar Brake section of the county. In 1858 brothers John H., George P., and David E. Dance purchased the two-story Aldridge house. In February of that year, the Dances paid $400 for lots 29, 33, and the lower half of lot 28 directly across the street and built a machine shop there. Their shop housed a large boiler and steam engine along with a forge, presses, drills, and lathes. J. H. Dance & Co. cut patterns for metal pieces, built grist mills and cotton presses, and made coffins.

The Dance house was later sold to Travis L. Smith, the organizer of the Columbia Transportation Company. In 1917 his son, T. M. Smith, purchased the home and added huge, white columns and a small balcony to the mansion. (T. M. Smith, Jr., moved into the home in 1965 and his widow still lived there as the 1990s opened.)

In 1846, Columbus Patton built a large, rectangular-shaped brick sugar processing house with eight-foot walls and a double set of kettles across Varner Creek from his home. Next to the sugar house was a bricked underground cistern to store water used in making cane sugar. Some 150 yards to the north were four brick slave cabins with wooden floors, each one a duplex in design with a fireplace at one end. In 1849 Patton produced 275,000 pounds of sugar and 22,000 gallons of molasses, ranking him as the fifth greatest sugar producer in Brazoria County. His last good year on the plantation would be 1852, as he ranked fourteenth among county sugar producers.

In November 1854, Columbus Patton was declared insane by a duly constituted court in Brazoria County and placed in the Lunatic Asylum of South Carolina. At the time, Dr. J. C. Davis was treating him for "aurarosis" or "amarosis," a disease involving a tumor or disintegration of the optic nerve or brain and which was said to have brought on his insanity. John Adriance was named administrator of the Patton estate and placed in charge of running the plantation. On September 29, 1856, Patton died of typhoid dysentery at the asylum. In a controversial will dated June 1, 1853, he left the bulk of his estate to his nine-year-old niece, Mary Hester Aldridge. The will was litigated by the rest of the Patton family, who claimed that he was insane when he wrote it and that the slave Rachel had prejudiced him against the family and extorted the will from him.[11]

11. In the Patton will, Rachel was given $100 a year and was allowed to live wherever she chose. Columbus also instructed that $5,000 be invested at ten percent per annum, with the proceeds given to "my Dutch boy Henry Patton" until the principal was

In 1849, two Danish immigrants, Henrich Adolphus Jansen and his wife Maria, settled in Columbia. Three years later this craftsman built a workshop and became renowned for building fine furniture for the residents of East and West Columbia. Some of his pieces can be seen today, including a beautiful cedar canopy bed in the east bedroom of the Varner-Hogg plantation house and some cedar bedroom furniture in the Underwood house. During the Civil War, Jansen fought with Hood's Texas Brigade.

By the 1850s there were forty-six plantations in Brazoria County. Nineteen produced sugar, sixteen grew cotton, and three combined the two crops. According to the 1840 census of the Republic of Texas, only Red River County in East Texas had more slaves than Brazoria County, 1,872 to 1,316. In that year the last shipment of slaves illegally imported into the United States arrived at the mouth of the San Bernard River. Among those slaves smuggled in from Cuba was Ned Thompson, who had been taken prisoner after his tribe was defeated in battle and purchased by an African slave trader. When Ned was in his nineties and living near East Columbia, he was interviewed by Joseph P. Underwood in 1913. At the time, Ned could still speak his native African dialect and was described by Underwood as being "an interesting man, dignified, polite, well preserved and happy."

On September 1, 1856, Brazoria County planters and Houston merchants obtained a charter for the Houston Tap and Brazoria Railway Company. John Adriance was among the active promoters of this new rail line formed to link Houston and Columbia. The name "Houston Tap" originated when the city built a seven-mile track to Richmond to connect with the Buffalo Bayou, Brazos and Colorado, tap-

---

paid.

Rachel was a slave who had been with the family since 1833. When Columbus's mother died and his sister left home, Rachel assumed the role of mistress of the house and his concubine. She wore fine clothes, had charge of the house and premises, and sat and talked with Patton as an equal. The other slaves had to call her "Miss Rachel." The intimate relationship between master and slave was known in Columbia as early as 1844. Henry Patton is now known locally as the illegitimate son of Rachel and Columbus, who referred to him as an adopted or foster son born in Germany. Whatever his roots, Henry disappeared from the records about 1870. After the death of Columbus, Rachel became a dependent of the estate and moved to Cincinnati about 1860, only to return to Brazoria County after the Civil War. In the 1880 census, she was listed as Rachel Patton, black, widowed, age sixty, and born in Kentucky.

In April 1857, the Patton family survivors agreed to make a partial settlement of the estate, with the undivided interest managed by John Adriance. However, the two special requests of Columbus Patton regarding Rachel and Henry were honored.

ping that route at Pierce Junction. Brazoria County planters later purchased the Houston Tap road for $72,000, and track work was started from Pierce Junction to the east bank of the Brazos at Columbia, a distance of fifty miles. Half the road was completed by June 1857, with planters providing free slave labor and live oak lumber for ties and bridges, thus cutting the construction cost to $9,950 a mile, only one-half the cost of the Houston Tap. Equipment included two engines, a passenger coach, seven boxcars, and eighteen platform freight cars. Known locally as the Columbia Tap or "Sugar Road," the new railroad made its first run from Columbia to Houston in late 1859. During the Civil War its tracks furnished steel for the Dance revolvers, and the line was abandoned due to unsafe wooden rails.

When war came the Confederacy received staunch support in Brazoria County. On February 11, 1861, secession was approved by seventy-six percent of Texas voters. In Brazoria County the only two negative votes were cast by the sons of Josiah Bell, Thaddeus C. and James Hall. Sixty men from the county joined Company B of Terry's Texas Rangers in September 1861. Known officially as the 8th Texas Cavalry Regiment, this famed unit of 1,170 men was commanded by Col. Benjamin F. Terry. Of the thirteen counties in Company B, Brazoria County furnished fifty-nine percent of the men and all of the officers, including Capt. John A. Wharton.

The Columbia Blues, 101 men led by Capt. S. W. Perkins, were sworn into Confederate service on October 5, 1861, at the warehouse of John Adriance, who served as a deputy for the commissary department. Although not actually enrolled in the army, the Alamo Guards were a home guard of patriotic boys led by Capt. Orlando Phelps. In 1864, John W. Brooks of Columbia served as the Confederate tax collector for Brazoria County (District 41).

During the war, brothers James H., George P., David E., and Isaac Dance were detailed to their own company to perform contract work for the Confederacy. After initially finishing and mounting cannons, the firm of J. H. Dance and Brothers decided to convert their machine shop into a handgun factory in the winter of 1861–62.

On May 2, 1862, George Dance wrote a letter to Texas Governor Francis Lubbock requesting a loan of up to $5,000 to purchase equipment for the manufacture of army revolvers. The basic patterns for the Dance six-shot revolver were the .44-caliber Colt 1848 Dragoon and the .36-caliber Colt 1851 Navy model. On October 2, 1862, the

Dance brothers sold their first eleven six-shot pistols to the Ordnance Office of the San Antonio Arsenal.

Soon after Anderson and Samuel Park were detailed to the Columbia "pistol factory" in March 1863, five enlisted men from Jacob Brown's regiment were added to the work force. On September 12, 1863, the partnership of Dance and Park received Special Order No. 190 for 100 pattern Colt six-shooters for Graham's Rangers, the personal bodyguards of Maj. Gen. John Bankhead ("Prince John") Magruder.

On November 2, 1863, Union General Nathaniel Banks began a sweep up the Texas coast at Brazos Santiago on the Rio Grande. Once he occupied Matagorda Island, Columbia became an inviting Union target. On December 10, the last Dance revolver was produced there, and the Dance brothers relocated further inland at Anderson in Grimes County.

The new Dance factory was on a tract of land two miles north of Anderson. Forty-six pistols were produced there by June 1864. The last shipment was sent to Houston in April 1865, and revolver making ended the next month. At that time George and David Dance, along with A. R. and Jessie W. Park, returned to their prewar trades at Columbia.

During the Civil War, the Dances produced 365 revolvers for Confederate cavalry in the western theater. In the years that followed, these scarce handguns were highly prized for their superior quality. When Texas desperado Bill Longley, the killer of thirty-one men, was arrested at De Soto Parish, Louisiana, in May 1877, he was armed with a .44-caliber Dance revolver.

The Dance factory in Columbia converted from weapons production to the making of fine furniture and beds after the war. The factory operated continually until the buildings were destroyed in the 1900 storm. Members of the Dance family continued to live in the fine home across the street until 1917. Today a state historical marker locates the site of the Dance factory; only the factory forge remains hidden in the background scrub.

On Washington's Birthday in 1863, the women of East Columbia put on a tableau and concert to raise funds for the Confederate wounded. Merchant Ammon Underwood wrote the script and served as both narrator and master of ceremonies. As a "fair lady" appeared on stage to represent each Confederate state, Underwood described its contribution to the Southern cause.

Ammon Underwood lost much of his fortune in the war since his investments were mainly in cotton. His son Joe joined the Confederate army as a private at age seventeen. Writing to Joe on July 3, 1864, Ammon said in part:

> . . . I have paid the government all the confiscated debt which they would take of me amounting to $30,000. We have but few goods on hand and unless we get them by Borden's train from the Rio Grande, shall probably close out what we have and discontinue business until after the war. All blockade running out and into this river seems to be effectively ended . . . There are now seven schooners laying up here not thinking of getting out; a number of them having taken their cargoes of cotton out of them . . .

Joe Underwood came home from the war on May 31, 1865. Although Brazoria County had been spared invasion and physical damage, he noted in his journal that everyone seemed "despondent and disheartened." In Joe's journal entry for July 1, 1865, he noted

> . . . the arrival of our conquerors commanded by Maj. Gen. [Gordon] Granger, to take possession of the State of Texas. He assumed command . . . on the 19th day of June. And on that day he issued his order liberating the slaves. He advised them to remain with their masters and informed them that they will not be supported by the government.
>
> Some of the slaves are leaving, but the majority of them are quietly remaining at home. Father informed his negroes, that are in town, of their freedom. They did not seem to rejoice over the information . . . None of our negroes have left us yet. [12]

---

12. When Ammon Underwood died in 1887, his oldest son, Joseph P., inherited the mercantile business and moved into the Underwood house with his family. In 1922, he could boast of the oldest business in Texas run continuously by the same family at the same location. Joseph's children lived in the Underwood house until 1958, when it was finally vacated.

As the Brazos River has caved in, this historic home has been moved three times, although always on the same lot. Shortly after the Civil War, the family discovered a wide crack running from the river to under the house. The resourceful Ammon promptly mustered all his plantation hands, who moved the home back a full width of the Brazos. Just before 1900, the river bank crumbled again, and the house was relocated and divided, with half of it being placed on an adjoining lot. It was this section that was destroyed in the 1900 storm. The remaining half was altered to face the street with an ell and kitchen wing added to the rear. During World War II, the Underwood house was moved to its present site almost on Main Street (now County Road 703).

Although it is just a remnant of the original place built in 1835, most of the home

After the war an ex-slave named Charlie Brown purchased 900 acres of the Cedar Brake plantation from the Dances. After marrying Isabelle, a young slave girl of the Dance family, Charlie built a two-story house with double galleries on the west end of Main Street in West Columbia. Eventually he owned 3,000 acres in the Cedar Bayou area and another 200 acres near town. When Charlie Brown died on December 31, 1920, at the age of ninety, the *Houston Post* referred to him as the wealthiest Negro in Texas.

In February 1869, the Houston Tap and Brazoria railroad was purchased by W. J. Hutchins of Houston. The new service consisted of one light passenger car pulled by mules with the trip from Columbia to Houston taking two days. Passengers carried huge baskets of food and were allowed to hunt and pick berries along the track while the train waited. In August 1870, the state legislature authorized the governor to sell the road to the highest bidder to satisfy a debt, some $402,000 the road had earlier borrowed from the State School Fund to buy rails.

In July 1871, the line was bought at public sale by Masterson and Wagley of Houston for $130,000. They sold the road to the International and Great Northern Railroad Company in December 1872. The new owner provided an engine and a mixed passenger and freight train. In 1924 the old Columbia Tap became a part of the Missouri Pacific system. Service on the historic line was discontinued in 1956.

---

material is original, including the hand-hewn cedar logs and studs that frame it and the whole cedar trunks spanning the ceilings. The furniture in the house includes a parlor rocker Catherine Carson brought to Texas in a covered wagon in 1824, some cedar bedroom furniture made by the Jansen family of craftsmen, and Ammon Underwood's tilt-top chess table and carved wooden chessmen. The Underwood house is among the oldest frame houses still standing in Texas.

Catherine Munson Foster, an area historian and the great-granddaughter of Ammon Underwood, was born in East Columbia and now lives in Angleton. When she and her brothers and sisters inherited the Underwood house, they generously donated the place to the First Capitol Historical Foundation of West Columbia, an area historical preservation group. The house is now vacant.

Behind it is the Sweeny-Waddy log cabin, built about 1850 and moved from the old plantation of John Sweeny, Sr., in western Brazoria County. This cabin was home to slaves Mark and Larkin Waddy, who continued to live there after their emancipation. It was occupied by the Waddy family until 1953; George S. Waddy was the last person to live there. The log cabin has been purchased and restored by the First Capitol group to resemble an early Texas kitchen.

Today arrangements to tour both the Underwood house and the Sweeney-Waddy log cabin can be made through the West Columbia Chamber of Commerce.

In June 1869, estate administrator John Adriance offered the 4,200-acre Patton plantation for sale, including 700 acres cleared and fenced, a two-story brick house, tenant houses, stables, a gin house and press, a sawmill, and a "brick sugar house with 1st class mill & engine." A month later it was purchased for $47,000 by John Q. Jackson, the son of a prominent county planter, and his wife, Patton heir Mary Hester Aldridge Jackson. The couple promptly sold the place to W. J. Hutchins and William R. Baker for $50,000. Hutchins, a Houston banker, merchant, railroader and former mayor, never lived there but owned the plantation for three years as part of his real estate empire.

Hutchins sold the Patton place to Moses Taylor, a New York banker and trustee for the Brazos Internal Improvement and Navigation Company, in October 1872. Convicts were put to work there making bricks and growing sugar in 1874 and 1875. They were leased for their labor by private companies who contracted to operate the Texas prison system from 1868 to 1882.

The plantation was sold again on March 31, 1876, this time to the Texas Land Company, a speculator in state land grants made to the railroads. Beginning in 1879, the new owner leased the Patton place to Capt. Thomas B. Yale, who grew sugar cane, cotton, and corn and raised livestock. After 1882 Yale continued to manage it for the New York and Texas Land Company, a New York-based land speculation firm. The plantation umbrella shed, where the slaves washed and waited for meals, and the stables were lost through the years. The hurricane of September 1900 destroyed the sugar house, brick slave cabins, cotton gin, and mule barns.

In the late 1870s, Carry A. Nation, the soon-to-be-famous saloon smasher, ran a hotel at Columbia. Shortly after their marriage in 1877, David A. Nation and his new bride Carry left Holden, Missouri, pooled their resources, and purchased 1,700 acres of land on the San Bernard River. Carry's first husband, Dr. Charles Gloyd, had died of alcohol abuse, leaving the buxom young widow alone to raise their daughter Charlien. David Nation, an attorney and minister of the Christian Church, was nineteen years older than Carry. A widower with his own family, David wore a long, white beard and always dressed in a black, high-crowned hat and black suit.

The Nations moved to Brazoria County to learn to farm cotton. Soon, however, an irate neighbor threw David's plows and farm tools into the river, his horses died, and a farm hand ran off with the family cash. Nation then went to Columbia and loafed around town trying to drum up some legal work.

Meanwhile, back on the farm, Carry and Charlien, Mother Gloyd, and stepdaughter Lola subsisted on side meat (fat bacon), corn-meal, and sweet potatoes. All the women were sick when David Nation sent word that he needed money. Carry then led her faint charges into Columbia, where they were saved from starving by an Irish ditch-digger named Dunn. Unable to find a job, Mrs. Nation noticed the dilapidated, rat-infested Columbia Hotel and persuaded Dunn to loan her his total savings — three dollars and fifty cents — so that she could invest in it.

After spending $2.50 cleaning up the place and the other dollar on groceries, Carry went into business as the tenant-operator of the hotel, hoping to corner the transient trade. Working from before dawn to midnight, she did all the cooking, dining room work, washing, and laundering for the guests. For their part, Mrs. Gloyd and Lola cleaned and made beds, Charlien did the buying, and David dined with the guests or sat in the lobby, looking thoughtful and giving the place some class. The hotel's cash flow problem was so acute that when the Oastram family gave an advance of ten dollars, Charlien cried out, "Now we can buy a whole ham!"

The strain of running the hotel caused Carry to have memory lapses and disturbing dreams and "visions," but she still managed to find time to teach Sunday school at the Columbia Methodist church. In 1881 the Nation family moved to Richmond, where Carry took charge of a twenty-one-room hotel and six cottages.[13]

---

13. In the late 1890s, Carry Nation won national fame as a prohibitionist after wrecking some Kansas saloons with a hardware store hatchet. After her first arrest in Wichita, she was regularly jailed on charges of common assault (Carry called the judge "Your Dishonor") and left a trail of smashed liquor bottles, mirrors, and windows in a succession of saloon raids. Armed with only her little hatchet, Mrs. Nation drove burly men from beer joints, challenged bartenders to step around and fight, and once threw a giant cash register out into the street. Amazingly, she was never shot.

Carry considered herself an instrument of God singled out to free the country of alcohol. Her weekly newspaper was called *The Smasher's Mail*. In her heyday, British feminists fought to attend her meetings, and one headline stated that "Mrs. Nation Carries Glasgow by Storm." She was even invited to lecture to Yale University undergraduates in 1902.

This disturbed crusader died on June 2, 1911, at Leavenworth, Kansas, and was buried in an unmarked grave beside her mother in Belton, Missouri. Two years later, some supporters raised funds for a granite shaft which bears these words:

CARRY A. NATION

The 1870s brought new economic development to the area. On March 1, 1871, a countywide meeting was held in Columbia which resulted in an association formed "to aid and encourage emigration." Ammon Underwood was elected president, and John Adriance was on the executive committee.[14] That year a nineteen-year-old Virginian, Travis L. Smith, arrived from New Orleans by water to clerk in the Columbia mercantile business of his uncle, John W. Brooks, and his two older brothers. Blessed with a brilliant, mathematical mind, Travis worked for salary a few years, then acquired the local ferry and went into the mercantile business with his brother, John G.

In the late 1880s, Travis purchased the Dance house and organized the Columbia Transportation Company along with brother John and brother-in-law Branch T. Masterson. The company owned a fleet of seven steamboats — the *White Water, Christie, Emily P., Alice Blair, Hiawatha, Mascot,* and *Justine* — and exercised a virtual monopoly on the lower Brazos between 1888 and 1895.

In December 1891, the company purchased the passenger steamer *Alice Blair* in Missouri. At the time she was the finest looking boat on the Brazos and was fitted for twenty cabin passengers and 200 deck passengers. The steamer was equipped with an electric search light which allowed for safe operations after dark. Initially, the *Alice Blair* and the *White Water,* a slow-moving sternwheeler built for hauling cotton, alternated on the weekly round-trip from Columbia to Galveston. Early in 1892 the *Alice Blair* began to make daily trips from Houston to the new town of La Porte. The boat also operated on the Sabine and Trinity rivers in the spring months before returning to the Brazos in 1893. After being driven hard aground in Christmas Bay on December 15, the *Alice Blair* was used in the cotton season of 1894, then was retired and dismantled at the company landing near Columbia.

Faithful to the Cause of Prohibition
"She Hath Done What She Could."

In 1987, East Columbia's newest and ninth state historical marker was dedicated on the site of the Old Columbia Hotel, located at the intersection of Front and Austin streets (now County Road 300E).

14. Before coming to Texas, Adriance had married Lydia Cook of New York. After her death in 1871, John married her sister, Mrs. D. E. Nash. He was the father of three children. In his twilight years, Adriance had an active role in the affairs of the Agricultural and Mechanical College of Texas and Prairie View College. He was also the Grand High Priest of the Texas Royal Arch Masons. John Adriance died in Galveston on December 10, 1903.

The *Hiawatha*, the last and most beautiful sternwheeler owned by the company, was built in Marietta, Ohio, in 1890, then sold while brand new to some St. Louis operators. After being purchased there by Branch T. Masterson, the vessel arrived on the Brazos in late November 1891. It was immediately put into service carrying 100 to 150 land investors daily from Columbia to the new deepwater boom port of Velasco.

This luxurious steamboat was 140 feet long, thirty feet wide, and was driven by two immense steam engines; the cylinders were nine feet long and seventeen inches in bore. It had two tall smokestacks, a brilliant electric search light that made the dark countryside appear like morning, and two large whistles that could be heard for eight or ten miles. The last word in passenger comfort, the *Hiawatha* offered the accommodations of a first-class hotel, including forty staterooms with upper and lower berths like Pullman beds on the sides. The upper deck Grand Saloon was a hundred feet long with a red-carpeted floor and multicolored, stain-glassed skylights. Near the center were two huge dining tables with a piano in the rear. Passengers could dance to the music of a seventeen-piece orchestra.

The *Hiawatha* also carried freight and could fit 1,500 bales of cotton on her broad decks; only the pilot house and smokestacks were visible above the piled cotton on the sides. Making weekly round-trips from Columbia to Galveston hauling cotton and cotton seed, on the return trip the steamer brought cargo for the general country stores, including sides of bacon packed in large wooden boxes and sugar, flour, and crackers in wooden barrels. These hefty loads were carried up the Brazos bank by black deck hands.

The *Hiawatha* was the swiftest boat on the river. With Capt. Andrew McFarland at the wheel, the paddlewheeler set a new Brazos speed record of eighteen miles per hour and once tried to beat a passing oyster boat through the cut near Red Fish Bar.

Once a short railroad connecting with the International and Great Northern at Anchor was built to Velasco, this rail link from Houston eliminated travel by boats. The *Hiawatha* was thus left idle in the slack summer months and Captain McFarland was transferred to the *Alice Blair* in 1895. By then Velasco had become a fashionable summer resort with a new hotel booked to capacity.

In July 1895, Capt. Travis Smith invited forty friends to join his family on the *Hiawatha* for two weeks on the beach. For this summer excursion, Smith took along two cows for fresh milk and butter, a surrey and team of horses, two servants, and a cook. The Brazos had been on a big rise, but the water level was falling fast when the steamboat returned to Columbia and docked near the Smith store. Shortly after she was moored on August 5, 1895, a grinding thump and the gurgle of water were heard in the hold at midnight. The *Hiawatha* had settled on a huge oak stump which had ripped a gaping hole in her bottom. After the boat careened, turned on her side, and sank, the company managed to sink barges on both sides with a connecting chain slung beneath her hull. When the barges were pumped out, the steamer rose with them, and its fittings and engines were swung ashore. At that critical point the securing chain snapped, the ship sank again, and no further attempts were made to refloat her. Today the bell of the sunken *Hiawatha* is owned by Randolph Smith of Sweeny.

Travis Smith also suffered lost tonnage and idled boats when the boll weevil came after the 1900 storm and destroyed cotton growing in the Columbia area. His business was almost destroyed, but Smith recouped his transportation losses and made another fortune through oil discoveries on his property before his death on September 25, 1927.

On May 23, 1901, former Texas governor James S. "Jim" Hogg purchased the historic Patton property for $30,000 in cash. Hogg was born on a plantation near Rusk and lost both parents before he was thirteen. He first heard of the old plantation when he was eighteen, while living with and working for Martin Varner's daughter and her husband, C. F. "Chris" Haines, in southern Wood County. Chris, the founder of Hainesville, hired Jim Hogg to help at his cotton ginhouse. He made Hogg one of the household and gave him access to their library. The ambitious orphan went on to become a typesetter, editor, lawyer, Texas attorney general, and the first native-born governor of the state. While serving in that post from 1891 to 1895, Governor Hogg was responsible for creating the Texas Railroad Commission.

After retiring from public life, Hogg began to speculate in oil lands and was convinced that oil in quantities rivaling Spindletop lay beneath the Patton plantation fields. Even before his wife Sallie died of tuberculosis in 1895, Hogg had dreamed of owning a big country home. "The Varner," as he called it, was to be a model for progressive farming and a "home place" during holidays and summer vacations for his four motherless children — Will, Ima, Mike, and Tom.

In 1902 the Hogg family first gathered at Varner for Christmas. The governor moved his Austin furnishings there and amused himself with a favorite hobby, horticulture, by growing a profusion of watermelons, peaches, tomatoes, beans, and squash in his Varner gardens. Ima, his only daughter, loved to ride horseback, to hunt duck and coon, and go fishing on the grounds. Following up on a hunch, Hogg drilled four oil wells on the place between 1901 and 1903, but with no success.

Governor Hogg's health began to fail in January 1905, after he was injured in a train accident and developed an abcess in the throat which put him to bed for two months. While en route to Battle Creek, Michigan, for treatment, he and Ima spent the night in Houston with his law partner, Frank C. Jones. Jim died there in his sleep of a heart attack on March 3, 1906, and was buried in Oakwood Cemetery in Austin. Convinced that there was oil on his property, the governor specified in his will that the family could not sell any land at West Columbia for at least fifteen years after his death. Ima was to receive two-thirds of the value of the Varner plantation property with Mike receiving the remaining one-third; Tom and Will were to share the mineral rights.

On January 4, 1918, the Tyndall-Wyoming Oil Company's Hogg #2 well came in near West Columbia. The field yielded 186,350 barrels in 1918 and jumped to 5,611,000 barrels the next year. Since the Hogg children owned most of the field, they became independently wealthy from oil. From the Varner main house, they could see row upon row of oil derricks beyond the fences. Hogg #3 produced 1,500 barrels a day. In 1920 Will Hogg wrote brother Tom and told him that their average monthly gross income from the oil was $225,000.

West Columbia's best well was the Texas Company's Abrams #1, completed July 20, 1920. In its first seventy-six days, it produced 1,275,000 barrels valued at $3,825,000. In its peak years, the West Columbia field produced 8,128,809 barrels in 1919; 10,563,150 barrels in 1920; 12,573,450 barrels in 1921; and 11,631,750 barrels in 1922.

During this boom period, the sleepy village of West Columbia mushroomed from three stores owned by W. C. Faickney, Zeno Gayle, and Ed Hagemeier to a bustling oilfield town. Almost overnight, makeshift shanties, poorly built homes, and boardwalks appeared. The Palace Cafe, owned by Jack Renfro, boasted of never closing its doors day or night for three years. The tidal wave of traffic on Main Street created mud so deep that a big barefoot black man rolled his pants above his knees and carried citizens across in his arms at ten cents a trip. The fare by wagon between East and West Columbia was $1.50, but when the mule team reached the Mud Hole, passengers had to alight and walk across, then board the empty wagon on the other side. When eighteen hardy souls wanted to build a Baptist church during the boom period, some local rowdies threatened them with bodily harm until a man on horseback, gun in hand, announced to all, "You fellows do the building and I will do the shooting if necessary."

After striking it rich from oil, Will and Mike Hogg undertook an extensive remodeling of the Varner main house and outbuildings in the spring of 1919. They replaced the second-floor rear gallery with a two-story veranda supported by six square white columns, reorienting the house to face the West Columbia road rather than Varner Creek. Permanent white stucco was applied to the antique brick exterior of the main house. The old dining room was enlarged, the original kitchen became part of the smokehouse and butler's pantry, and a new kitchen building was added with a new breezeway connecting it to the parlor of the main house. The Varner renovation project was completed in June 1920, at a cost of $40,974.28. For the next thirty-seven years, the house was reserved as a weekend and vacation resort for the Hogg family and guests.

Will Hogg also began to collect furniture and art and to buy antiques for the family home at Varner in 1920. During this period, four frame houses, a barn, and a four-bay garage were added to the plantation grounds by the Hogg family. Large groves of pecan trees were also added, some of them planted by the governor himself.

After Will died in 1930, Ima Hogg decided to repair and restore the old Varner home and give it to the State of Texas as a state park. Over a number of years, she furnished it with pieces dating from 1835 to 1850, along with Hogg family furniture and Governor Hogg's memorabilia. This was Ima's first effort at historic preservation, and she took a more personal interest in the park than her other collection projects at Winedale or Bayou Bend. Her extensive collection of historic furnishings at Varner concentrates on two styles then popular, Empire and Rococo Revival. "Miss Ima," as she was affectionately called, had two objectives in mind: to exhibit furniture available to an antebellum family of means and to commemorate such important state and national political figures as George Washington, Zachary Taylor, Sam Houston, and her father.

In December 1956, Ima Hogg donated the Varner house and fifty-three acres of land to the State Parks Board, reserving the use of the cottage nearest the main house for herself. On March 24, 1958, the 107th anniversary of Governor Hogg's birth, the Varner-Hogg State Historical Park was formally dedicated. In 1966, Miss Ima donated the furnishings collection, and her cottage passed to the State after her death in 1975. Today when visitors approach this beautiful park off FM 2852, they will see a personal family memento: twenty magnolia trees the Hoggs planted as a rectangular border for the front lawn.

The oil derricks which once dotted the West Columbia area are gone today. The town has a population (in 1991) of 5,000 and is best known for Columbia Lakes, an adjacent planned community and resort owned and operated by Tenneco until 1989.[15] It is an impressive symbol of a progressive town looking to the future, but West Columbia is also proud of its past. The capitol replica, the Varner-Hogg plantation, the Patton family cemetery, and the old Columbia cemetery remind visitors of the town's remarkable founders and rich heritage.

Two miles east off State Highway 35 is County Road 300E (formerly Austin Street), which leads only to East Columbia. Today this former bustling, wealthy port town lies hidden and obscure. Now a tiny, quiet residential settlement, it has no city government, stores, or schools. Remarkably, the community has more state historical markers (nine) than streets. The Bell's Landing marker is located where County Road 300E intersects Front Street; across from it is the old Columbia Hotel marker. Most of the scenic old homes are clustered together at one end of shady Main Street (now County Road 703), including Dr. Weems's house, the Underwood house, and the Aldridge-Smith house. Like her sister town to the west, East Columbia is a treasure trove of Texas history and offers a rare glimpse of the bygone Republic and plantation era.

---

15. On January 1, 1989, Jerry Moore, a shopping-center developer, purchased Columbia Lakes from Tenneco Realty. This 750-acre golf resort and conference center includes a lodge, complete conference facilities, eleven tennis courts, two bass lakes, and 325 beds. Moore acquired an additional 1,200 acres for expansion, including two more golf courses.

T. M. Smith, cadet at Texas A&M, 1901.

— Courtesy of Mrs. T. M. Smith, Jr.

Aldridge-Smith House, built between 1837 and 1841.
— Courtesy of Mrs. T. M. Smith, Jr.

The Hiawatha.
— Courtesy of Mrs. T. M. Smith, Jr.

The Alice Blair *docked at Front Street; second from left is the Columbia Hotel operated by Carry Nation.*

— Courtesy of Mrs. T. M. Smith, Jr.

Weems House, built about 1839.

— Photo by J. C. Hoke, Wharton, Texas;
courtesy Everett and Bonnie Maynard

Original fireplace in Weems House.
— Photo by J. C. Hoke, Wharton, Texas;
courtesy Everett and Bonnie Maynard

Carriage House of Weems House.
— Photo by J. C. Hoke, Wharton, Texas;
courtesy Everett and Bonnie Maynard

David E. Dance
— Taken by permission from the book A *Window To The Past:*
A *Pictorial History of Brazoria County, Texas* (1986)

Dance Gun and Machine Shop, destroyed in 1900 storm.
— Taken by permission from the Book A *Window To The Past:*
A *Pictorial History of Brazoria County, Texas* (1986)

Plat of East Columbia (Marion).
— Taken by permission from the Book *A Window To The Past: A Pictorial History of Brazoria County, Texas* (1986)

Ruins of structure where House of Representatives met when the capital was located at Columbia.
— Taken by permission from the Book *A Window To The Past: A Pictorial History of Brazoria County, Texas* (1986)

State Historical Survey Committee Marker, Bell's Landing.
— Photo by J. C. Hoke, Wharton, Texas

Orozimbo plantation, home of Dr. J. A. E. Phelps.
— Courtesy Mrs. Ruth Munson Smith, Angleton, Texas

Bethel Presbyterian Church, organized June 13, 1840. The land and original church were given by Mrs. J. H. Bell. The new church was acquired in 1932.
— Photo by J. C. Hoke, Wharton, Texas

Ammon Underwood House. First portion built in 1835; enlarged in 1838–1839.
— Photo by J. C. Hoke, Wharton, Texas

State Historical Survey Committee Marker, Ammon Underwood. Columbia Cemetery.
— Photo by J. C. Hoke, Wharton, Texas

Varner-Patton-Hogg House, 1835.
— Photo by J. C. Hoke, Wharton, Texas

Patton Family Cemetery, Varner-Hogg State Historical Park.
— Photo by J. C. Hoke, Wharton, Texas

Site of Sugar House built by C. R. Patton in 1846; destroyed in 1900 storm.
— Photo by J. C. Hoke, Wharton, Texas

Replica of first capitol, Republic of Texas. Built at site in 1976–1977; original destroyed in 1900 storm.

— Photo by J. C. Hoke, Wharton, Texas

II

Egypt:
Crossroads Town of Plenty

Egypt, the oldest town in Wharton County, is located some ten miles northwest of Wharton. The fertile alluvial plains of the Colorado River inspired its biblical name.

The planter class of Egypt produced a remarkable number of leaders in the 1830s, including a signer of the Texas Declaration of Independence, a company commander at the Battle of San Jacinto, a pioneer sugar producer and refiner, and one of the earliest stagecoach operators in Texas. Egypt's founder and his slave mistress became unwitting parties to a famous lawsuit. The tiny crossroads settlement was also a headquarters for the Methodist missionary effort in the Republic era. Today only the antebellum plantation big house on the hill reminds the visitor of Egypt's bygone days of glory.

Egypt is rooted in a Mexican land grant made to John C. Clark on July 16, 1824. Clark was one of Stephen F. Austin's original "Old Three Hundred" colonists, and his league of land (4,428 acres) ran to the Colorado River. Born in South Carolina in 1798, Clark came to Texas in 1822 and joined a militia company led by Robert Kuykendall, another of Austin's first colonists whose league of land along Peach Creek was south of and adjacent to Clark's land. John soon had his first encounter with the fearsome Karankawa Indians, who roamed the area at the time. The incident was described by W. B. Dewees, a founder of Columbus, in a letter to a friend dated August 29, 1823:

> We have had one severe engagement with the Carancohua Indians. Three of our young men had been down the river in a canoe to secure

corn . . . The Carancohuas had come up country and camped at the
mouth of Skull Creek, about fifteen miles below our settlement.
They saw the young men as they returned with their canoe load of
corn, and lay in ambush for them; when they were sufficiently near,
fired upon them and killed two, a Mr. Loy [H. W. Law] and Mr.
Ally [John Alley]. Mr. Clark, the only one now remaining, leaped
into the river and endeavoured to save himself by swimming. By the
time he reached the shore, he had seven severe wounds from arrows.
He succeeded in escaping by crawling into a heavy cane brake . . . .

In July 1824, Clark, Kuykendall, and Alexander Jackson were involved in another Indian fight near Peach Creek.

Life was harsh for these early settlers. One such man, a Mr. Parker, lived on the west side of the Colorado. After suffering a leg
wound, it became infected and a terrible sore developed. For two
months Parker begged his neighbors to cut off the leg. Finally, four
friends agreed to amputate the limb. Each was assigned a part of the
operation: Tom Williams was to cut the flesh; Mr. Bostick would saw
the bone; Robert Kuykendall was to tie off the arteries and sew the
flesh back in place with a dull needle; Jesse Burnham would use his
suspenders and a stick as a tourniquet to slow the blood flow. All went
well until Kuykendall's hands began to shake; then Burnham had to
finish the sewing procedure. The rugged Parker survived the ordeal
and "rested easier" for a time before dying on the eleventh day.

In 1827 Clark cleared and planted fifteen acres in corn. A severe
drought struck the Texas Gulf Coast that year with the only significant
rain in present Wharton County falling on Clark's land. As news of his
good fortune spread, other Austin colonists looked to him for assistance and talked of "going down into Egypt for corn" (Genesis 42:2–
3). The name stuck and a small settlement called "Egypt" developed
near Clark's place at the intersection of the mail routes connecting
Richmond with Texana and Columbus with Matagorda.

In 1849 John Clark built a three-room brick house, and his holdings evolved into a large plantation worked by 116 slaves. A single
man who made only unkind remarks about his relatives, Clark had an
antisocial nature and seemed to be preoccupied with making money. In
1833 he purchased a comely mulatto named Sobrina, who was kept on
the plantation with his other slaves. Sobrina had three children —
Bishop, Lorinda, and Nancy — by her master, and they later brought
a famous lawsuit which established the validity of the common law
marriage in Texas.

Among the first settlers at Egypt was Eli Mercer, a prominent farmer and Baptist preacher's son from Amite County, Mississippi. His oldest daughter, sixteen-year-old Penelope, married a local surveyor and teacher, Gail Borden, Jr., in March 1828. After visiting his older brother Tom, the surveyor for Austin's colony, Borden returned to Mississippi and persuaded his father-in-law to join him in moving to Texas. Bringing his wife Ann Nancy, five children, and three slaves, Eli Mercer traveled by boat to Natchitoches, Louisiana, then came overland by wagon and arrived at Egypt on November 29, 1829. Since Penelope Borden was pregnant, she and her husband came later by boat, and their baby Mary was born on Galveston Island on Christmas Eve of 1829. After joining the Mercers at Egypt, Gail Borden lived there for a time and made a half-hearted attempt at farming and stockraising before turning to surveying. In early 1830 the future dairy king moved his family to San Felipe, which was nearer his land grant in present upper Fort Bend County.

Egypt was also known as Mercer's Crossing since Eli's land along the Colorado was one of only three sites to cross that river in Austin's colony. Mercer was the first settler to plant sugar cane in the area and to manufacture his own white sugar. With the help of two sons and a slave, he was cultivating enough cane fields to supply all of Egypt with sweetening by 1833. Mercer designed his own sugar mill, using live oak stumps as a rolling mill and large fleshpots as an evaporating battery. The article he produced was described as being similar to the "Mississippi alluvion, steeped in molasses," and Mercer sold it to his neighbors for a good price. The quality of this sugar was praised by Gail Borden in a November 1836 issue of *The Telegraph and Texas Register*. Mercer also started one of the first cotton gins in Texas on his plantation that year; little wonder that Rufus Burleson later described him as being "a prince among farmers."

Another prominent pioneer in the Egypt area was Maj. Andrew J. Northington. A native of Christian County, Kentucky, he was raised by wealthy parents who provided him with a good education. The surveyor was well read and a brilliant, witty speaker. After death claimed two wives, Northington decided to start a new life in Texas with his two children, Rachel Ann and Mentor. On April 29, 1831, he was granted a league and labor of land near the San Bernard River. Two years later, he took his family to "Buffalo Grove" plantation, their new Texas home. Rachel Ann served as his hostess and kept an open house, feeding and lodging a steady stream of travelers who were entertained by Andrew's humorous anecdotes. The major also saved the life of James L. McKenzie, one of his Egypt neighbors. When a storm hit while they were hunting, both men squatted against a tree until the rain passed. As McKenzie arose, a coiled rattlesnake bit the underpart of his thigh. After killing the snake, Northington scarified the wound and sucked out the blood and poison, leaving his hunting partner "suffering no serious inconvenience." In July 1835 Northington married Nancy George, a union that would produce four children.

In 1832 William Jones Elliott Heard bought land near Mercer's plantation in the Egypt area. Heard was born on August 16, 1801, near Knoxville, Tennessee, and was the oldest of ten children of Stephen Rhodes and Jemima Menefee Heard. William attended school in the same log cabin at Merryville where Sam Houston taught his mother and uncle, William Menefee, for a term. Finding that the land of central Tennessee was not productive enough to support his large family, Stephen Heard moved to near Tuscumbia, Alabama, when William was a boy. In 1824 young Heard married America Morton, daughter of Rev. Quinn Morton, a stout-framed and popular revivalist. Since Tuscumbia was staging area for Austin's Second Colony, a five-man committee including William Heard, William Menefee, George Sutherland, Jesse White, and Anthony Winston came to Texas in 1829 to look over the country. On February 19, 1830, George Sutherland signed a contract at Austin's headquarters town, San Felipe, which authorized eleven Alabama families to receive land in Texas.

On October 30, 1830, the Heards were among a caravan of families which left Alabama by land. On December 9 they reached their destination, a league of land on the left margin of the Navidad River seven miles above Texana. This league was granted to the recently widowed Jemima Heard on November 24 and was next to that of George Sutherland. The poor quality of the land and Indian problems caused William to be dissatisfied with his mother's location. After hearing of the more fertile lands of Egypt, he decided to inspect the area by horseback. Once Heard stood on that hill and gazed over the rich, alluvial plains of the Colorado River, he knew he had found his dream farm. In 1832 he purchased 2,222 acres of land from John Clark for fifty cents an acre, then moved the Heard family there the next year after selling their holdings in present Jackson County. Heard called his spread the Egypt plantation and grew sugar cane, cotton, and corn. Like his neighbor Eli Mercer, "Uncle Billy" had both a cotton gin and sugar mill on his place. He was also a breeder of fine saddle horses, and his

"Crescent 69" cattle brand was known throughout the region. During these early years, Heard sold 1,211 acres of his Egypt land to his uncle, William Menefee, a lawyer by trade who brought his wife, Agnes Sutherland, and their seven children to Texas as part of the Alabama Settlement in 1830.

Two Egypt residents played key roles in the political phase of the Texas Revolution. Eli Mercer served as a delegate from Mina (Bastrop) to the Conventions of 1832 and 1833 at San Felipe, gatherings which demanded political concessions — including separate statehood — from the Mexican government. William Menefee also attended both conventions as a delegate from the Lavaca district. Judge Menefee was a delegate from San Felipe to the Consultation of 1835, where he was appointed to a committee of twelve (one from each municipality) charged with preparing an address "setting forth to the world the causes that impelled us to take up arms and the object for which we fight." He also served as a member of the General Council of the provisional state government. As one of the two elected delegates from Colorado Municipality, Menefee signed the Texas Declaration of Independence at Washington-on-the-Brazos on March 2, 1836, then joined the civilian flight known as the "Runaway Scrape" and took his family to safety near the Louisiana border.

After Texas declared its independence from Mexico, and ad interim President David G. Burnet ordered the government moved to Harrisburg, Eli Mercer provided a wagon and team so that Gail Borden and Joseph Baker could haul their revolutionary printing press there. Before leaving Egypt, Mercer supplied the Texas army with beef and hid corn in the cane brakes so that his neighbors would have food and seed when peace came. In the Battle of San Jacinto, Mercer served as first sergeant of Company F, fighting alongside his seventeen-year-old son, Elijah, the second corporal of the company.

Major Northington was placed in charge of the women and children fleeing from the Egypt-San Bernard area. While he headed a train of wagons and crude sleds pulled by oxen, his fourteen-year-old son, Mentor, drove a supply wagon with Rachel Ann caring for the infant son of James McKenzie, who had just lost his wife. This forlorn train was only a short distance from the Texian and Mexican armies when the Battle of San Jacinto was fought; Rachel wrote that they "could hear the cannon fire and they were getting away fast." Upon hearing of the Texian victory the next day, April 22, 1836, the Northingtons returned to their San Bernard homestead. The McKenzie baby died from exposure and poor diet early that summer. Rachel married his father in January 1839.

When war came, William Heard joined the volunteer company of Capt. Thomas J. Rabb, his neighbor above Egypt. After Rabb left the Texas army to take his family to safety, Heard was elected captain of Company F, First Regiment of Texas Volunteers, on April 2, 1836. When he left home to join General Houston's retreating army at Gonzales, Heard left instructions for the women to put all the family jewelry and heirlooms in a trunk, then bury it in a fresh grave under a wooden cross in the front yard of his home (the trunk is displayed in the entrance hall of the Heard home today). The ruse fooled General Filisola and the invading Mexican army that came through Egypt in early April. They also failed to find the Heard family furniture hidden on the creek banks.

After joining the Texas army at Gonzales on February 28, 1836, Captain Heard wrote to his mother at Egypt, commenting that the country was in critical condition and that men had left there to go to the relief of the Alamo. He was obviously concerned about provisions for his family; the words "ground planted in corn" are still legible in the faded letter.

Once General Houston ordered a retreat from the Colorado River, Heard and Eli Mercer wrote a joint letter highly critical of their leader. The two noted that the men had been anxious to engage the outnumbered Mexican army of General Sesma there. Both asserted that Houston intended to take the road to the Trinity when his army arrived at a major crossroads. His dissatisfied men had arranged that if he did, the volunteers would call out for a new leader to take them to Harrisburg to meet the enemy. According to Heard and Mercer, it was advance knowledge of such a scheme that caused Houston to turn in that direction. When General Santa Anna and a division of Mexican cavalry reached San Felipe on April 7, Capt. Moseley Baker's company so resisted his crossing that the Mexicans turned down the Brazos River and camped at Cole's on the ninth and tenth. At that time Santa Anna sent a foraging party back to Egypt to pillage the fine Heard and Mercer plantations of provisions and sugar.

As commander of Company F during the Battle of San Jacinto, Captain Heard was involved in several important episodes. When General Cos arrived with 550 Mexican reinforcements on the morning of the battle, it was William Heard who reported that Deaf Smith said to Houston, "General, they're following in our tracks. Let me go cut down Vince's Bridge so they can't get any more help that way from the other Mexican armies." When Houston inspected the Texian battle line at 3:30 P.M., he was mounted on a white stallion named Saracen. Realizing what an obvious target he offered the Mexicans, Old Sam tried to swap horses with Captain Heard, who was riding a half-thoroughbred bay gelding. Heard rebuffed his leader by saying, "This old bay is a pet, General. I couldn't any more trade him off than I could a child." Once the Texians charged, Heard's company was among those attacking the area around the Mexican twelve-pound cannon, the Golden Standard. His men would fall to the ground when they thought it was about to be fired, then "sprint like bucks" before it could be reloaded. It was said that Heard's company fired their long rifles sixteen times; the same number of Mexican corpses were found near the captured artillery pieces.

Santa Anna's war chest of $12,000 was captured after the battle. Captain Heard contended that the booty was really much larger, about forty-five boxes with each containing $1,000 of "silvery money." He claimed that Commissary General John Forbes secreted and made off with much of the money for himself. According to Heard, the men of his F Company got $10.25 each as their share of the San Jacinto spoils, which was not bad pay for eighteen minutes' work. One member of Heard's company, Joel Robinson, was in the party of six who captured Santa Anna the morning after the battle.

Years later, Captain Heard revealed an interesting fact about the timing of the battle in a letter to Sidney Sherman. Writing from Egypt plantation on June 15, 1859, Uncle Billy recalled that there was a major difference of opinion as to when to attack at San Jacinto. When the Texas army was paraded out to fight at 3:30 P.M., Col. Edward Burleson polled all the company captains in his First Regiment. The majority of them, including Heard, wanted to wait until morning to attack so that their wounded would not have to suffer by being out in the night. However, with both General Houston and Colonel Sherman, leader of the Second Regiment, determined to go into battle that evening, the attack occurred at 4:00 P.M.

The end of the war brought new responsibilities to the men of Egypt. In February 1837 the Republic of Texas authorized the first elections for officials of the three districts of Colorado County. Eli Mercer and Gail Borden were elected justices of the peace in the Lower District. In 1838 Captain Heard was elected chief justice of Colorado County. From 1835 until 1841, Eli Mercer served as the first postmaster at Egypt. An 1835 mail route — one of the first in Texas — included San Felipe, Mercers, Texana, and Victoria, with mail service once every two weeks. The relative affluence of Mercer's customers is revealed in the following statistic: On January 8, 1840, the money return from the Egypt post office was $111.50, ten times higher than other towns of comparable size. In 1843 a new mail route was begun from Egypt to Victoria via Menefees (Jackson County).

From 1837 to 1839, the Egypt post office also served Post West Bernard, a major ordnance depot for the Republic of Texas Army. Founded soon after the mass furlough of troops in May and June of 1837, this wilderness military outpost was eight miles from Egypt. The handful of men on duty there had no permanent shelter and spent their time repairing the hundreds of damaged muskets and other artillery captured from the Mexican army at San Jacinto. The majority of these guns were .75-caliber India Pattern Brown Bess flintlock muskets, the standard arm of the British army until 1815, when the Mexican army purchased these outdated weapons. Once these guns were reconditioned, they were sent to the new armory at Houston. During its brief two-year history, Post West Bernard was a busy place: Of the 988 muskets owned by the Texas army in 1838, 653 of them were sent there after being listed as "out of order."[1]

Egypt residents played leading roles in several unsuccessful efforts to clear the Colorado River raft, a series of floating and sunken log and debris obstructions near the mouth of the river. By 1838 the head of the raft was twelve miles above Matagorda, and it was reported as being from three to eight miles in length. Because of this huge raft, keelboats such as the *David Crockett* that brought cotton downriver from Bastrop were forced to unload at the raft, then haul their cargo overland to Matagorda. On December 14, 1837, the Republic of Texas Congress incorporated the Colorado Navigation Company with its main office at Matagorda. The company was authorized to issue capital

---

1. This old military post was located west of Hungerford and near the West Bernard River. In 1981, Joe D. Hudgins, a rancher and avocational archaeologist, discovered the site when he found metal gun fragments in the plowed rows of a field. Since that time, more than 2,000 artifacts have been recovered by the Houston Archaeological Society, which surveyed the site and salvaged both metal and non-metal artifacts. The former were taken to the Department of Nautical Archaeology at Texas A&M University, where they were cleaned by electrolysis and treated to prevent further rusting. These artifacts were then photographed, identified, and catalogued. Permanent exhibits of these artifacts can be seen at the Wharton County Historical Museum and in the J. M. Hodges Learning Center at Wharton County Junior College, Wharton, Texas.

stock of $125,000 in shares of $100 each "for the purpose of clearing a channel susceptible of navigation by steamboats or other craft for the Colorado River." The company was allowed four years to open a channel permitting steamboats to pass fifty miles upstream; otherwise, the charter would be forfeited.

In 1838 the town of Columbus and the Egypt home of Eli Mercer were designated to receive subscriptions for stock in Colorado County. The three commissioners appointed to sell stock at Egypt were Thomas Rabb, William Heard, and Eli Mercer. On June 1, 1842, delegations from nearby counties met at Columbus, with Captain Heard representing Egypt. This committee estimated that the cost to clear the raft would be $30,000. The Colorado Navigation Company was rechartered in January 1844 and in September 1850, the final effort, with Eli Mercer among the three representatives from Wharton County. (The raft problem was finally solved between 1925 and 1930 when a dredging company cut a deep, wide channel along the east bank of the Colorado.)

Another Egypt resident, Judge William Menefee, achieved political prominence during the Republic era. In December 1836 President Houston appointed him the first chief justice of Colorado County. Menefee then represented Colorado District for five terms in the House of Representatives of the Republic, serving in the Second, Third, Fourth, Fifth, and Ninth Congress. Under terms of an Act of Congress passed at Houston on January 14, 1839, three commissioners were elected by the House and two by the Senate to choose a site for the capitol of Texas. The law specified that the site to be named Austin must be between the Trinity and the Colorado rivers and above the Old San Antonio Road. Judge Menefee was elected to the five-man commission, which chose a trading post on the Colorado called Waterloo, the capital site favored by President Lamar. He also carried out his duty as a citizen-soldier by taking part in the Vasquez Campaign of 1842.[2]

In June 1837 Andrew Northington sold his Buffalo Grove league to William Houston of Harrisburg for $4,000. Relocating near pres-

---

2. After Texas was annexed by the United States, Judge Menefee moved in 1846 from Egypt to Fayette County, where the town of Oso developed around his home. Menefee's son, John L., also lived there and used the initials "O.S.O." as his cattle brand. William Menefee represented Fayette County in the House of Representatives of the Fifth Legislature, serving from November 1853 until February 1854. The town of Oso died in 1873–1874 with the coming of the railroad to nearby Flatonia. Judge Menefee died on October 29, 1875, and was buried beside his wife Agnes in the Pine Springs Cemetery six miles from Flatonia. Their remains were reinterred in the State Cemetery at Austin in 1936.

ent Hungerford, Northington settled on the south side of West Bernard Creek on the trail leading to Richmond. The sandy creek crossing near his new home became known as the "Northington Crossing." In November 1837 he was among the signers petitioning the Texas Congress to create Fort Bend County. In July 1839, he established a stagecoach line route connecting Houston, Richmond, and Egypt. The stage left Houston at 7:00 A.M. every Friday and arrived at Richmond at 4:00 P.M., then departed Richmond at 7:00 A.M. and reached Egypt at 5:00 P.M. on Saturday. The fare was five dollars per person in Texas currency. Major Northington later extended his stage line to Texana and developed many of the early mail routes in Texas.

Even as his agricultural fortunes increased, Captain Heard responded to the call to perform militia duty. After the great Comanche raid to the Gulf Coast against Victoria and Linnville in August 1840, William Heard was among those taking part in the retaliatory Moore raid that October. Ninety volunteers led by Col. John H. Moore destroyed a Comanche camp on the upper Colorado, killed 128 men, women and children, and captured 500 horses. In September 1842, Gen. Adrian Woll and a Mexican army of 1,300 captured San Antonio for nine days and took fifty-three civilian prisoners, including the entire district court in session there. Captain Heard was among the 210 Texan volunteers under Matthew "Old Paint" Caldwell, who dealt a stinging defeat to Woll's forces in the Battle of Salado before expelling him from the city.

Deeply religious like his mother, Jemima, Heard made Egypt a focal point for the Methodist missionary effort in the Republic of Texas. In August 1835, William Barret Travis wrote the *New York Christian Advocate and Journal* to request a subscription and plead for five young Methodist circuit ministers in Texas. Three such preachers were sent to Texas to begin mission work in 1837. Their superintendent was Dr. Martin Ruter, president of Berea College in Kentucky. Dr. Ruter had moved to Egypt that year and used Captain Heard's home as headquarters in organizing the first Methodist mission west of the Trinity. In 1837 Dr. Ruter and Rev. J. W. Kinney organized a church in the Heard home and held the first Methodist services in Wharton County. Ruter dreamed of establishing the first Methodist college in Texas, but died at Washington-on-the-Brazos in May 1838 while recruiting students and soliciting money and land. In 1840 the Texas Congress granted a charter and donated four leagues of land for Rutersville College, which was established near LaGrange. Among its supporters were Captain Heard and William Menefee, who donated $100 and was named an "honorary trustee." The school had a peak enrollment of 194 students and lasted until 1859, when it was separated from the Methodist Conference and merged with the Texas Military Institution of Galveston under a new state charter.

On March 17, 1839, Methodist circuit riders Jesse Hord, I. L. G. Strickland, and Fowler organized a Bible Society for Colorado County at Egypt. Among the three vice-presidents of the society were Eli Mercer and William Heard. Reverend Hord made Egypt his headquarters and also taught school there until he retired for health reasons in 1848 and moved to Goliad. After volunteering for missionary work in Texas in October 1842, John Wesley DeVilbiss was assigned to the Egypt circuit, which included the area from Fayette County to Matagorda and the entire valleys of the Lavaca and Navidad rivers. In February 1845, Reverend DeVilbiss married one of William Menefee's daughters, Talitha Ann.

Homer S. Thrall, D.D., the noted Methodist minister and Texas historian, had his first circuit between Galveston and Matagorda in 1842, but later traveled over most of Texas by horseback and spent much of his time in Egypt. In his twilight years at San Antonio, 1892–93, Dr. Thrall wrote a series of newspaper and magazine articles, including a "Life of Reverend J. W. DeVilbiss." In writing of his co-worker, Thrall said:

> In the spring I was urgently solicited to attend a camp meeting in the Spanish springs camp ground on Bro. DeVilbiss' circuit . . . I copy from my private journal under date May 26, 1843: "Arrived on the Camp Ground, six miles below Egypt, to learn that the meeting was postponed on account of the incessant rains. I had ridden a great distance and swam rivers five times to reach it." At Egypt, Dr. DeVilbiss and myself met for the first time in Texas and had a most (interesting) interview. Then and there I formed acquaintance of some of the best men I ever met in my life: Capt. Heard, Judge Menefee, Col. Hodges, Dr. Sutherland, the father of A. H. Sutherland, Tom Read, the Mercers, etc. The Egypt Society had been organized by Dr. Ruther {sic} and was composed of as good material as they had in Texas.

Jemima Heard was a staunch Methodist, and a mother who heeded the admonition of Jesus to love all children. The youngest of her ten children, Stephen Rhodes, Jr., was born in August 1822, long before the family came to Texas. Jemima was an old lady when she

took in a baby boy named Lee McLaughlin. Shortly after the family
came to Egypt from Mississippi, Lee's mother died and the distressed
father decided to go home. Since the long trip was simply too much for
an infant, two of Jemima's daughters persuaded their mother to keep
little Lee, who was raised as a member of the Heard family and later
married Virginia Young. One of Gail Borden's children was also born
in Jemima's Egypt home.

That prince among farmers, Eli Mercer, was a devout Baptist and
an original trustee of Baylor University at Independence, chartered by
the Republic of Texas on February 1, 1845. Judge R. E. B. Baylor,
the namesake of the school, later recalled the circumstances of Mercer's
conversion to Christianity. According to Judge Baylor, Mercer was
digging a friend's grave when "he began to think seriously of time,
death, and eternity and was immediately struck under conviction of sin
. . . ; so he mounted his horse, rode up the Colorado until he found a
Baptist church, made a profession of faith, and was duly immersed."
After the town of Wharton was founded in 1846, Mercer joined the
Baptist church there and worshiped in the courthouse.

Mercer was on the trustee committee that named Henry Lee
Graves as first president of Baylor University; in fact, it was he who
"marked Dr. Graves' qualifications and standards" and recommended
him to the committee. When the Baylor trustees met at the end of the
first school term in June 1848, the struggling college had no funds to
pay the salaries of President Graves and Professor Henry F. Gillette.
This crisis was resolved when the trustees agreed to pay twenty dollars
each in partial compensation "with Eli Mercer to pay the residue, providing it did not exceed $150." When the Baptist State Convention
met at Independence in June 1851, the Baylor trustees submitted a
plan for endowing the presidency. Mercer was one of those making a
personal plea for the proposal, and the convention pledged $5,355 for
that purpose. Mercer died at Egypt on December 7, 1872, and was
buried in the family cemetery a half mile from town and near the Colorado River.[3]

---

3. Eli's uncle, Jesse Mercer, was the greatest Southern Baptist revivalist of his day.
This Georgia preacher founded Mercer University at Macon and donated the princely sum
of $2,500 to maintain a Baptist missionary in Texas. This gift was sufficient to keep a man
in the field for ten years. On January 24, 1840, the *Neptune* arrived at Galveston with Rev.
James Huckins on board. This missionary was bound for Houston but was persuaded to
stay over a day and preach to 200 souls hungry for the gospel. With Reverend Huckins
taking the lead, a meeting was held in the home of Thomas Borden for the purpose of or-

On April 3, 1846, the First Legislature of the State of Texas created Wharton County, an area of 1,079 square miles formed out of Matagorda, Jackson, and Colorado counties. Captain Heard was one of five commissioners appointed to locate the county seat, and he assisted Virgil Stewart in surveying the township of Wharton. When the new county's commissioners' court met in September 1846, Heard was chosen as presiding officer.

James McKenzie, the son-in-law of Major Northington, died at Egypt on October 4, 1845, leaving Rachel Ann alone with two little girls and six months pregnant with a baby boy later named James Mentor. A road project would soon bring a suitor into the young widow's life. Joel Hudgins, a Mississippi native and carpenter by trade, had lived in the West Bernard area since November 1839. After the commissioners' court ordered him and Andrew Northington to lay off County Road No. Five from Wharton to the Northington Crossing on the West Bernard, Joel met Rachel while working with her father, and the two were married in March 1847.[4] A town named Quinan (pronounced Qui-nine) soon developed on the new county road. Named in honor of Judge George Quinan, a prominent Wharton County lawyer and plantation owner, the settlement was renamed Hungerford in 1883 with the coming of the New York, Texas and Mexican Railway. The town was named in honor of the railroad's president, Daniel E. Hungerford.

The 1850 census of Wharton County showed Andrew Northington as possessing a net worth of $9,300. He suffered from poor health in his final years and was frequently treated by Dr. W. C. Veasey of Quinan. A lifelong indifference toward religion ended at a camp meeting in October 1853, when Andrew joined the church as a seeker of

---

ganizing a Baptist church in Galveston. At the conclusion of the meeting, Gail and Penelope Borden stepped forward and asked to be baptized. On Tuesday afternoon, February 4, 1840, fifty spectators stood on the beach as Brother Huckins waded into the Gulf of Mexico to baptize husband and wife. This was the first such baptism in the Gulf west of the Mississippi River. It is noteworthy that the first lost sheep brought into the fold as a result of Jesse Mercer's contribution were his own relatives.

4. In October 1850, Hudgins purchased from Andrew Northington all the land in the Alexander Jackson league to the east of the West Bernard River. Joel and Rachel built a fine, fourteen-room, two-story home on their new property near present Hungerford. The house featured cypress doors, handmade bricks, wide front porches on both floors, and a picket fence enclosure. The couple had nine children, five of whom lived to maturity. Joel Hudgins and his descendants pioneered the development of one of the world's largest herds of registered beef-type Brahman cattle.

salvation and set up an altar of worship in his home. After six weeks of suffering, the new Christian died at home of abcess of the spleen on October 23, 1854. Since he left no will, his son Mentor was appointed administrator of his estate, which included a tract of 900 acres between the West Bernard and Peach Creek. Mentor Northington had married William Heard's oldest daughter, Elizabeth, in December 1845, and was living in Egypt.

In 1847 Captain Heard started construction of the most historic "big house" in Wharton County. Built on the highest point of his land on the Egypt prairie, this classic Georgian home was inspired by his childhood memories of fine homes in Tennessee. There were no plans on paper; he and his wife, America, built it as they went along, with "pillow talk" often determining the next day's work. The original home was four rooms — a parlor, dining room, and two bedrooms — with a dogtrot (open breezeway), a loft, and twin chimneys in the gabled ends. The walls were twelve inches thick and extended four feet into the ground. Metal ceiling rods extended through the house to the outside, thus keeping the walls in alignment. The slave-made pink bricks came from the banks of Caney Creek, the cypress doors and beams were brought from Galveston, and the pine was hauled from East Texas by ox-cart for the hand-adzed, one-and-a-half-inch-thick plank floors and ceilings. The German carpenters from Galveston who built the house planted cedar trees in the front yard as was their custom (three of these magnificent trees still shade the home today). Known locally as the Red Brick Ranch, the home was completed in 1849 and became a center for dances, social activities, and deer and bear hunting parties on the San Bernard prairie.[5]

---

5. Each generation of the Northington-Heard family added various pieces of furniture to the home. Today it is primarily furnished with pieces of the Empire Period. A heavy bed of carved walnut dominates the Victorian Room, while the entrance hall features burls of curly pine wainscoting on the stairway and walls.

Between 1975 and 1978, the Egypt big house was professionally restored and renovated through the efforts of George Heard Northington III and his wife Anita, then opened to the public for the first time. The couple also added a new bedroom, kitchen, and "keeping room" (family living room) to the back of the original house. The keeping room displays hundreds of antique Texana books, maps and letters, including the framed Mexican land grant to Jemima Menefee Heard in Jackson County, signed by Estevan F. Austin and dated November 24, 1830. Among the special attractions are George's closet, a china collection, and a sixteen-foot Brunswick wet bar, circa 1875.

Public tours of the Egypt Plantation big house and the Northington-Heard Museum behind it are by advance arrangement only. Further information may be obtained by contacting Mrs. Anita Northington, Box 277, Egypt, Texas 77436 (713/677-3562).

Just down the lane from the "big house" was the Heard-Nor-thington family cemetery. The early graves were covered with crypts made of handmade brick to prevent tampering by Indians. The first to be buried there was the youngest of Heard's four children, George S. Heard, who died on January 8, 1854. Uncle Billy put his wife, America, to rest there on June 18, 1855, followed by his mother, Jemima, who passed away on January 27, 1859.

The 1850 census showed Captain Heard as owning real estate valued at $16,888. He owned forty slaves by 1860 (one of his slave cabins and a slave bell are still on the grounds of Egypt plantation today). In 1853 Heard and Eli Mercer were the second and third largest sugar growers in Wharton County, producing 106 and 80 hogsheads, respectively, compared to the 491 hogsheads produced by former Lieutenant Governor Albert Clinton Horton, who lived in a "big house" on the edge of Wharton. Horton was a large-scale planter who also produced an average of 650 to 700 bales of cotton and 1,600 barrels of syrup annually.

Heard's feelings about the master-slave relationship are revealed in a letter he wrote to Gail Borden on January 1, 1855. At the time, Uncle Billy owned two servants, Daniel and Ellen, who were the former property of Borden. It seems that the two had produced free papers in which Gail had promised their freedom if he proved to be successful in his meat biscuit enterprise. In his letter Heard contended that the paper was worthless since the two servants now belonged to him, then proceeded to lecture his old friend on the dangers of being too familiar and lenient with slaves. Like the typical planter, Heard saw no contradiction between his professed Christianity and slave ownership; he concluded the rather harsh letter by saying, "I do want us to spend our last days in loving and serving our Creator and preparing to meet our Savior when we come to die . . . ."

On February 28, 1859, Senator Sam Houston delivered his farewell speech on the floor of the U.S. Senate, saying he intended to refute the calumnies made against his character as commander-in-chief of the Army of Texas. Much of the speech was a diatribe against Col. Sidney Sherman's conduct in the Battle of San Jacinto. During his speech, Senator Houston read a vicious letter written to him by Lt. Col. Joseph L. Bennett, a former officer under Sherman. The letter, written in September 1841, had accused Sherman of cowardice in the battle. According to the writer, when the men of Sherman's Second Regiment were paraded, the colonel asked Bennett to take command since he had some experience in fighting, and Sherman had never been in a battle. Bennett said he agreed to do so. He also said that Sherman left in great haste when the enemy commenced firing, going to a small island of timber 300 yards to the rear and staying there until all the enemy had fled.

Sherman reacted to these charges by writing his San Jacinto comrades and asking their opinion of his actions during the battle. All of the replies commended him highly, and many were included in a small pamphlet he compiled titled a "Defence of Gen. Sidney Sherman." Writing from Egypt on June 15, 1859, Captain Heard endorsed Sherman's character and said in part:

> Dear Friend,
> . . . It will give me pleasure at all times to assist in establishing truth, and doing justice to a fellow soldier that has been most shamefully abused and vilified by malice and falsehood . . .

He went on to defend Sherman against charges that he gave up his command to Colonel Bennett, acted cowardly, and was anxious for property or plunder.

Heard's letter to the *Galveston News,* dated May 18, 1859, was included in Sherman's "Defence" pamphlet. In addressing the charge of cowardice made against his friend, Heard said:

> When we had formed our army for battle, Col. Sherman's regiment was on the extreme left of the line. When the order was given to march, Col. Sherman marched his regiment to a point of woods, where the Mexicans had taken position and attacked them. A sharp fire took place at that point. In a few moments, I looked in that direction, and saw the Mexicans running along the edge of the woods and Sherman after them. This greatly encouraged me and others. We shouted at the top of our voices, 'Yonder they go, boys, and Sherman after them.' This happened when our regiment was some distance from the enemy, and before we had fired a single shot. Sherman and his men pursued them in hot haste, and crossed near where the breastworks joined the timber. This circumstance had more to do in gaining the victory than any other that took place on that day.

During the Civil War, Heard was appointed a captain for patrol duty in Beat (precinct) One. His responsibility included visiting slave quarters once a week and reporting those privates who refused his orders or neglected their duties. He was empowered to administer up to twenty-five lashes to those slaves found to be traveling without passes.

In November 1861, Uncle Billy was appointed as the Confederate postmaster at Egypt. Confederate soldiers flocked to Egypt plantation to enjoy his special brand of hospitality. According to family legend, the Heards cared for a seriously wounded soldier, an amputee with a wooden leg who died in an upstairs bedroom. Ever since that time stories have been told of eerie tapping sounds coming from that room, as if some ghostly presence was pacing the floor.

Captain Heard moved to Chappell Hill in 1866 to enjoy the advantages offered by two Methodist schools, Chappell Hill Female College and Soule University.[6] He married a local widow, Esther F. Glass, and in April 1867 purchased a thirteen-acre tract on the west side of Main Street and bounded on the south by the Soule University lot. While building a home there, he sealed a broad hatchet in the wall over the front door so people would know that he had "buried the hatchet" and had no animosities toward General Houston or anyone else. This simple story-and-a-half dogtrot structure had fireplaces in the two front rooms. When the house was torn down in 1953, it was in such poor condition that only a walnut mantle could be saved.

In 1872 the editors of the *Texas Almanac* requested the names of old Texas veterans for publication, and Heard was among those who responded. In his letter he noted that he was quite feeble, and that his eyes were so dim he could not see the lines when writing. He lamented that some of his books and papers had burned in a recent house fire, including his discharge papers, but that he managed to save his land certificate for services rendered from February 28 to May 30, 1836.

After serving as a trustee of Chappell Hill Female College, Heard died of dropsy on August 8, 1874, and was buried in the old Masonic Cemetery there. Upon his death Dr. R. J. Swearingen wrote the following tribute:

> The State has lost a worthy patriotic citizen, who has followed her fortunes from revolution to revolution, through nights of sorrow and

6. Chappell Hill Female College existed from 1852 until 1912. After Dr. R. J. Swearingen donated a ten-acre plot for the school, Soule University received a charter from the state legislature in February 1856. A three-story stone building with nine classrooms was completed in May 1861. Senior Methodist Bishop Soule officiated at the ceremony, and the institution was named for him. During the Civil War, classes were suspended and the school was turned into a Confederate hospital. The university reopened in 1865, and Dr. Francis Asbury Mood became the new president four years later. In 1872, the college moved to Georgetown, Texas, and was renamed Southwestern University in February 1876. Dr. Mood continued as president until his death in November 1884.

days of glory, and no son more faithful than he. He rests now among the gallant dead.

Captain Heard's second wife died in June 1878, and was also buried in the Masonic Cemetery at Chappell Hill. In 1936 the Texas Centennial Committee erected a monument at Heard's grave.

When Captain Heard moved to Chappell Hill in 1866, his daughter Elizabeth and son-in-law Mentor Northington moved into the Egypt big house. On November 8, 1873, Heard agreed to sell Egypt plantation — some 1,165 acres — to James R. Dillard for $10,000 in gold. Under terms of the agreement, Dillard was to make five annual payments of $2,000 each at ten percent interest starting on January 1, 1874. When Dillard was unable to meet the payment schedule, Heard's grandson, William A. Northington, took up the payments, took possession of the plantation, and the place was conveyed to him on March 11, 1881.

For Indian service in the field under General Green, Mentor Northington received a land grant in Jones County, and he died there at Anson on September 18, 1888. Both Mentor and his wife, Elizabeth, who died in 1892, were buried in the family cemetery at Egypt. Of their eight children, only two survived infancy, William A. and George Heard Northington. Will, the older brother, married Pauline Jones, and the couple had no children. After attending school at Randolph Macon in Virginia, George H. Northington married Jessie Virginia Simmons of Chappell Hill on February 7, 1875, assumed the active management of Egypt plantation, and started a family that would number eight children.

John C. Clark, the founder of Egypt, died in 1862, leaving an estate of land, slaves, and personal assets valued at $478,000. Dennis and Whitten were appointed administrators of the Clark estate, sold all of the land and personal assets, and turned over the proceeds to the state treasurer in 1866. By this time Clark's three mulatto offspring were not living in Texas. On March 28, 1871, a suit was started in the District Court of Wharton County, with Bishop Clark and his two married sisters as plaintiffs. The three brought suit to recover their father's property, claiming to be John Clark's children by the slave Sobrina and his legitimate heirs. The suit alleged a marriage between the two known as a "common law" marriage under the Constitution of 1869, which provided that "all persons who at any time heretofore live together as husband and wife, and both of whom, by the law of bondage, were precluded from the rites of matrimony, and continued to

live together until the death of either party, shall be considered as having been legally married," and legalized their offspring. In this suit the
state treasurer answered that other parties — all of them white people
— also claimed to be Clark's heirs and that by a judgment rendered in
the District Court of Fort Bend County, all of said assets were awarded
to Joseph B. Wygal and others.

The Wharton County District Court held, however, that the
three blacks were the lawful heirs of John Clark. The following evi-
dence was introduced in the case: Clark was a single man when he came
to Texas; he bought Sobrina in 1833, and she became the mother of the
three; several blacks testified that the two occupied the same bed, and
that Sobrina carried the keys to the house and exercised authority as
mistress of the house, with Clark speaking of her as his wife; and black
witnesses also said that Clark distinguished between Sobrina's children
and others, and that he claimed them as his own. It is interesting to
note that no white witnesses, some of whom were overseers on the
plantation, ever heard Clark speak in such terms or observed anything
to indicate that Sobrina was his wife.

In a lengthy opinion the Supreme Court of Texas affirmed the decision of the lower court and awarded Clark's assets to the three children of Sobrina (37 _Texas Reports_, 686). This so-called "semi-colon"
court was controlled by Reconstructionists at the time. The supreme
court ruled that Clark and Sobrina had lived together as husband and
wife before January 16, 1837, when a Republic of Texas law prohibited marriage between whites and blacks, and that neither "race,
order, nor social rank appears to constitute an impediment to marriage
at the common law."

Bishop Clark and his two sisters took possession of as much land
as they could while other claimants, including Joseph Wygal and
George Dorman, took other portions. Finally, four different suits were
consolidated, and a judgment was rendered by agreement in November 1893 (_Wharton County District Court Minutes_, Vol. F: 497). Neither
side established heirship, and all claimants took what they actually
possessed. However, vigilante lawlessness prevented the blacks from
staying on the Clark property. Some armed men surrounded their
home and ordered them out of the county. The house was set on fire,
and three people either burned to death inside or were shot while
trying to escape the flames. The few family members who survived
promptly left Wharton County.

During this postwar period of turmoil, the torch was passed to a new generation of leaders at Egypt. In 1872 Green Cameron Duncan settled there. He was born in Bloomfield, Kentucky, on October 10, 1841, and his mother died when Green was only a baby. Since his father's next wife did not want a stepchild, the boy went to live with his uncle, Ellis Duncan, and his wife, Mary Wilson, a sister of Green's mother. Young Duncan always considered them as his real family. At age eighteen he joined the Confederate army and had four horses shot from under him while serving with a cavalry company commanded by Gen. Nathan Bedford Forrest. His half brother, Isaac Runnells, died in 1855 and left Duncan 500 acres of land in south Wharton County. When the war ended, an extended visit left Duncan stunned by the beauty and lushness of Texas. In February 1872 he paid John B. (Jack) Walker $10,000 in gold for 1,332 acres in Egypt, part of the old John Clark league. The following January, Duncan purchased an additional 1,312 acres for the same price and named his holdings the Spade Ranch.

While visiting Bowieville, the site of George J. Bowie's Caney Creek plantation in Matagorda County, Green met Mary Jane (Mamie) Bowie, the fifth of eight children of George and Frances Sophie Bowie. Green and Mamie were married at her plantation home in July 1872. The newlyweds first moved into Clark's original three-room brick house in Egypt, then made additions through the years. All of their five children except the eldest, Nancy, were born in this stately white colonial home, which is still owned by the Duncan family. Green and Mamie lined the driveway with magnolia trees and added expansive, elegant gardens while son Bowie and his wife, May, made such improvements as a tennis court and swimming pool.

George H. Northington's land was adjacent to that of Green Duncan, and the two became partners in the mercantile and stock business in 1881. When Northington initially expressed some concern as to whether the two could "get along," Duncan replied, "Doggonit to hell, if I put my money in it, and you run it, of course we'll get along!" The partners used the initials "DN" to brand their Hereford and Durham cattle and built a general store in 1881 which stands today. The Northington-Duncan store included a meat market and sold coffins, shoes, boots, Stetson hats, yard goods, and groceries. Since the general store was both the commercial and social center for the Egypt area, the post office also was located there. A lumber yard stood behind the store and a cotton gin next door. For years the Northington and Duncan families also hired a teacher for the white children of Egypt.

Green Duncan was elected to the 22nd State Legislature in 1891 with his 66th House District including Wharton, Brazoria, Matagorda, and Galveston counties. He also served on the committee that drafted the constitution and bylaws for the White Man's Union Association of Wharton County, organized on November 25, 1889. This arm of the Democratic party was open only to whites, and those who opposed its principles and objectives were considered and treated as political outcasts. Within a month, more than 700 joined the White Man's Union in the county.

The first sheriff of Wharton County elected by the White Man's Union was to suffer a tragic fate in Braddock's thicket near Egypt. H. B. (Hamilton Bass) Dickson, a former cattleman and organizer of the union, was elected county sheriff in 1890 and 1892. A stocky man with a booming voice and heavy mustache, Dickson lost his first wife, Clementine, to tuberculosis in April 1892. Their two sons, Raymond and Pierce, gained a stepmother when Sheriff Dickson married Belle Faires of Edna in January 1894, but that happy union was to be short-lived.

Early the next month a desperado named Dee Braddock was removed from a train near Weimar for misconduct. The angry Braddock then fired into the sleeper car and was arrested at Weimar. When Constable Townsend brought supper for him the next evening, Braddock killed him with a knife, escaped, and went into hiding on the H. H. Moore place near Egypt. After being tipped off about Braddock's hiding place, Sheriff Dickson sent a telegram to Sheriff J. L. "Lite" Townsend of Colorado County, requesting that he bring a posse and meet Dickson at the Northington-Duncan store. The two lawmen arrested Moore there and left him in the custody of George Northington. Two blacks then led the sheriffs to the dense thicket where Braddock was hiding. After walking a short distance along a narrow trail, Dickson spotted something, raised up, and whispered to Townsend, "Here he is." At that instant he was hit by a single rifle shot; mortally wounded, his last words were, "Townsend, he has killed me." What Sheriff Dickson mistook for Braddock was actually a dummy lying on the ground near a log. Lite Townsend then opened fire with his Winchester, wounding and killing the desperado. As the posse returned to Egypt, they met Moore and a companion on horseback. Moore ignored an order to surrender, pulled his gun, and was killed by the peace officers.

The body of Sheriff Dickson first lay in state in the parlor of

George Northington's home at Egypt. When his funeral was held in Wharton on February 9, 1894, a special train came from Richmond and sixty-one vehicles accompanied the body to the cemetery, the largest funeral procession in Wharton County history. In December 1894 a twenty-one-foot marble shaft was erected in Dickson's memory on the courthouse square.

As the community of Egypt became more affluent in the late 1890s, Northington and Duncan ended their partnership and divided their stock and property. As one family member later recalled, "They each knew exactly what they had, and they sat there on the front porch or in the office of the store and divided their cattle, shook hands, and that was it." Once they divided the stock, Duncan used the Spade brand while George retained Captain Heard's old Crescent 69. Duncan kept the general store and cotton gin, and Northington built a new and larger store down the street in 1900. He added a meat market in 1914, which included a cold storage meat room and equipment for making ice, and customers came there from Wharton and Eagle Lake to buy meat.[7]

The Cane Belt Railroad, known as the "sugar line" from Eagle Lake to Bonus, was chartered in March 1893 and reached Bay City in June 1902. When the line was sold to the Santa Fe the next year, Northington and Duncan paid the railroad $2,500 to build a depot in Egypt. The structure was originally located directly across from the present state historical marker.

Green Duncan died August 5, 1910, in New York City following surgery for cancer of the stomach. At the time of his death, he owned property valued for tax purposes at $108,510, second only to the A. H. Pierce estate. Both Duncan and his wife, Mamie, who died on July 3, 1903, are buried in the Bowie family cemetery at Cedar Lane (formerly Bowieville) in east central Matagorda County. Their sons, Francis Bowie and Donald, assumed joint ownership and management

---

7. The store built by George H. Northington, Sr., in 1900 is now known as John's Country Store and owned by John W. Northington. The old meat market was converted to a family museum in 1946. The museum began in a slave cabin on Egypt plantation when George H. Northington III started to gather documents, farm equipment, books, and other items from old family trunks and storerooms and from the Northington Store in Egypt. Today the Northington-Heard Museum is housed in the old Santa Fe Depot, which was purchased and moved behind the big house. The museum houses one of the largest private collections in Texas.

of the Duncan Brothers Spade Ranch and Farm.[8]

Green Duncan's longtime friend and partner, George Northington, died in a Houston hospital on March 13, 1938, leaving an estate of land and improvements valued at $139,016. At that time George H. Northington, Jr., took over management of the family farm and ranch interests and the general store at Egypt. The death of Green Duncan and George Northington, Sr., marked the end of an era; the last of Egypt's pioneer builders were gone.

Approaching Egypt from Wharton on Farm Road 102 in the early 1990s, one has a real sense of stepping back in time. Making a right turn near the historical marker, one first sees John's Country Store, the place built by George Northington, Sr., in 1900. Farther up the street is the old Northington-Duncan general store on the hill, now standing empty and dilapidated. Another right turn up a narrow country lane takes the visitor by the Northington-Heard family cemetery before Egypt plantation comes into view. Nestled in the trees is the big house built by Captain Heard in the 1840s; directly behind it is the Northington-Heard museum and an old slave cabin. Six generations of the family have lived on these storied grounds. A short distance up the road is the white colonial mansion still occupied by the Duncan family. Truly, a visitor to this tiny town will discover a treasure trove of Texas history, a proud heritage nobly preserved.

---

8. Francis Bowie Duncan, who was born at Egypt in September 1887, later earned a special niche in the athletic history of the University of Texas. On November 10, 1906, he caught the first forward pass for a touchdown against the Haskell Indians, then repeated the feat against Texas A&M on Thanksgiving Day. Both passes were thrown by Winston McMahon, who later became a Houston attorney. This was a daring play at the time, since the penalty for an incompleted forward pass was loss of the ball. Bowie Duncan served as captain of the Longhorn football team in 1907 and, like his father, was elected to the state legislature in 1922.

As of 1974, the Spade Ranch covered some 12,000 acres. A thousand head of Hereford cattle grazed on ten percent of the land, while rice, cotton, corn, and maize were grown on the remaining acreage.

Capt. William J. E. Heard   *Mentor Northington*
— Courtesy Mrs. Anita Northington, Egypt, Texas

George Heard Northington
— Courtesy Mrs. Anita Northington, Egypt, Texas

Sheriff Hamilton Bass Dickson
— From *The History of Wharton County*,
by Annie Lee Williams

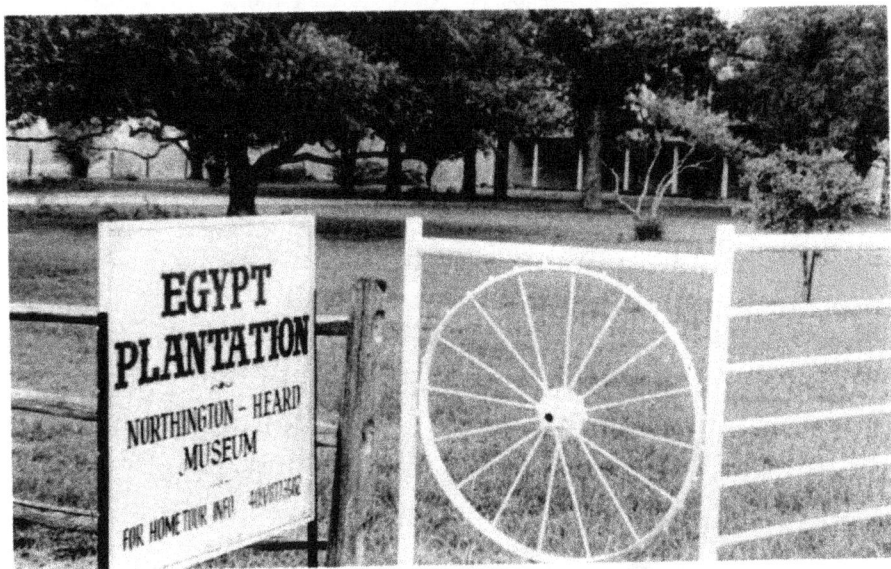

Egypt plantation
— Photo by J. C. Hoke, courtesy Mrs. Anita Northington,
Egypt, Texas

Big House, Egypt plantation.
— Photo by J. C. Hoke, courtesy Mrs. Anita Northington, Egypt, Texas

Slave cabin, Egypt plantation.
— Photo by J. C. Hoke, courtesy Mrs. Anita Northington, Egypt, Texas

Northington-Heard Museum, Egypt plantation.
— Photo by J. C. Hoke, courtesy Mrs. Anita Northington, Egypt, Texas

Northington-Heard Family Cemetery, Egypt, Texas.
— Photo by J. C. Hoke, courtesy Mrs. Mary Louise Dobson

Northington-Duncan General Store, built in 1881, Egypt, Texas.
— Photo by J. C. Hoke, courtesy Mrs. Mary Louise Dobson

Northington Store, built in 1900, Egypt, Texas.
— Photo by J. C. Hoke, courtesy Mrs. Mary Louise Dobson

Entrance to Duncan House and Spade Ranch, Egypt, Texas.
— Photo by J. C. Hoke, courtesy Mrs. Mary Louise Dobson

Green Duncan House
— Photo by J. C. Hoke, courtesy Mrs. Mary Louise Dobson

III

Matagorda:
Commercial and Cultural Hub of Early Texas

In the 1830s, Matagorda was a major seaport and one of the largest towns in Texas. The Matagorda Cemetery displays nineteen historical markers; among the Texas notables buried there are Albert Clinton Horton, S. Rhoads Fisher, Ira Ingram, Richard R. Royall, and George M. Collinsworth. Matagorda can boast of the oldest Episcopal church in Texas and the finest hotel of its time. Before the Civil War, the city was renowned as a cultural, social, and educational center. Prominent planters maintained fine homes there for entertaining their guests. Unlike such towns as Columbus and Jefferson, today's residents of this small coastal resort have done little to promote a glorious past. Thus Matagorda remains one of the best kept secrets in Texas history.

In January 1821, Spanish Governor Antonio Martinez authorized Moses Austin to bring 300 families to Texas. Empresario Austin intended to bring twenty-five men and lay off the town of Austina at the mouth of the Colorado River, a port that would rival New Orleans in importance. When Moses died of pneumonia at Potosi, Missouri, in June 1821, his eldest son, Stephen Fuller Austin, was waiting to meet him at Natchitoches, Louisiana. Upon learning of his father's death, Stephen traveled to San Antonio and was confirmed by Governor Martinez as legal heir to the Austin grant.

After selecting the rich coastal prairie between the Colorado and Brazos rivers, Stephen Austin and his partner, Joseph Hawkins, purchased the schooner *Lively* at New Orleans. On November 20, 1821, the *Lively* sailed for Texas with eighteen colonists and a load of provisions. In accordance with his father's plans, Austin ordered the vessel to proceed to the mouth of the Colorado, where the first colonists were to travel upriver and find a suitable site for building a stockade and growing corn. Traveling overland to meet them, Austin arrived at the mouth of the Colorado in January 1822 and waited in vain for three weeks. After living on catfish and wild onions, he finally gave up the watch. In the meantime the *Lively* had mistakenly landed at the mouth of the Brazos River.

After missing the departure of the *Lively*, another group of immigrants, including William Kincheloe and his son-in-law, Capt. Horatio Chriesman, purchased the schooner *Only Son* and sailed from New Orleans on February 7, 1822. Many of the ninety passengers died of yellow fever en route and were buried at sea. The *Only Son* reached Matagorda Bay in late March and was followed a few days later by a second ship from New Orleans, with Samuel May Williams and Jonathan C. Peyton on board.

The colonists from both ships made camp on the west bank of the Colorado three miles above its mouth, made a peace treaty with the Karankawa Indians, and were led into the interior by James Cummings. The first settler in the area, Cummings brought two brothers and two sisters to Texas in ox-drawn wagons in the fall of 1821. While camped near the mouth of the Colorado, the party fed the oxen corn and pumpkins. When Cummings returned to the campsite the next summer, he found an uncultivated crop of corn and pumpkins growing on the virgin prairie and built a double log cabin there, thus becoming the first permanent resident of what became Matagorda.

While Kincheloe and the other colonists explored the interior, they left three men behind to guard their stores. After hearing that the Karankawas had murdered the three and taken their supplies, the Kincheloe party moved up the Colorado and settled at different locations along the river.[1] Another member of the group, Capt. Jesse Burnham, led a surprise attack on the Karankawas before building a cabin on a bluff near the Cummings place.

In June 1822, the two were joined by Thomas M. Duke and other passengers from the *Lively*, which had wrecked on west Galveston Is-

---

1. On July 6, 1824, William Kincheloe received two leagues of land, one of which was on the east bank of the Colorado River near Peach Creek in present Wharton County. After his death in 1835, sons Daniel and Lawrence donated land from this league for a courthouse square on the banks of the Colorado in 1846. This "Monterey Square" was the focal point for the new town of Wharton, the county seat of Wharton County, created by an act of the Texas legislature in April 1846.

land on a return voyage from New Orleans. The stranded colonists were picked up by the *John Motley* and landed at the mouth of the Colorado. Duke, a native of Lexington, Kentucky, was a nephew of Chief Justice John Marshall and had studied law under him. In 1821 he became one of Austin's "Old Three Hundred" colonists and received a league of land on Caney Creek on July 24, 1824.

In November 1822, the new governor of Mexican Texas, José Felix Trespalacios, authorized two districts, one on the Colorado and the other on the Brazos, with each to elect its own officials. The Colorado colonists chose John Tumlinson as *alcalde,* Robert Kuykendall as captain, and Moses Morrison as lieutenant. In January 1823, a formal request was made of Governor Trespalacios to raise a company to guard the coast at the mouth of the Colorado. A ten-man company commanded by Moses Morrison was mustered on May 5 to scout and control the Indians. This first company of Texas Rangers made its headquarters at Wilson's Spring, a branch of Tres Palacios Creek.

In the meantime, Stephen Austin traveled to Mexico City in April 1822 to have the Mexican Congress confirm his father's grant. When he returned a year later, two factors caused Austin to change his mind about locating his colony headquarters at the mouth of the Colorado: The Mexican Colonization Law of 1824 prohibited settlement within ten leagues of the Texas coast except for the first 300 families brought in by Austin, and Austin favored a site more central to the inland settlement taking place. As a result he established the headquarters town of San Felipe de Austin on the west bank of the Brazos in July 1823.

The Austin colonists who settled in the Matagorda area had to contend with the cannibalistic Karankawa Indians, who had enjoyed a long, undisputed claim to the hunting and fishing grounds along Matagorda Bay. In March 1822, the "kronks" had killed three members of William Kincheloe's party from the *Only Son.* In August 1824, James Cummings, the first Matagorda settler, sent a letter to Austin warning of an impending Karankawa attack along the lower Colorado. After organizing a company of sixty-two men, Austin took to the field on a futile search for Indians, going as far west as the Lavaca River. On September 25, his company made a gruesome discovery on a stream emptying into Tres Palacios Creek. In this former Karankawa camp, they found the bones of two men who had been cut up and boiled. Their remains were buried, and the stream was named Cannibal Creek.

In the winter of 1826, the Flowers-Cavanah Massacre occurred on

Liveoak Bayou. Charles Cavanah and three unarmed slaves were working some distance away when the Karankawas attacked his house. At
the time, a neighbor, Mrs. Elisha (Polly) Flowers, and her daughter
were visiting Mrs. Cavanah and her four girls. During the surprise attack both mothers and three of the Cavanah girls were killed. The
other two daughters were wounded, thrown on a brush pile with the
others, and left for dead. Both recovered. When Mr. Cavanah returned
to the grisly scene, he went for help and raised a company of sixty men
to pursue the marauders. Led by Capt. Aylett C. "Strap" Buckner, the
settlers overtook the Indians at a small grove near the Cavanah home.
The "kronks" put up a brave fight until young Jimmie Jameson shot
down their chief. At that point the demoralized warriors fled down the
shore of Matagorda Bay toward the mouth of the Colorado. Two miles
northeast of present Matagorda, they made a stand at the mouth of Little Boggy Creek. All but five of them were killed there, and the site
was later renamed "Battle Island." Those managing to escape in canoes
were overtaken and killed six miles inland. Ever since then that area
has been called the "Dressing Point," the place where some brave settlers saw to it that the Karankawas were "properly dressed." (The
Flowers-Cavanah Massacre was the last recorded Indian raid in Matagorda County.)

Moses Austin's dream for a port at the mouth of the Colorado was
realized by Elias Wightman, the founder of the town of Matagorda.
Wightman was born in Herkimer County, New York, in 1792. His
father, Benjamin, was a Baptist minister and served as a private in the
New York Tryon County Rangers during the American Revolution.
Elias taught school as a young man and later married a former pupil,
Mary Sherwood. By July 1825, he was in Texas employed as a surveyor
by Austin.

On August 2, 1826, Wightman, H. H. League, James C. Lud-
low, and Richard Matson petitioned Austin for permission to build a
town on the beautiful bluff east of the Colorado overlooking Matagorda
Bay. It was Wightman who suggested that the town be called Matagorda, a Spanish word meaning dense brush. In another petition
Wightman proposed to put up houses and warehouses for the conven-
ience of immigrants.

In 1827, Austin obtained permission from the Mexican government to build the town of Matagorda as a military post to protect the
colonists. Once this approval was granted, Elias Wightman was

granted title to town league number eleven of Matagorda on May 25, 1827.

Austin received a contract from the state government in July 1828 to introduce an additional 300 families within the ten-league coastal reserve. After building a small fort at the site of Matagorda to protect the expected colonists, he sent Wightman and David G. Burnet to the United States to recruit immigrants.

While Elias was in Cincinnati waiting for warmer weather before going north, he made a draft of the first map of Texas and its coastline from his field notes and information gathered from travelers and traders. He was able to recruit twelve families from New York and Connecticut, a total of thirty-five settlers including his parents and sisters Jerusha and Margaret. Other recruits included Asa Yeamans, his wife, and five children; Noah Griffith, his wife, and five children; Henry Griffith, his wife, and three children; and Emilius Savage, his wife and son. On November 2, 1828, they joined other immigrants at Olean Point, the head of navigation of the Allegheny River. After boarding two large flatboats, lashed together, the Wightman party floated down the Ohio River to Cincinnati, where they took a steamer to New Orleans.

On December 26, 1828, the Wightman recruits sailed for Texas on the twenty-two-ton schooner *Little Zoe.* On its first attempt to enter Matagorda Bay, the vessel was blown out of Pass Cavallo. Short on provisions, the colonists survived on seagull soup and one-half pint of daily water rations before taking refuge at Aransas Pass for six days. Leaving the women and children on land, twelve of the men took their rifles and went up Matagorda Island to hunt for deer. The *Little Zoe* anchored 200 yards offshore with only Captain Alden, the mate, immigrant Thomas Pilgrim, and one musket left on board. When they saw canoes of the Karankawas approaching, Pilgrim and the mate grabbed the old musket, jumped into a little boat, and headed straight for the Indians. When Pilgrim pointed the weapon at the chief, the latter made signs of peace and agreed to trade his fish. (When Joe Yeamans was interviewed years later at age eighty-three, he said that the curious Indians actually boarded the ship but made no attempt to harm anyone. When they saw the white men returning, they made for their canoes and went up the bay.) Shortly after this confrontation, the hunters returned and the passengers were taken back on board.

Several days later, the *Little Zoe* set sail for Pass Cavallo. Pilgrim and the mate went ahead in a boat and used a long rope to sound Matagorda Bay and guide the schooner into it. The wind was fair this time, and the ship arrived at Matagorda on January 27, 1829. James Cummings and Jesse Burnham were already living there in good log cabins, and Austin had built a fifty-foot-square stockade equipped with mosquito netting and had sent a small party of militia to the site.

In the winter of 1829, the Matagorda pioneers built a log schoolhouse with dirt floor for the teacher, Josiah P. Wilbarger. For the next two and a half years, he was assisted by Mrs. Mary Wightman, who also organized a Sunday school upon their arrival, the first one in Texas.

On June 20, 1830, Elias Wightman's mother, Esther, died of typhoid fever after drinking river water. She was the first to be buried in Matagorda Cemetery. Six weeks later, her husband, Benjamin, died of the same cause and was buried beside her. Their coffins were made by Daniel Decrow with lumber brought from New Orleans, and their hearse was an ox-drawn cart. On October 28 of that year, a league of land on the eastern end of Matagorda Peninsula was granted to Benjamin's heirs. In 1833 Elias and Mary Wightman built a home there, twenty miles east of Matagorda, and traveled by skiff across Matagorda Bay on their trips to town.

On July 8, 1830, Thomas Barnett, *alcalde* of San Felipe de Austin, witnessed the signing of the "Constitution of the Proprietors of the Town of Matagorda" by the four owners of the town league. According to the document, Elias Wightman owned one-fourth of the said league, Stephen F. Austin (representing the estate of his deceased brother, James Brown Austin) owned one-fourth, H. H. League owned three-eighths of the league, and Ira Ingram owned one-eighth — all being a common undivided interest in the said league.

Under terms of the constitution of Matagorda, the proprietors met on August 1, 1830, and elected H. H. League as president, Ira Ingram as secretary, Seth Ingram as treasurer, and Elias Wightman as surveyor. From January 29, 1831, until his death in 1837, Ira Ingram served as president.

Ira and his younger brother Seth were born in Brookfield, Vermont. Both served in the War of 1812, and Ira suffered a severe bayonet wound at the Battle of Lundy's Lane from which he never completely recovered. Seth Ingram came to Texas in the spring of 1822 as Austin's first surveyor of public lands. It was Seth who laid out the town of San Felipe de Austin. His brother Ira married the beautiful and accomplished Emily P. Hoit in New Orleans in March 1823. After losing their first child in April 1824, Emily died of yellow fever that

October. Ira had idolized her, and Seth persuaded him to move to Texas to help recover from the loss. The Ingram brothers were merchants in San Felipe for two years beginning in 1828. After moving to Matagorda, Ira received the next adjoining league of land east of town and was agent for the other owners in the town league. Seth's league was west of Matagorda across the Colorado.

On September 2, 1830, Seth Ingram killed a lawyer named John G. Holtham to uphold his brother's honor. It seems that the drunk Holtham had entered Ira's yard and been forcibly evicted. He then posted lampoons on the *alcalde*'s door calling Ira a coward, rogue, and man without honor. When Seth confronted Holtham and demanded that he remove the lampoons, Holtham refused. A duel ensued, in which Seth killed him with one shot. Hosea League was arrested as an accomplice since he was armed and had served as Seth's second. Both he and Seth were held in chains for sixteen months, released on bond, arrested again, and held until the summer of 1833.

On April 2, 1831, the Matagorda proprietors met to donate town lots to individuals for services rendered the town. Jesse Burnham received five lots as one of the earliest settlers and for constructing a salt factory; Elias Wightman received three lots as founder of the town; James Cummings received two lots for guiding the immigrants and driving away the Karankawas; his daughter, Maria Ross, received a lot for braving Indian danger to make her father a home.

Two days later, town lots were auctioned off at $30 each, producing a net revenue of $1,511. On August 16, 1831, this amount was declared as the first dividends, with Stephen F. Austin receiving the largest dividend ($344) based on his two shares. For their one share, Elias Wightman, Seth Ingram, Ira Ingram, H. H. League, S. S. Veender, and S. R. Fisher received dividends of $172 each.

One of the most prominent of the early Matagorda settlers was Samuel Rhoads Fisher, who was born in Philadelphia on December 31, 1794. He and his wife, Ann Pleasants, were reared as Quakers. After living for a time in Missouri and Tennessee, Fisher left his wife and four children with Ann's father in Philadelphia and came to Texas with Austin's third colony in 1830. After starting a small mercantile business in Matagorda, Fisher brought his family to Texas from New Orleans on a small, dirty schooner in the winter of 1832. He had left plans and money behind for building a house of their own, but his agent used the money to clear his brother of some "difficulty." Thus, the Fisher family was put up in one corner of the MacFarlane cabin, a small, one-room structure built on posts five feet off the ground. The place had no floors, but clapboards and a rag carpet were laid between two rough bedsteads nailed to the wall in opposite corners of the room.

In her memoirs, Fisher's daughter, Annie P., recalls that her father soon persuaded two young men named Grassmeyer and Cazneau to relinquish their fifteen-by-twenty-foot frame building with fireplace in return for taking their meals with Mrs. Fisher. For the next three months, the family lived there while the young men stayed in their Matagorda store, where they received bales of cotton from the upper country.

Fisher hired ships carpenters and skilled woodworkers to build him a two-story frame house made from cypress and cedar. The foundation blocks were made of sea shells and oyster shells and were belled underground four feet square and six feet deep. The walls were three-ply cypress: one course of boards was fastened vertically, another horizontally, and the other diagonally. This type of construction helped Fisher's "Old House" withstand many storms, hurricanes, and tidal waves. On May 29, 1833, he and his family moved into their new home on St. Mary's Street.[2]

Little Annie Fisher recalled that Mexican traders would come to Matagorda and camp around her father's house. They brought herds of mustangs to be broken into pack horses for the tobacco and salt they carried away. One such trader, Don Flores, was invited to eat with the Fishers and gave Annie a pet pony named Lapapeachy. On their way back to Mexico, the Flores party was ambushed, robbed, and killed by Karankawas near Corpus Christi.

An early landmark in Matagorda was built by Dugald Mac-Farlane, Jr., who was born in Scotland in August 1797. After immi-

2. Mr. Fisher's heirs sold the "Old House" to John T. Sargent in 1875. A hurricane that September demolished the family ranch house at Sargent, Texas, and led to the death of John's wife, Sarah Ann, and father George. After moving his children and housekeeper into the Fisher house, John added a wing to be used as a schoolroom. He remarried, and the Sargent family lived in the house for twenty-nine years.

In 1904, Gustave Gottschalk purchased the Old House and moved his family there from their ranch house on Little Boggy Creek. By then the place was also known as the "Cool House" since its construction and location maximized the effect of breezes from Matagorda Bay. The Gottschalk family and heirs lived in the house until 1979, when Grady and Virginia Dansby purchased the place and began the nine years of restoration and remodeling.

In October 1987, J. C. and Babe Stanley purchased the historic home and continued the renewal project. Much of the original Fisher house still survives, including the shutters, the wide inside trims with hand-carved scroll, ceiling, flooring, and staircase.

grating to South Carolina about 1815, he later moved to Alabama, where he married Eliza Montgomery Davenport in Mobile on March 25, 1825. The MacFarlanes settled near Tuscaloosa and had two children. Coming to Texas in 1830, they first lived at San Felipe before deciding on Matagorda as a permanent home. MacFarlane received a league of land on the Colorado just above Selkirk's Island and built the first two-story house in town, a structure tall enough to be seen by ships at sea. Sailors on lookout duty referred to it as "MacFarlane's Castle."[3]

Stephen Austin believed that Matagorda and Galveston would become the most important ports in Texas. Writing to his cousin, Henry Austin, in 1829, he predicted that the two towns would attract all the trade from Chihuahua, Sonora, and New Mexico if roads were built from the interior to the coast. His confidence in Matagorda's future was demonstrated on December 18, 1830, when he patented 5,580 acres of land in present Matagorda County. The lake adjoining his land was later called Lake Austin.

During a two-year period of time, eighteen individuals were given town lots in Matagorda for making certain specified improvements. At a proprietors' meeting held on March 29, 1834, it was agreed to give a lot to any person building a "substantial house of timber, well fitted together or of brick." Such a house had to have well-hinged doors, sashed and glazed windows, plank floors, at least one chimney, and was to be completed within six months. No more town lots were donated by the proprietors after that date.

The last proprietors' meeting recorded in the minute book was held on June 6, 1835. By special resolution, lot number four (just over six acres), located just east of Center Street, was donated as a public burial ground. This was the area where Esther and Benjamin Wightman had been buried in 1830, thus providing officially for the Matagorda Cemetery. At this last meeting, each of the proprietors was granted one additional town lot.

Matagorda could boast of the only known woman colonizer in

---

3. Dugald MacFarlane later served with Philip Dimmit's company at Goliad and was an artillery captain during the Texas Revolution. In 1842, he joined the volunteer Texas army for the campaign against Gen. Adrian Woll. After representing Matagorda County in the Ninth Congress (1844–1845), Dugald served with the United States Army in the Mexican War. A man of considerable literary skill, he wrote for newspapers and magazines and left a history of Freemasonry in manuscript form. In partnership with his son-in-law, Joseph Theall, MacFarlane also published a newspaper called the *Chronicle of the Times*.

Texas. Jane Maria McManus, the daughter of a United States congressman, was born on April 6, 1807, near Troy, New York. After her first marriage to William F. Storins ended in divorce, Jane and her younger brother Robert came to Texas in 1832 on the advice of Aaron Burr to engage in land speculation. The beautiful Jane stayed for several months in the home of S. Rhoads Fisher. During this time William L. Cazneau, one of the two storekeepers in Matagorda, fell in love with her.

In 1833 Jane traveled to Mexico and received certificate number 411 for eleven leagues of land and contracted to bring fifty European families to Texas. On February 3, 1834, she was granted another league and labor of land. After chartering a schooner in New York, Jane sent some German immigrants to Matagorda at her own expense. Since she had exhausted her funds and could go no further, the dissatisfied colonists broke their contract, settled in Matagorda, and the colonizing enterprise failed.

Jane's brother, Robert McManus, surveyed the David G. Burnet, Lorenzo de Zavala, and Joseph Vehlein grant. He remained in Texas to serve under William Logan at San Jacinto, then joined the scouting force raised by Deaf Smith before returning to New York.

Matagorda men were active in all phases of the Texas Revolution. On the morning of June 26, 1832, news reached there of an all-night battle between 112 colonists and a Mexican garrison of 150 troops stationed at Fort Velasco. Ira Ingram rushed there to join the fray; before his arrival, Col. Domingo de Ugartechea surrendered the fort to Capt. John Austin at 11:00 that morning.

On August 4, 1832, a Texian force led by Col. James Bullock defeated Colonel Piedras's Mexican garrison at Nacogdoches. The victory was celebrated with a public dinner at the Matagorda home of James Cummings on August 22. Special guests were the Irish Bayou volunteers, who took part in the Battle of Nacogdoches. A number of prepared and volunteer toasts were offered at the dinner, including this one by Ira Ingram:

> The settlers of Texas — Hand in hand, shoulder to shoulder, they have expelled the savage, subdued and planted the forest — The enemies of their country may read their future history, at Velasco and Nacogdoches.

The following October, Ira Ingram and Silas Dinsmore represented Matagorda at the Convention of 1832 held at San Felipe.

In January 1834, Mexican Vice-president Gomez Farias sent Col.

Juan Almonte to conduct a political and military survey of the province of Texas. He found the people of Matagorda peacefully going about their business. Indeed, they had little to complain about. On March 6, 1834, Decree No. 265 of the Congress of the State of Coahuila–Texas extended local self-government by establishing the municipality of Matagorda. Its boundaries ran from Caney Creek north to the southern boundary of the municipality of Austin, then west to the Lavaca River and to its mouth. When Almonte reported to the Mexican government in 1835, he said that Matagorda was the third largest town in the Department of the Brazos with 1,400 residents; only San Felipe with 2,500 and Columbus with 2,100 had a larger population.

When armed conflict with Mexico appeared inevitable, a Committee of Public Safety was organized at Matagorda on September 25, 1835. Committee members were Hamilton S. Cook, Ira Ingram, Seth Ingram, Richardson Royster Royall, and W. J. Russell. Five days later, the Matagorda committee authorized the raising of a volunteer company to rendezvous at James Kerr's place, Old Station on the Lavaca River, and cooperate in the defense of Texas.

Traveling on foot, Capt. George M. Collinsworth and his forty-seven-man Matagorda and Bay Prairie Company arrived at Victoria tired and hungry. While being hosted there by Mrs. Margaret C. Linn, they learned that General Cos had passed through Goliad en route to San Antonio and left a small detachment at Presidio La Bahia. Rather than join other volunteers gathering at Gonzales, the Matagorda men resolved to capture the Mexican troops at Goliad and thereby cut the line of communications between San Antonio and Copano, the port of entry for the Mexican army.

Collinsworth sent three men ahead to reconnoiter Goliad and find a guide to lead them into Presidio La Bahia. The main part of his company reached Manahuilla Creek after dark. Just as they passed a clump of mesquites, Ben Milam emerged from hiding and identified himself. He had just escaped from prison in Monterrey and agreed to join Collinsworth's men as a private. After a forced march the Matagorda men reached Goliad at 11:00 P.M. on October 8, 1835. Shortly before entering town, the company members signed a pledge to protect the citizens of Goliad and other towns they might enter subject to one condition: the citizens of "said towns (must) stand firm to the Republican institutions of the Government of Mexico and of Coahuila and Texas under the Constitution of 1824."

Captain Collinsworth then divided his force into four groups of twelve men each. While one unit stayed with the horses, the other three groups attacked the twenty-four-man Mexican garrison at the presidio. Protected by an early morning fog on October 9, the Texians caught the enemy by total surprise. The single sentinel on duty fired only a few shots before being killed. Some Texian axemen broke down the door of Lt. Col. Francisco Sandoval's quarters and took him prisoner before his troops could even return fire. In only a few minutes, one Mexican was killed, three were wounded, and the rest of the garrison surrendered. The only Texian casualty was Samuel McCulloch, a freed black from the Navidad who was slightly wounded in the shoulder. Collinsworth's men captured $10,000 worth of military stores, including two brass cannons, 100 muskets, and 600 spears. This total victory was relished by Ben Milam, who was heard to say that "the events of this night have compensated me for all my losses and all my sufferings" (at the hand of Mexico).

After Collinsworth was promoted to major in late October and removed to San Antonio, the Matagorda men elected Philip Dimmit as their new captain. On November 18, 1835, Stephen Austin relieved Dimmit of command and reprimanded him for the alleged harsh treatment of former state governor Augustin Viesca and the residents of Goliad.

After taking part in the Siege of Bexar, Dimmit returned to La Bahia, where he and Ira Ingram drafted the first Texas Declaration of Independence from Mexico on December 20, 1835. Among the ninety-two members of Captain Dimmit's company who signed this historic document were the following Matagorda men: Albert Pratt, Alvin Woodward, D. M. Jones, J. C. Hutchins, E. B. W. Fitzgerald, Hugh McMinn, Wm. Robertson, Horace Stamans, Peter Hynes, Dugald McFarlane, Benj. Noble, M. Carbajal, Thomas Hanron, John Johnson, Edward Quirk, Robert McClure, Andrew Devereau, Charles Stearn, J. B. Dale, Ira Ingram, John Dunn, Walter Lambert, Miguel Aldrete, Wm. Quinn, B. H. Perkins, Benj. White, Jr., Edward St. John, D. H. Peeks, Philip Dimmit, Francis P. Smith, Thomas M. Dennis, and John Duncan.

To celebrate the signing, Dimmit's men made and ran up the first Texas flag of independence. Two yards long and made of white domestic cotton, it was centered by an arm and hand holding aloft a drawn sword that was painted with red dye. The flag was unfurled from a sycamore pole in the center of the La Bahia quadrangle.

A committee of six was delegated to present the Goliad Declaration of Independence to the provisional government meeting at San Felipe. However, the General Council there declared the document to be premature and ordered it suppressed.

When the General Consultation met at San Felipe on October 16, 1835, the Matagorda delegates were Richardson R. Royall, Ira R. Lewis, and Charles Wilson. The Royalls were among the eleven prominent families from the area of Tuscumbia, Alabama, who arrived at Matagorda on the schooner *Emblem* in the spring of 1832. A man of considerable means, Richardson and his fashionable wife, Ann, sent their two oldest daughters and a governess by coach back to Alabama for school that autumn.

There was no quorum when the Consultation met, and Royall was elected president of the so-called Permanent Council, the governing body of revolutionary Texas until November 3, 1835, when the Consultation finally organized itself and elected Branch T. Archer as president. During this critical interim period, Royall and the Permanent Council closed all land offices, authorized a force of Texas Rangers for defense against the Indians, provided funds for the Texas army, appointed Thomas F. McKinney as agent to secure a loan for $100,000 from the citizens of New Orleans, inaugurated the Texas postal system, appointed John Rice Jones as first postmaster general, granted letters of marque and reprisal, and took steps to organize a Texas navy.

On November 12, 1835, Royall was elected to represent the Matagorda municipality on the General Council of the provisional state government, and he arrived to take his seat on December 6.

On February 1, 1836, an election was held to choose two delegates from the Matagorda municipality to serve at the convention meeting a month later at Washington-on-the-Brazos. Each voter was to select two delegates from the seven on the ballot: Bailey Hardeman, S. Rhoads Fisher, R. R. Royall, Ira Ingram, Daniel Elam, Thomas Cayce, and S. Allen Sanders. The top four vote-getters were as follows: Royall–83, Fisher–79, Hardeman–75, and Ingram–74. On February 22, the election was contested by Fisher, who charged voting irregularities. As a result the Committee on Privileges and Elections recommended that sixteen votes cast for Royall by volunteer soldiers in Goliad were invalid, as were five votes cast by members of the New Orleans Grays in the Tres-Palacios District. The committee report was approved, Royall was denied his seat, and Fisher and Hardeman remained to represent Matagorda at the signing of the Texas Declaration of Independence on March 2, 1836.[4]

Richardson Royall returned to Matagorda, resumed his role as president of the Committee of Public Safety, and sent word to Austin that he could "count on Matagorda." On April 1, 1836, he joined Thomas McCoy's Company of Mounted Riflemen (Spies) and served with the Texas army until his discharge on July 1. Richardson then served in the cavalry company of John P. Gill from July 16 to October 17, 1836, when he was discharged at Columbia. Royall later submitted claims against the Texas government for $15,000 for supplies he furnished the Texas army in 1835 and 1836. The Texas Congress eventually voted him the sum of $3,717 in relief.[5]

In addition to the Collinsworth company, one other Matagorda unit participated in the Texas revolutionary war. This cavalry company was led by Albert Clinton Horton, a former Alabama state senator. Leaving his wife Eliza and family behind, Horton sold his eighty acres in Greene County and left for Texas in January 1835. Soon after arriving at Matagorda that April, Horton met Abner L. Clements, and the two began the retail firm of Horton & Clements, operating out of a large general store on the corner of Fischer and Cedar streets in Matagorda. Horton's home there, a two-story wood frame cottage known as the Rugeley-Sisk House, was built in 1830 and still stands today.

---

4. Bailey Hardeman was born near Nashville, Tennessee, on February 26, 1795. After serving as an officer in the War of 1812, he was admitted to the bar and married Rebecca Amanda Wilson in 1820. Hardeman came to Texas in 1834 and received land grant #128 on Caney Creek. He built a home there before returning to Tennessee for his family and kinfolks in 1835. In late November, Bailey organized a seventy-five-man militia company from Matagorda municipality. When Gen. Martín Perfecto de Cos heard that Hardeman's company was bringing an eighteen-pound cannon from Dimmitt's Landing to San Antonio, the news prompted the Mexican leader to surrender the city on December 10, 1835.

Hardeman was a delegate to the Convention of 1836 and signed the Texas Declaration of Independence. He also served as ad interim secretary of the treasury and was among the signers of the Treaty of Velasco with Santa Anna. On September 25, 1836, Hardeman died of congestive fever at his Caney Creek plantation near present Van Vleck. Hardeman County was named for Bailey and his brother, Thomas J. On August 29, 1936, his body was reinterred in the State Cemetery at Austin.

5. After Royall's wife, Ann, died at Matagorda in February 1836, he used Vice-president Lamar as an intermediary in a futile effort to win the hand of James Walker Fannin's widow, who lived at Quintana. Richard then married Elizabeth Ann Allen Love of Houston in January 1839. This planter-merchant died at age forty-two on June 29, 1840, at the family home in Matagorda and was buried in the Matagorda Cemetery. Fortunately, the large file of letters in his Matagorda home was released for publication by his young widow. Much of the Royall correspondence is now in the State Archives. In 1936 a Texas Centennial Marker was placed beside his grave.

In mid-October 1835, Horton returned to Alabama to help James Butler Bonham organize the Mobile Grays and was back in Texas with the unit in late December. A month earlier the firm of Horton & Clements donated $500 to help the Matagorda Committee of Public Safety purchase the privateer *William Robbins*. In January 1836 Col. James W. Fannin, Jr., at Copano, ordered 23 barrels of flour, 646 pounds of rice, and three sacks of corn from Horton & Clements.

In early February 1836, Horton raised, mounted, and armed a cavalry company of thirty-one men from Matagorda at his own expense. The unit then galloped off to Goliad, where Colonel Fannin and his 390 volunteers from the United States had taken over Presidio La Bahia and renamed it Fort Defiance. One of Fannin's companies, the Alabama "Red Rovers" of Capt. (Dr.) John Shackleford, was made up of sons of Horton's Alabama friends.

On March 13, 1836, Fannin received orders from General Houston at Gonzales to destroy Presidio La Bahia and quickly retreat to Victoria. Instead, Fannin chose to wait for two units to return from helping families at Refugio. On March 16, Captain Horton's cavalry company arrived at Goliad with a strong yoke of oxen to transport the Texian cannons.

On the morning of March 18, Horton's men gave chase to a Mexican cavalry patrol found near the presidio. When Mexican reinforcements appeared, Horton's company dashed to the protection of old Mission Espiritu Santo and held off the attackers from behind its walls. At this point Shackleford's "Red Rovers" forded the San Antonio River, came to Horton's rescue, and the Mexican cavalry retreated. Although Fannin's garrison at La Bahia enjoyed watching the "fun," Horton's men were left bone-tired and with jaded horses.

Shortly after dawn on March 19, Captain Horton was sent ahead to scout the country and examine the crossing at Coleto Creek. At 9:00 Fannin's men finally began their retreat from Goliad on foot and with no provisions saved for the march. Fannin was urged to make a forced march to Coleto Creek and the shelter of its woods. Instead, he marched only six miles, then stopped on an open prairie to feed his animals, allowing Mexican General Jose Urrea and his army of 1,300 to overtake and surround the Texians at about 3:00 P.M.

Horton had left four of his horsemen in the rear of Fannin's line to warn him of the Mexican approach. When they dismounted to rest, the lookouts fell asleep, and the enemy was upon them before they knew it. Three of the four fled in panic and passed only a hundred yards to the right of Fannin's men, cursed by those they were supposed to warn. The only rider who stopped with the Texian army was the German volunteer Herman Ehrenberg, who later escaped during the Goliad Massacre.

After hearing the gunfire, Horton's company returned to find Fannin's men completely surrounded and standing off a fierce attack. It was said that Horton circled the battlefield three times trying to find some way to join Fannin, but only four volunteers agreed to join him in the hopeless effort. When he heard the warlike bugle sounds of the Mexican cavalry, Horton quickly decided to save his men and arms for the Texas cause. His cavalry company then galloped off to Victoria, thus escaping the massacre of Fannin's men on March 27, 1836. Where Horton went is a mystery; he is not recorded as fighting in any other battle in the revolution. On April 13, his company was dispersed to care for their families during the Runaway Scrape. On May 9 Horton arrived at New Orleans on the steamboat *Caspean,* where he confirmed General Houston's victory at San Jacinto before visiting his family in Alabama.

In February 1836, a small Matagorda company led by Capt. Thomas Steward was organized. Other members included J. Q. Hoyt, William Freum, Benjamin Loins, Daniel Yeamans, Hamilton Cook, George Elliot, John Plunket, William Russel, Joseph Yeamans, William Robin, Samuel Brigam, John Devoit, J. Burnit, and John Krowlin. After the company sailed to Cox's Point on Lavaca Bay, General Houston ordered them to retreat and take families from General Urrea's line of march. When the Matagorda men reached Velasco, they served two weeks as artillerymen under Capt. T. Bromley, the commander of Fort Velasco. The company was then ordered to Galveston on the steamboat *Yellowstone,* where they served out their time protecting the interim government of President Burnet and the mass of civilians on the island.

In early 1836, John Duncan of Matagorda joined Capt. Moseley Baker's Company D of Burleson's First Regiment of Texas Volunteers. After serving as a steamboat captain in Alabama, Duncan left his family behind and came to Texas at age forty-five in 1835. During the retreat of General Houston's army, Company D prevented Santa Anna from crossing the Brazos River at San Felipe. Baker's unit also fought at San Jacinto, and Matagorda County legend has it that Private Duncan's mule, Ulysses, was the real hero of that historic battle. After his mare stepped in a pothole and broke her leg, Duncan was on foot a week before coming upon a piebald farm mule on the Harrisburg Road on April 16, 1836. When General Houston ordered his Texian army to charge across the plain of San Jacinto at 4:00 P.M. on April 21, the stubborn Ulysses refused to budge, even when Duncan spurred and beat him with a branch and the blunt side of his sword. Suddenly, the mule was accidentally jabbed in the rear by a comrade's bayonet point. The startled animal bolted away, with Duncan clinging to his back, and reached the Mexican barricades seventy-five yards ahead of the rest of the Texian army. As he knocked over Mexican tents and sent men and equipment flying, this crazed mule began the demoralization of the Mexican army. Because of Ulysses' exploits, he lived a life of pampered ease on the Duncan plantation.[6]

Matagorda was a hotbed of naval activity during the Texas Revolution. The *William Robbins* was owned by the Matagorda Committee of Public Safety and won fame as a privateer. On November 20, 1835, Capt. William A. Hurd and a volunteer crew from Matagorda captured a Mexican prize crew from the warship *Bravo*, which had boarded the *Hannah Elizabeth*, a New Orleans schooner carrying $35,000 worth of powder and munitions for the Texas army. Fortunately for the crew of the *William Robbins*, the *Bravo* was blown out of Pass Cavallo by a fresh norther after seizing the *Hannah Elizabeth*. Once they recaptured the American ship, Hurd and S. Rhoads Fisher sold some of the ship's cargo at auction to members of the expedition, a sale that was con-

---

6. "Captain" John Duncan, so called because of his background as a steamboat pilot, received a league and labor of land bordering Caney Creek ten miles north of present Bay City in 1837. He then brought his family and slaves there from Alabama and built a three-story home. (Today only two huge crepe myrtles mark the location of this mansion.) Eventually, the Duncan plantation sprawled over 16,000 acres. Julia Duncan died on May 3, 1846, and the body was returned to Mobile, Alabama, for burial.

The Matagorda County census of 1850 showed John Duncan as owning real estate valued at $100,000. By 1860 he owned 3,000 head of cattle — the largest herd in the county — and ninety-four slaves. One group of slaves was led by a tribal chief from Zululand named "Podo." Even after emancipation and the sale of the plantation, this Kaffir slave continued to lead. Thus the sugar cane area and the shipping and switching point on the Southern Pacific Railroad which ran through the plantation were known as "Podo."

John Duncan died at age ninety in 1878 and was buried on the plantation grounds. In 1936, the State of Texas erected a granite marker there under an oak tree, but it has since disappeared.

In 1882, the only surviving child, John Duncan, Jr., sold the plantation to the famed cattleman, A. H. "Shanghai" Pierce. It is still in the possession of his heirs as the Runnells-Pierce Ranch.

demned by Col. James W. Fannin, Jr., the Texas military commander in the area.

On November 25, 1835, the General Council of the provisional state government passed a bill to create a navy and to purchase four schooners. Charles E. Hawkins was named as first commander of the Texas Navy. In early January 1836, the navy purchased the *William Robbins* from the Matagorda Committee of Public Safety and renamed it the *Liberty*. The three other navy ships were the *Brutus,* the *Independence,* and the *Invincible.* To protect the flank of General Houston's retreating army, Commodore Hawkins kept his tiny fleet in Matagorda Bay, thus making Matagorda the first homeport of the Texas Navy. In mid-April 1836, the fleet base was moved to Galveston Island to protect the ad interim Texas government there. After being sent to New Orleans for repairs, the eighty-ton *Liberty* was sold there when the Texas government was unable to pay the repair bill.

Silas Dinsmore, a Matagorda ship owner and master, became a "legalized pirate" on December 1, 1835, when he was issued three letters of marque and reprisal to seize Mexican ships and cargoes. Dinsmore then served as a captain in the Texas Navy from March 30 to May 10, 1836.

Upon hearing news of the fall of the Alamo and General Houston's retreat from the Colorado River, most Matagorda residents boarded ships and sailed for New Orleans or the East Texas coast. Many of these families, including that of Elias Wightman, joined thousands of other refugees encamped at Beaumont. S. Rhoads Fisher was attending the convention at Washington-on-the-Brazos, and his family took passage on the *Brutus,* which sailed for Galveston on March 17, 1836. When Fisher last left Matagorda, he hid $300 in an unlocked trunk in their home. The night before the family sailed, the mate on the *Brutus* stole the money from the room where he slept. After the Battle of San Jacinto, Fisher joined his family at Galveston and sailed with them on the *Brutus* to New Orleans, arriving there on May 2, 1836. He soon returned to Texas but sent his family on the *Saratoga* to Philadelphia, where they remained until November 1838.

After hearing of Houston's victory at San Jacinto, the people of Matagorda returned to find their homes ransacked and empty, their fences down, and livestock and crops stolen or destroyed either by General Urrea's Mexican army, the Karankawas, or opportunistic neighbors.

In the tense weeks that followed, another Mexican army at Matamoros made plans to land a division of 2,000 at Copano Bay on the Texas coast. Upon hearing of the planned invasion, Gen. Thomas J. Rusk ordered Maj. Isaac Burton and his company of twenty mounted riflemen to patrol 400 miles of coast and prevent the landing of any Mexican ship. Several men from the Matagorda area were in Burton's company, including John Duncan.

On June 2, 1836, Burton's scouting party sighted a suspicious vessel lying in Copano Bay. After concealing his men, Burton used a Spanish-speaking member of the company to signal the craft to send its long boat ashore. When the five Mexicans in the landing party were seized, sixteen Texians took their places and rowed out to the surprised captain, who surrendered the *Watchman* without a shot. A search revealed that the vessel was loaded with provisions for the advancing Mexican army. Burton ordered the captain to sail the ship to Velasco, but the absence of winds detained any departure for two weeks. During this time two other ships with similar cargoes, the *Comanche* and the *Fanny Butler,* anchored off the bar. Major Burton used pistol persuasion to force the captain of the *Watchman* to lure the skippers of the other two ships aboard his vessel, where Burton demanded complete surrender. All three ships were then taken to Velasco, where their $25,000 worth of cargo was condemned and turned over to the Texas army. Because of their unusual victory at sea, Burton's mounted riflemen were known thereafter as the Texas "horse marines." Due to the vigilance of these men, the Mexican army canceled its coastal invasion plans.

On October 3, 1836, the First Congress of the Republic of Texas assembled at Columbia, the temporary capital. Ira Ingram represented Matagorda County and was elected Speaker of the House of Representatives. He served in that key post until his resignation just prior to the convening of the second session of Congress at Houston on April 1, 1837.[7] Albert Clinton Horton of Matagorda represented Matagorda,

---

7. Ira Ingram died on September 22, 1837, and was buried in the Matagorda Cemetery. In his will he named Seth's wife, Susannah Rice Ingram, as his major heir. This may explain why Seth refused to make any provisions for Susannah after they divorced on October 15, 1840.

Ira left $15,000 and his land on the San Bernard and Brazos rivers to the town of Matagorda to create a school system. Although this school fund was estimated at $75,000, the Ingram will was not probated until July 28, 1856. On three different occasions, in 1838, 1856, and 1859, five commissioners were elected to manage the Ingram School Fund. What happened to the fund after 1859 is unknown.

Seth Ingram married the widow Mary Susan Davis in Christ Church on February 9,

Jackson, and Victoria counties in the Senate of the First and Second Texas Congress (1836–38).

On October 22, 1836, President Sam Houston and Vice-president Mirabeau B. Lamar were inaugurated in the hall of the House of Representatives. Once Houston finished his inaugural address, he paused a few seconds, then dramatically removed the sword he wore at San Jacinto and presented it to Speaker Ingram. Among President Houston's cabinet choices was another Matagorda man, S. Rhoads Fisher, as secretary of the navy.

On November 7, 1836, Houston sent a message to both houses of Congress suggesting that the government should move to some point with better housing and office accommodations. On November 30, the two houses met in joint session to decide on a new site for the capital. Fifteen towns entered the competition. On the first ballot, Matagorda received eight votes to eleven for Houston, the new town going up on the banks of Buffalo Bayou. Houston finally won out on the fourth ballot, defeating Washington by a vote of twenty-one to fourteen.

Secretary of the Navy Fisher proved to be a very controversial cabinet member. In April 1837, he took a furlough and went on a sea voyage, supposedly for his health. Fisher's real intent was piracy, both to swell the coffers of the depleted treasury and to call attention to the unpopular navy, which needed to fight its way into public respect.

After Fisher ordered the *Invincible* and *Brutus* to prepare for a cruise, the two navy schooners sailed out of Galveston on June 10, 1837. They rendezvoused at the Isle of Mugeres on the tip of the Yucatan Peninsula. There the two ships looted and destroyed a large number of Mexican pirogues, released one Mexican boat in return for a ransom, and cannonaded the town of Sisal. The Texas schooners then sailed up and down the coast, making repeated landings to burn nine Mexican villages to the ground.

During these raids Secretary Fisher had a narrow escape when he and Capt. James D. Boylan of the *Brutus* went ashore with a boat crew of six to obtain fresh water. Leaving their muskets in the boat, the sailors walked toward a village where a troop of Mexican cavalry was camped. When the dragoons charged, the Texians dashed for the beach. Luckily, Fisher had a pistol and dropped one horseman from his saddle before the sailors reached their arms. When the other wary Mexicans retreated, the navymen escaped to their ship.

1846. He died of consumption on May 12, 1857, and was buried beside his brother Ira. In 1936, a Texas Centennial Marker was placed beside each of their graves.

In July 1837, Capt. Henry L. Thompson of the *Invincible* put a prize crew on board the English brig *Eliza Russell* off Alacran Island, Yucatan. The British contended that the ship was carrying merchandise, not contraband, and that seizing and taking her to Galveston was "an act of piracy." After capturing and stripping two Mexican schooners en route, the *Brutus* and *Invincible* arrived at Galveston on August 26. Both were destroyed the next day, after being attacked by two larger Mexican brigs.

An embarrassed President Houston released the *Eliza Russell* and suspended both Fisher and Thompson. The latter was also charged with cruelty by his crew but died before being brought to trial. In October 1837, the president ordered Fisher removed from office for directing a cruise "of a character not calculated to elevate us in the scale of nations."

Rhoads returned to private business at Matagorda, where he was shot to death by A. G. Newton. On March 21, 1839, the *Matagorda Bulletin* announced his death as follows:

> We are sorry to state that a fatal encounter took place in our city on the evening of Thursday last, between Mr. A. G. Newton and S. Rhoads Fisher, which resulted in the death of the latter gentleman. Under existing circumstances, we forbear making commentary. The survivor voluntarily surrendered himself to the authorities and . . . was held to bail for the sum of $3,000.00 for appearance at the next circuit court.

After being charged with the murder of Fisher, Newton was acquitted by a jury on March 3, 1840. The former secretary of the Texas Navy was buried in Matagorda Cemetery on March 16, 1839. His was the first interment by the parish of Christ Episcopal Church, which recorded the cause of death as "shot." (Fisher County was created and named in his honor on August 21, 1876. A Texas historical marker was placed at Fisher's grave in 1964.)

Another Matagordan, Senator A. C. Horton, was equally controversial during this period. The flamboyant Horton was six feet, seven inches tall, and nicknamed "Old Sorrel" because he often wore his sandy gray hair long and plaited in a queue.

On December 14, 1837, Senator Horton remarked that he "would thank God if the President [Houston] were dead." The next day Senator William H. Wharton took exception to the remark and declared his intention to challenge Horton once the claims of another old Horton adversary, S. Rhoads Fisher, were satisfied. Horton retorted that Wharton had first claim, but the duel was avoided by disagreement as to who should have the first shot at Horton.

A. C. Horton was later denied an appointment as postmaster general by President Lamar. After the post was awarded to Judge Edwin Waller, Horton picked a fight with him, and the brawl took place in front of the capitol with the president and a recessed Congress looking on. Once Horton began to get the worst of it, Lamar waved his hat in the air and shouted, "Do not interrupt them, let them fight, let them arrange it without interference."

On March 17, 1836, the Republic of Texas created Matagorda County out of the old Mexican municipality of Matagorda. The county was organized in July 1837, with Matagorda as the county seat. In 1849 a two-story wooden county courthouse was built on Market Street on a block of land given by Seth Ingram. The structure was destroyed by the 1854 hurricane and rebuilt using the original plans.

Mail route #11 was inaugurated from San Felipe to Matagorda in April 1836. Mail route #18 from Matagorda to Columbus began on a weekly basis in the fall of 1837. Local planters subscribed $500 to extend this route to San Antonio. A bi-weekly mail route from Galveston to Matagorda and Texana began in May 1838.

On August 2, 1837, the *Matagorda Bulletin* was started in Matagorda by J. W. J. Niles, editor and proprietor. He was the son of Jonathan Niles, the publisher of the renowned *Niles Register* in Washington, D.C. The *Bulletin* continued until 1839 and was a four-page weekly newspaper with an annual subscription rate of five dollars. Other early newspapers in Matagorda included the *Colorado Gazette and Advertiser* (1839), the *Weekly Dispatch* (1843), the *Colorado Herald* (1846), the *Chronicle of the Times,* and the *Matagorda Gazette* (1858).

On January 28, 1840, Matagorda and Houston were granted charters creating a chamber of commerce. The city of Matagorda was incorporated by a special act of the Texas Congress on February 5, 1841, and Harvey Kendrick was elected as first mayor.

In the early years of the Republic, Matagorda was the major seaport of Texas. In 1837 it was not unusual to see ten or twelve foreign vessels lying at anchor in the bay below Dog Island. A pilot would meet the *Cora, Amite,* or other ships at Decrow's (Decros) Point, Pass Cavallo, and guide them through Matagorda Bay to Dog Island Reef, an obstruction of shells crossing the bay at right angles four miles below Matagorda.[8] There the cargoes and passengers were sent ashore in small boats called "lighters."

Matagorda was designated as one of six ports of entry in 1837, and President Houston appointed George M. Collinsworth as the first collector of customs for the Matagorda revenue district. His deputy (clerk) was E. O. Connor. After locating his office on June 19, 1837, Collinsworth hired Hugh O. Watts as a deputy collector to work from the port of Lavaca. George's duties included the collection of import duties, enforcing rules and trade regulations, reprimanding ship captains for failing to follow regulations, and appraising damaged goods of ships wrecked at Pass Cavallo.

In 1840 a customshouse was built in Matagorda at the corner of Fisher and Market streets. Among the first items of merchandise to come through the customshouse were new record books for the county government. Shipped from the firm of Hotchkiss & Co. in New Orleans, the books arrived at Matagorda on the steamer *Convoy* on July 15, 1837.

By the spring of 1836, only about thirty Karankawa warriors were left along the shores of Matagorda Bay. Elias Wightman hired them to pick cotton on his plantation on Matagorda Peninsula. When he used his own skiff to search for a brave's runaway squaw and found her up the Colorado living with her mother, the grateful mate offered to help Wightman if *his* squaw ever ran away.

The Karankawas were not allowed in Matagorda and began to drift toward Mexico in 1839. Four years later, they suddenly reappeared in a drunken, pathetic condition and offered to trade fish for whiskey. After a bolt of lightning killed the chief and his squaw without harming the six-month-old boy between them, the tribe thought

---

8. Decrow's Point, on the western end of Matagorda Peninsula at Pass Cavallo, is rooted in the league of land granted to Thomas Decrow, Sr., in 1831. Thomas was one of six seafaring brothers who came to Texas from Maine before 1840. After serving as a boarding pass officer, Decrow was later appointed as a ship pilot at Pass Cavallo.

Captain Decrow hired an expert ship carpenter to construct a two-story home at Decrow's Point. Built to withstand hurricanes, this structure had corner posts extending six feet into the ground; each post had a crosspiece fastened to the bottom called an anchor. In addition to his home, Thomas also owned a wharf protruding into the bay and warehouses for storing cargoes.

The hurricane which destroyed Indianola on September 17, 1875, also washed the anchor posts of the Decrow home out of the ground. As a result, twenty-two people who had gathered there for protection were drowned, including Thomas, his wife Lucretia, and three of their children.

the incident was the work of the "Great Spirit," a punishment for their drunkenness and bad behavior. Leaving the little orphan behind, the Matagorda Karankawas joined one of two large bands leaving Texas.[9] One group migrated to South Padre Island, and the other band received land from the Mexican government near La Mesa in Reynosa.

A. C. Horton's family arrived in Matagorda in May 1837. Within four months, four of the six children were dead. By then Horton and his partner, Abner Clements, were engaged in retail merchandising, cotton trading, and land speculation. Within ten years the two land agents owned over 13,000 acres in Bexar and Comal counties.

In 1837 their advertisement in the *Matagorda Bulletin* read as follows:

> Have constantly on hand a general assortment of Staple and Fancy Goods . . . Ready made Clothing . . . Hardware . . . Drugs and Medicines, Crockery, Groceries, etc. . . . . They will also be prepared at all times, to purchase or make liberal advances on cotton.

At one time or other, Horton and Clements sold lumber and bricks, barrels of flour and beans, soap, salt, sugar, potatoes, powder, whiskey, coffee, "30,000 fine flavored cigars," and Southern Tonic, which claimed "the credit of effecting *a perfect and lasting cure* for Fever and Ague . . ."

On May 30, 1838, the citizens of Matagorda endorsed Mirabeau B. Lamar as president of the Republic and A. C. Horton as vice-president. In early June, Horton began a campaign trip to San Antonio and

---

9. Mr. D. E. E. Braman took in the orphan Indian baby and raised him in Matagorda until he was nine. Local residents referred to him as Tom Braman or "Indian Tom." He was a stoutly-built, healthy lad who loved tobacco, boats, fishing, swimming, and playing with Christian Zipprian. Braman later described Tom as being lazy to the extreme, wasteful with his clothing, untruthful, thieving in small things, wild, and incorrigible.

In May 1851, Chief Justice M. Talbot recognized Humphrey N. Gove of Matagorda Peninsula as the legal guardian of Indian Tom in order to keep him away from blacks and place him in a more rural, secluded environment. Gove signed a $1,000 bond to protect, feed, and clothe the boy, teach him to read and write, and make him a useful member of society until he was twenty-one.

During the Civil War, Tom was living with the Sterry family. In 1863, Union troops took the Sterrys and some twelve other Matagorda families to New Orleans as refugees, where they were kept in a large refugee camp outside the city. When a Yankee lieutenant ordered Tom to a work detail, the proud Indian refused and was run through with a sword. He was buried near the camp. Tom Braman of Matagorda is the last known survivor of the Karankawa Indians in Texas.

the principal western towns. His actions near Coleto Creek came back to haunt him during this time. In the July 14 issue of the *Houston Telegraph,* a man claiming to be "One of Fannin's Advance Guard" anonymously charged Horton with acting cowardly in not forcing his way to Fannin. A week later, nine members from Horton's company signed a statement at Matagorda. In defending their leader, they said the charges were false and slanderous; that Horton's conduct was brave and manly on that occasion.

In August, both Horton and fellow candidate Joseph E. Rowe helped suppress Vicente Cordova's rebellion near Nacogdoches. When Horton proceeded to canvass for votes dressed in military regalia, he was lambasted for such degrading opportunism. One newspaper referred to his hustling self-promotion as "strolling like a peddling Jew from village to village, and making stump speeches . . ." Evidently, such a campaign did not impress the voters. Horton collected less than thirty percent of the vote and finished a distant second to David G. Burnet.

Soon thereafter Horton built a three-story building in Matagorda with the intention of offering it to the Republic as the capitol building if Matagorda was chosen as the capital. When he was named chairman of a five-man committee to choose the site for a new permanent capital in January 1839, Horton promptly withdrew his Matagorda bid due to possible charges of conflict of interest. It was Horton who cast the deciding vote for President Lamar's choice, a trading post on the upper Colorado called Waterloo that was renamed Austin.

Matagorda could boast of one of the first Masonic lodges in Texas. On June 24, 1838, a petition for dispensation was signed by twelve town residents. The dispensation was granted on July 18, 1838, and signed by Anson Jones, Grand Master of the Grand Lodge of Texas. Matagorda Masonic Lodge #7 was chartered on December 2 that year, with Seth Ingram, Thomas M. Duke, and Charles W. Rice among the twelve charter members. They were later joined by A. C. Horton. A Masonic hall was erected in Matagorda in 1849, but the building, charter, books, and papers were destroyed by the 1854 hurricane. Lodge #7 finally disbanded in 1864.

On December 22, 1837, Jane and Robert McManus returned to Matagorda on the schooner *Himnora.* After being taken in by the family of I. R. Lewis, spinster Jane became a recluse for a time. On November 27, 1838, her protector, the chivalrous Mr. Lewis, wrote an indignant letter to the six managers of the "Cotillion Party" (ball) held the night before. Lewis demanded to know whether Jane's not being invited was an act of intentional disrespect; if so, he considered it a "wanton outrage" and "personal indignity" to him and his family since Jane had already suffered enough misfortune and injustice. Lewis went on to warn that further action might be direct and personal (possibly a duel challenge) if he did not receive a proper explanation. This controversy may account for Miss McManus's decision to leave Matagorda for good.[10]

Silas Dinsmore was the first chief justice of the county court at Matagorda. His wife, Amanda, moved to Matagorda in January 1833, after leaving their two children with her sister Julia, the wife of Capt. John Duncan, in Mobile. After returning to Mobile to "wait out" the war in 1835, Amanda Dinsmore brought the family back to Matagorda in August 1836. By then Julia Duncan was living at the family plantation on Caney Creek.

The two sisters joined other Matagorda residents and promised support in inviting an Episcopal minister, Rev. Caleb S. Ives of Mobile, to move there and establish a school.[11] On December 12, 1838, Reverend Ives arrived in Matagorda as the first foreign missionary of the Missionary Society of the Episcopal Church in the United States.

---

10. Jane returned to New York in 1839 to launch a career as a journalist and author. Among her credits was the series "The Presidents of Texas," published in the *Democratic Review* in 1849. She spent much of her time in Washington, D.C. observing the political scene in the 1840s. A staunch advocate of Texas annexation and the doctrine of "Manifest Destiny," she undertook a secret diplomatic mission to Mexico in 1847.

After marrying longtime suitor William Cazneau in 1850, the two lived on the Rio Grande for several years. During this time Jane wrote *Eagle Pass* (1852) under the pen name of Cora Montgomery. William carried out several successful diplomatic assignments during the next ten years, largely because of Jane's superior energy, personality, and statecraft.

Jane Cazneau died on December 10, 1878, when her ship was lost at sea en route to the family estate at Keith Hall, Jamaica. Her brother Robert married Sarah Spinks on July 18, 1838, and retired to a planter's life at his large estate, Moss Bluff, on the Trinity River. He died on September 1, 1885, and was buried in the State Cemetery.

Today a Texas historical marker, at the corner of Fisher and Laurel streets in the city park at Matagorda, commemorates the site of the "dream colony" of Jane McManus, the only woman colonizer in Texas history.

11. Caleb Ives, a native of Vermont, was educated at Trinity College in Hartford, Connecticut, and at the General Theological Seminary in New York City. He was ordained a deacon and priest in 1833. After developing tuberculosis, Caleb was appointed a missionary to Alabama by the Domestic Committee of the Missionary Society. He then moved to Mobile and founded three churches in five years. On September 25, 1838, Reverend Ives was appointed a missionary to the Republic of Texas by the Foreign Committee of the Board of Missions.

After celebrating Holy Communion for the first time on Christmas Day, Caleb organized Christ Episcopal Church on January 27, 1839, the oldest such church in Texas. Reverend Ives also established the Matagorda Academy the same day.

Initially, the services of Christ Church were held in the Masonic Hall. Judge Dinsmore was a member of the first Vestry. Since Silas believed that "total immersion" was the only true baptism, Reverend Ives baptized him in Matagorda Bay on May 31, 1840.

In 1841, A. C. Horton and Abner Clements donated land for a church (Lot 5, Block 12, Tier 1, Matagorda Front). At that time Reverend Ives traveled to the eastern United States to raise funds for a new church building, and the structure was shipped prefabricated from New York on a schooner. It was erected some 400 yards east of the present church site. The first services in this new building were held on Easter Sunday of 1841.

Christ Church was consecrated by The Right Reverend Leonidas Polk, bishop of Louisiana, on Sunday, February 25, 1844. That night Bishop Polk held the first confirmation ever held in his parish. Seventeen were confirmed, including Helen Milne Dinsmore, Seth Ingram, and the Rice twins, Elizabeth M. and Elanor M., who were namesakes of the two famed cannons used by General Houston in the Battle of San Jacinto, the "Twin Sisters."

On September 11, 1854, a hurricane destroyed Christ Church. The congregation moved to the present location in 1856 and built the church that still stands on Lots 5 and 6, Block 9, Tier 2. This property was purchased from James W. Granger for $250 on May 1, 1855. A new bell was obtained at the time, but many of the original church fixtures were salvaged, including the altar, altar cross, communion silver, baptismal font, communion rail, priest's chair, sedilia, supporting pillars, timbers, flooring, and many of the pews.[12]

On July 31, 1858, the *Matagorda Gazette* ran a notice that pews in this new Episcopal church would be rented to the highest bidder on August 6. Forty-one such pews were rented by 1860.

Reverend Ives and his wife, Katherina, had a home on the lot next to the original church (still standing in 1991). The couple estab-

---

12. Although damaged by several hurricanes, Christ Episcopal Church has been restored to the same design and condition as in 1856. The building has been designated as a recorded Texas Historic Landmark and received the official Texas Historical Building Medallion in 1962. In celebration of its 150th anniversary, a Texas Historical Commission marker was dedicated at the church on October 22, 1988.

lished and operated the Matagorda Academy from 1839 until 1849. Caleb also organized a Sunday school for slaves in Matagorda.

On February 4, 1840, Ives ran the following academy advertisement in the *Colorado Gazette and Advertiser*:

Tuition charges:

Spelling, reading, writing, and first lessons in arithmetic — $3 per month.

Arithmetic, Grammar, Geography, History and Composition — $6 per month.

Higher branches of Science and literature, and especially the Mathematics and the Latin and Greek language — $9 per month.

The academy would have at least one vacation during the year, which would last from July 1 to October 1.

On February 3, 1845, the Matagorda Academy was chartered by the Congress of the Republic of Texas as Matagorda University. Among the fifteen named as trustees were Caleb Ives, Seth Ingram, A. C. Horton, and John Duncan.

At the General Convention of 1841, Caleb Ives was proposed for but not elected bishop of Texas. In May 1843, he was among the three who proposed the organization of a diocese. Reverend Ives's dream was realized on January 1, 1849, when the Diocese of Texas came into being at the Primary Convention held at Christ Church, Matagorda. W. L. Sartwell, the first elected senior warden of Christ Church, Matagorda, donated three Longhorn steers to defray the cost of bringing Reverend Ives from Mobile to Matagorda. A Texas Longhorn is pictured on the seal of the Diocese of Texas to commemorate this first gift to the Episcopal church in Texas.

Hard labor as a minister and teacher caused Caleb Ives's health to fail, and he returned to his native Vermont in the summer of 1849. He died there on July 27, 1849, at the age of fifty-one.

On January 6, 1839, the Matagorda Methodist Church was organized by Jesse Hord, an itinerant Methodist preacher to the Rutersville missionary district. At 3:00 P.M. on January 3, Reverend Hord arrived in Matagorda with a letter of introduction for Colonel Horton, who was absent at the time. Eliza Horton graciously provided a room in their home for Hord, who said he was "well domiciled with this very refined and intelligent family."

In his journal entry for January 6, Hord noted:

I attended the Episcopal service at 11:00 P.M. At 3:00 P.M. I preached. We had much interest. I also preached at early candle

light with much liberty. I opened the doors of the church and four
came forward. This was the beginning of the first Methodist Class in
Matagorda.

That spring Rev. Isaac Strickland made a missionary journey, and
the Matagorda church was on his circuit. In a diary entry dated May 7,
1839, he noted that the "whole town turned out" for his Sunday night
appointment.

In late 1839, the Mississippi Conference organized the Rutersville District. Matagorda was one of the seven churches in the district,
and Rev. R. H. Hill was appointed pastor there.

The Texas Conference was organized on December 25, 1840, by
Bishop Waugh. Among the fourteen appointments in the Rutersville
District was D. N. V. Sullivan as pastor of the Matagorda church.
Reverend Sullivan held services in private homes and public buildings.

The Methodists built their first church in Matagorda in 1851
after James H. Selkirk sold Lot #12, Block #9, Tier #1 to the congregation for $100. This building was destroyed by the hurricane of
1854. It was said that the roof was blown out to sea and never found.
After losing their church building, the Methodists held services in the
county courthouse and then the "new" schoolhouse until 1893.[13]

An era ended for Matagorda with the passing of its founder in
1841. Elias Wightman lived in Matagorda County until then, serving
as county surveyor and justice of the peace. He and wife Mary then sold
their land and moved to Covington, Kentucky, in hopes of improving
his health. He lived only two months, however, and died in Covington

---

13. In 1891, Fred S. Robbins loaned the church money to build a parsonage. When
church members met at the schoolhouse for Thanksgiving services on a cold, rainy day in
1892, no one had a key to the locked building. Shivering and dripping wet, the worship-
ers decided on the spot that they *must* have a proper church. Robbins again loaned the
money, and the present church was finished in March 1893. It was built by Charles Baker
from longleaf yellow pine and cypress shipped from Galveston.

Two black members were on the church rolls at this time, Jackson Holt and Hannah
Carr. Aunt Hannah, a slave of the Carr family, moved to Matagorda after the Civil War.
She donated twelve dollars to the building fund and cleaned the church as long as her
health permitted. When she died, Hannah Carr left all her possessions to the Matagorda
Methodist Church.

In 1927, Sunday school rooms, a kitchen, and study were added to the church. A
hurricane in 1942 did extensive damage to the church and parsonage, but both were re-
paired. The sanctuary was remodeled in 1947, and the church's appearance was changed by
adding a large entrance porch in 1965. The original Bible and handmade cypress pews are
still in use today.

on October 26, 1841. On his monument is the phrase: "He had a head to contrive, a heart to conceive, a hand to execute, angels could do no more."[14]

By 1840 Matagorda had a population of over 1,500 and was the social, cultural, and educational center of the area. One impressed observer was Englishman William Bollaert, who spent over two years in Texas in the early 1840s. When Bollaert first visited Matagorda on April 19, 1842, he passed the evening in the home of Dr. Johnson Calhoun Hunter, an accomplished violinist and harpist. Bollaert's diary entry for that day included the following observation:

> . . . The society I met at his house, both of ladies and gentlemen, left nothing to be desired. Beauty, talent, and friendship. The "Belles of Bonavista" were there. They are mild and fair, gentle as a zephyr's sigh! . . .

Three days later, Bollaert attended a musical party hosted by Col. "L." and was impressed by the music, dancing, and elegance. On April 23, a local gentleman told the Englishman that the people of Matagorda had *all* they could wish for or want except a deepwater approach to town. Bollaert was in Matagorda again on May 24, 1842, and saw the local Thespian Company perform two plays "very well indeed in their pretty little theatre."

In 1847, many prominent families of Matagorda were among the sixty shareholders who contributed to the "social library tax." The contributors included George Burkhart, D. E. E. Braman, John Duncan, Sam W. Fisher, A. C. Horton, Galen Hodges, Caleb S. Ives, Seth In-

---

14. The original copy of Elias Wightman's *Field Notes, Book I, Matagorda County* is in the Matagorda County Clerk's Office. The frontispiece is a map of the county showing land grants in 1839. Written in beautiful penmanship and fine language, the book offers a thorough description of the land.

Wightman's compass, in good condition and working order, is still in the possession of a Matagorda County descendant. This compass was used to survey both Marion (East Columbia) in 1829 and Matagorda in 1832.

After her husband's death, Mary Sherwood Wightman returned to Matagorda for a brief visit. Several years later, she married Meredith Helm, a Kentucky native and founder of Connersville, Indiana. It is possible that Meredith was one of the young soldiers manning the stockade when Mary first arrived at Matagorda. Mary Helm spent the rest of her life in Connersville and died there in 1886 at age seventy-eight.

Before her death, Mary's invaluable memoirs, *Scraps of Early Texas History*, were published in Austin, Texas, in 1884. The book includes Elias Wightman's field notes and history of Texas from his writings.

gram, Ira A. Lewis, William J. Russell, John Rugeley, and James H. Selkirk.

In June 1849, the *Colorado Tribune* mentioned a dancing academy in town; W. T. M. Smithson was the instructor. By 1850 there were four seminaries of learning in Matagorda, the most important of which was the LaFayette Academy.

The most renowned Matagorda resident of this period was Albert Clinton Horton. From March 6 to April 13, 1842, Captain Horton and a volunteer company of forty men from the Matagorda area served under Col. Clark L. Owen in a campaign against Mexican General Rafael Vasquez, who was driven from San Antonio after occupying the city for two days.

When Gen. Adrian Woll captured San Antonio again on September 11, 1842, Horton mustered another company of volunteers, assigned this time to the command of Brig. Gen. Alexander Somervell. There is no record of Horton's command being involved in any combat.

In July 1845, Horton represented Matagorda County in the convention which drafted a new state constitution. In a behind-the-scenes caucus, he consented to run for lieutenant governor to balance the ticket with James Pinckney Henderson of San Augustine. The old charge of cowardice was revived against Horton, and the initial vote count went to Nicholas H. Darnell by a margin of 4,319 to 4,271. Following late returns from South Texas and a recount, the legislature declared A. C. Horton the first lieutenant governor of the state, and he was sworn in on March 26, 1846.

When the Mexican War erupted, Governor Henderson was granted a leave of absence on May 9, 1846, to take command of Texas volunteers as a major general. Horton then served as acting governor until December 15, 1846, and was paid as governor during that period. Since the legislature was not in session, Horton's only major problem was a battle with the federal government in which he unsuccessfully sought to enlist five companies to protect the Texas frontier from the hostile Comanches to the west. (In 1936 the Texas legislature declared that Horton *was* governor during that time. As a result his picture was placed in the capitol along with those of other Texas governors.) His term of office as lieutenant governor expired on December 21, 1847. [15]

---

15. In January 1837, Horton purchased 2,222 acres from Randall Jones and established "Sycamore Grove" plantation in present Wharton County. This sugar and cotton plantation extended from the eastern edge of present Wharton past Caney Creek and along

From 1840 to 1865, Matagorda ranked second to Galveston as the leading seaport on the Texas coast. However, its potential growth was limited by the shallow waters of Matagorda Bay, Dog Island Reef four miles below town, and the "river raft," a massive logjam along the lower Colorado River first noted by the Spanish in 1690.

In her book *Texas* (1836), Mary Austin Holley reported that the average depth of Matagorda Bay was only eight feet. William Bollaert

---

the only road leading to Matagorda.

In 1846, A. C. built the Sycamore Grove "big house" on the outskirts of the new town of Wharton. This two-story farm house was made of hand-hewn logs with slave-made bricks for the big double chimneys. Both stories were divided into two 20 x 20 rooms. The dining room and living room were on the bottom floor, and both bedrooms were upstairs. A middle hall and front galleries were on both floors.

The 1850 census of Wharton County showed Horton owning real estate valued at $105,610 — the highest listing in the county. He also owned fifty-five town lots in Matagorda and county real estate there valued at $13,937. In the 1850s, his Sycamore Grove plantation produced a yearly yield of 650 to 700 bales of cotton, 450 to 500 hogsheads of sugar, and 1,600 barrels of molasses.

Planter Horton was also a prominent Baptist layman during this period. He served for twenty years as a charter trustee of Baylor University at Independence. As a patron of the college, he contributed $5,000 and donated a large, costly bell to the Female Department in 1858. That same year, Horton and Charles L. Bolton purchased land on the corner of Burleson and Rusk streets in Wharton and built the First Baptist Church, a white frame structure with a gallery above the front section of the sanctuary for slaves.

In the 1850s, A. C. maintained homes in both Wharton and Matagorda, where he kept a pew in the Episcopal Church and was a member of the Matagorda Masonic Lodge #7, AF and AM. In an 1858 will, Horton deeded Sycamore Grove to his daughter, Patience Louisiana Texas, and her husband, Col. Isaac Dennis. Patience died before her father and was buried in the Sycamore Grove family cemetery.

By 1860, Horton owned 170 slaves and was one of the wealthiest men in Texas, with $319,000 in real and personal property. That year he served as a delegate to the Democratic National Convention in Charleston, South Carolina. He planned to endow a $50,000 Baylor professorship, but the Civil War wrecked his fortune.

On September 1, 1865, A. C. Horton died of pleurisy at his home in Matagorda. Buried in the Matagorda Cemetery, his grave was marked by a "conservative stone." A Texas historical marker was dedicated at the gravesite on October 10, 1987.

Six generations of the Horton family occupied the Sycamore Grove "big house" through the daughters. In 1960, Mrs. Lida Croom Hodges Shryer had it torn down due to continued breaks in the gas line, deterioration, and the cost of needed repairs.

On March 19, 1988, a Texas Historical Commission marker was dedicated at 500 Park Drive, the site of the Albert C. Horton Mini-park just opposite where his home stood. This land was given to the city of Wharton by attorney Thomas H. Abell, a great-grandson of Horton and former Wharton County judge, and his wife Frances. Among those taking part in the program was another great-grandson, Horton Foote, the famous playwright, screenwriter, and author.

noted in his journal entry of April 19, 1842, that his vessel anchored off Matagorda in only six and a half feet of water and that it took an hour to run in their boat from the anchorage to town. To the Englishman, this was "rather inconvenient for the shipment of goods, etc."

The head of the massive driftwood obstruction on the Colorado was located twelve miles above Matagorda in 1838. On April 14 of that year, the keelboat *David Crockett* arrived at the raft after a five-day trip downriver from Bastrop. From that time on, Matagorda teamsters met boats there and shuttled cotton bales and other freight into town, where the cargo was loaded onto other boats.

The first attempt to remove the raft came when merchants and planters from Matagorda, Columbus, and La Grange persuaded the Texas Congress to pass a special law incorporating the Colorado Navigation Company on December 14, 1837. The company had its main office in Matagorda and was empowered to issue capital stock of $25,000 in shares of $100 each "for the purpose of clearing a channel susceptible of navigation by steamboats or other craft for the Colorado River." The company was required to open a channel permitting steamboats to pass fifty miles upstream within four years or forfeit its charter. Once the fifty-mile channel was completed, the company could levy tolls on craft using the river. Such tolls would be used to clear obstacles in the river. Although the company hired a civil engineer to survey the raft in 1839, no further action was taken due to lack of funds.

On June 1, 1842, delegates from counties along the lower Colorado met at Columbus to discuss the raft problem. J. R. Lewis and G. W. Ward represented Matagorda County on a five-man committee which reported that $30,000 would be required to remove the raft. They recommended that the money be raised by subscription through county committees and that the work start once $10,000 was raised. After two years this effort also ceased.

On January 18, 1844, the Texas Congress rechartered the Colorado Navigation Company with minor changes. In June of that year, Samuel Ward of La Grange agreed to build a steamboat for the company at the head of the raft. Ward purchased the engine and equipment in Pittsburgh, and his steamboat, the *Kate Ward*, arrived at Austin on March 8, 1846. She drew only eighteen inches of water without cargo and could carry 800 bales of cotton. During highwater in 1848, the *Kate Ward* escaped around the raft and reached Matagorda Bay.

The company was rechartered for a third and final time on September 5, 1850. With $17,000 raised in stock sales, engineer W. T. Ward used the *Kate Ward* as a snag-boat to clear a channel from the mouth of the Colorado through the seven-mile-long raft in December 1852. By that time, however, the company had been forced to suspend operations because none of the six counties involved had paid their subscription pledges.

The most successful approach to the raft problem was undertaken by the U.S. Army Corps of Engineers. Between November 1853 and March 1854, the Corps dug a bypass channel around the raft and through a series of lakes. For the first time a steamer from Matagorda could ply directly to Columbus and La Grange through safe, navigable waters. The years between 1854 and 1860 marked the best period of navigation on the Colorado. During this time the steamer *Betty Powell* regularly carried 500 bales of cotton downriver from La Grange.

During the 1840s, Matagorda Peninsula was known as the health resort of South Texas because of its pure air and sea-bathing. An invalid when she moved there from near La Grange in 1844, Mrs. Mary A. Maverick was soon restored to good health. She found Matagorda to be the most cultured society in Texas. Mary's husband, Samuel A. Maverick, was an attorney and signer of the Texas Declaration of Independence. On June 24, 1846, the five Maverick children — Sam, Lewis, Agatha, Augusta, and George Madison — were all baptized in Christ Church at Matagorda.

The family settled on a farm at Tiltona, across the bay and southwest of Matagorda. In 1845, a neighbor who owed Samuel $1,200 paid up by giving him 400 head of cattle valued at three dollars a head. Samuel never wanted the herd and left them in the care of a black family when the Mavericks moved to San Antonio in 1847. For the next six years, the neglected cattle were left unbranded and were allowed to multiply and run wild on Matagorda Peninsula. Such poor management by the caretaker resulted in numerous complaints from Matagorda County cowmen. Neighbors assumed that stray, unbranded calves were Maverick's cattle and began to call them "mavericks." Finally, in the spring of 1855, Samuel moved his herd to the Conquista Ranch fifty miles below San Antonio. The cattle fared no better there; only one-third of the calves were branded. When Maverick sold all his cattle to Mr. Beauregard for six dollars per head in 1856, the entire branded herd totaled only 400, the original number. Samuel thus retired from the cattle business with a 100% profit. His indifference also resulted in a new international word. Today all stray cattle bearing no brand and found alone without proof of parentage are called "mavericks."

The so-called German Settlement adjacent to Tiltona began when John Zipprian emigrated from Germany to Matagorda County in May 1846 and purchased 320 acres of land on Matagorda Peninsula. A chimney maker and stonemason by trade, Zipprian used these skills to assist a colony of Germans from Hanover in building a dozen homes. This settlement produced the best-known cowboy author in the United States, Charles A. Siringo. On February 7, 1855, Siringo was born in one of its little cottages.

In 1867 the Faldien family moved from the mainland to the German Settlement for health reasons and rented part of Tom Siringo's home. That spring twelve-year-old Charles was hired to run cattle on the Faldien ranch on Big Boggy Creek northeast of Matagorda. His first job was branding wild cattle at Lake Austin. Siringo hired out as a cowboy to "Shanghai" and Jonathan Pierce at Rancho Grande in the spring of 1871. Each winter, from 1872 until 1875, Charles and his partner, Horace Yeamans, skinned dead cattle at Hampton's Point on Tres Palacios Bay and sold their hides for five dollars each. After driving cattle up the Chisholm Trail, Siringo returned to Matagorda County to visit with friends Wylie Kuykendall and Yeamans. [16]

In the 1850s, slave labor became increasingly important to planters in the Matagorda area. During the decade the number of slaves and their value in Matagorda County increased from 1,208 worth $500,520 to 2,265 worth $1,130,300.

On August 6, 1849, a planter signing his name "Sangborn Cultivator" wrote a letter to the editor of the *Colorado Tribune* at Matagorda. Noting that the time was long past for a planter to kill and wear out one Negro to buy another, the pragmatic Sangborn recommended that beginning with working the cotton crop on April 15, hands and mules should be allowed two hours of rest at noon with the rest period extended to three hours by July 1. He had found that his crop was as large as the year before since both mules and hands were in better condition. Sangborn also recommended having a cook with well-prepared food ready for the field hands at the end of their work day.

Evidently, there was much fear of bad behavior or possible insur-

---

16. Charles Siringo wrote a book titled *A Texas Cowboy or 15 Years on the Hurricane Deck of a Spanish Pony* in 1885. He was the first authentic cowboy to write an autobiography. His book is still considered the best and most realistic record of life on the range. Will Rogers, a Siringo fan, said the book was the "cowboy's Bible" when he was growing up. Charles also wrote *Lone Star Cowboy* and *Riata and Spurs*.

rection by slaves. On April 19, 1850, a series of Matagorda city ordinances signed by Mayor T. C. Steward included the following curfew provisions: The city constable would ring a bell at 9:00 in the evening; all slaves or free persons of color had to be at their respective houses within fifteen minutes of the bell ringing; such persons found in the street after 9:00 without a pass would be punished with from five to twenty stripes; and the constable had authority to disperse four or more male slaves at the same house not belonging to the same person who gave the appearance of disorderly conduct.

The wealth produced by slavery and the plantation system made this period the "golden days" of Matagorda. The "Belle of Old Matagorda" society was Frances McCamley Gordon Newsom. Fannie's father, John W. McCamley, came to Texas from Long Island, New York, with Austin's second colony. After Mexicans and Indians raided and burned his Goliad mercantile store in 1836, McCamley moved to Matagorda and served as an Indian scout. When he was sure that Texas would be annexed by the United States, he brought his family to Matagorda on the steamer *New York* in 1845. His daughter Frances was a student of Reverend Ives at the Matagorda Academy. In 1912, Fannie's reminiscences appeared in the *Galveston News* under the title, "Early Days in Texas." In recalling the elegance of Matagorda society, she noted:

> . . . In those years Matagorda was the seat of Texas wealth and aristocracy. The people were wealthy, cultured and sociable, and entertained with the most liberal prodigality. Their guests were treated as members of the family. Their fine homes were elegantly furnished and supplied with numerous well-trained servants and every convenience necessary for making life gay, happy and delightful.
>
> It was famous as a winter resort, and during that season the pleasure-seekers and society devotees came there from all sections of the Union. George Ludlow, who became governor of Ohio, had a wealthy aunt living there, and he was quite a familiar figure in society circles in Matagorda during the gala season. John Donelson and other nephews of President Andrew Jackson were also numbered among the annual winter visitors.
>
> The wealthy citizens kept open house, and dancing, balls, social visiting and gatherings, riding parties, excursions on the bay, etc. following one after another, made society life in the old town one continual round of pleasure . . .

On August 9, 1853, an article appeared in the *Indianola Bulletin* describing a flying visit that fourteen residents made to their sister town of Matagorda, a place "populated by a people noted for their sociability, hospitality, and intelligence." The Indianola visitors observed that Matagorda "displays more evidences of wealth and comfort than any other [town] in its handsome residences, fine walks, and beautiful yards and gardens . . . The Colorado House, kept by Mr. Galen Hodges, is one of the best buildings and best conducted hotels in the State . . . We also visited the courthouse and the Daguerrean gallery of Mr. James H. Selkirk. In the latter we were shown the likenesses of eleven of Austin's 'Old Three Hundred' . . ."

The James Selkirk mentioned was one of the most prominent Matagorda businessmen of this period. His father, William, was one of Austin's "Old Three Hundred," coming to Texas from Albany, New York, in 1822. He surveyed much of the Gulf Coast and on August 10, 1824, received a league on Selkirk's Island, formed by two branches of the Colorado River just above Matagorda. After he died in 1830, squatters occupied his land.

Soon after the Battle of San Jacinto, William's only son, James Henry, a skilled "ornamenter" of post coaches, came to Texas and recovered the Selkirk land through legal proceedings. By 1843 he was operating a ferry just above Selkirk's Island. In August of that year, he married Lucy Hall, a union that produced six children. James and his cousin built the first dock in Matagorda on the south side of town. In addition to his profitable shipping and warehouse business, Selkirk opened a daguerreotype studio in January 1848. He made many likenesses over the next few years, often trading them for services for his family. James H. Selkirk was a member of Masonic Lodge #7 and served as city clerk and treasurer, as well as county clerk, surveyor, and treasurer. He was a victim of a yellow fever epidemic and died on October 31, 1862. Both James and his wife, Lucy, who died in 1892, were buried in the Matagorda Cemetery.

Matagorda's Colorado House, one of the finest hotels in Texas, was built by John Ives in 1852. This celebrated hotel and social center was located in the heart of town on Main Street. Built of cypress lumber imported from the East as ship ballast, this twenty-room showplace had copper and brass fixtures and mahogany, walnut, and cherry furniture. Each of the fourteen guest rooms upstairs had a private dressing room. The dining room had Chippendale chairs, silver with the marking "Colorado House" on the handle, and beautiful candlesticks. Downstairs were two great rooms separated by a folding door, which opened to form a large dancing floor for balls, soirees, and evening parties. At one end was a huge fireplace with a large mahogany-framed mirror above it.

Since Matagorda was a thriving seaport, captains, sailors, and businessmen from New Orleans, Mobile, New York, Connecticut, and Pennsylvania stayed at the Colorado House. A frequent guest was the famed Texas cattleman, A. H. "Shanghai" Pierce. Foreign guests from England, Germany, Ireland, France, and the Netherlands were also registered there. The stagecoach arrived and departed from the hotel, and mail carriers made overnight stops there.

In late 1852, Galen Hodges purchased the Colorado House and the block on which it stood, including the private home of John W. McCamley, a mercantile store, drug store, and slave quarters at the back of the block.

After Helmuth Hotz, a German artist, visited Matagorda in the early 1850s, he returned home and painted a town lithograph from memory. His picture of town scenes included six Matagorda buildings: Christ Episcopal Church, the Masonic Hall, the courthouse, the Robert H. Williams home, the George Burkhart store, and the Colorado House.[17] Hotz sent the lithograph to Hodges, who used it as the letterhead on his hotel stationery.

---

17. Among the area planters having second homes in Matagorda was Robert H. "Gentleman Bob" Williams, who came to Texas form North Carolina as one of Austin's "Old Three Hundred" in December 1823. His league of land on Caney Creek was known as Rotherwood Plantation. Caney Crossing, where the road from Matagorda to Brazoria crossed Caney Creek, was on Williams's plantation.

In December 1826, he was elected *alcalde*. The next year, he built the third cotton gin in Austin's Colony. In June 1832, Williams fought in the Battle of Velasco and was blinded by a splinter in one eye. He wore an eye patch the rest of his life. Williams represented the Matagorda municipality in the Convention of 1833 and was listed as postmaster at Caney Crossing as early as September 1838. He served in that capacity again from May 1847 until September 1851.

After the death of his first wife, Anna, Williams married Mary Lawson White of Texana in May 1833, and they had five children. The Williams family entertained and spent much of their time in a fine, two-story home in Matagorda. Gentleman Bob died on September 11, 1880.

George Burkhart and his wife, Catherine Dorothy Robideaux, were both natives of Philadelphia, Pennsylvania. They raised a family of seven sons and five daughters, one of whom married D. E. E. Braman of Matagorda in April 1844.

In 1838, Burkhart received land grant #176 for 640 acres in Matagorda County. He was among those who contributed to the Social Library Tax for 1847. In 1854, the town of Matagorda appointed Burkhart, John W. Gibson, and Galen Hodges to a new "com-

In 1858, Hodges became the owner and editor of a new newspaper, the *Matagorda Gazette,* with a motto of "Truth Fears Nothing But Concealment." Two years later, E. J. Lipsey became editor of the paper. [18]

A house of unique design was built two miles due west of Matagorda by the Robbins brothers, Frederick Wells and Chester H., in the late 1850s. Their father, Samuel A. Robbins of Petersburg, Virginia, went $3,000 in debt in 1832 after losing his ship and cargo to a Gulf storm near Mobile, Alabama. This misfortune brought the sailor to Texas in the spring of 1836, and at that time he helped women and children to safety during the Runaway Scrape. After returning to Virginia, the fifty-six-year-old Robbins and his eighteen-year-old son, Frederick Wells, sailed for Matagorda from New Orleans on the schooner *Pocomoke* on March 12, 1838. The two first settled near Caney Creek and present Sargent, then moved to Frederick's 320-acre headright across Selkirk Island west of the Colorado in 1844 and built a wooden cabin near its banks. Frederick raised cattle, sheep, and goats there, and his father purchased a small sailboat for trading along the Gulf Coast.

In early June 1848, Samuel Robbins was murdered in his sleep and robbed of eighty dollars in silver on a return voyage from Corpus Christi. After the boat washed ashore at Port Aransas, his body was spotted and the remains were buried in the Robbins ranch family cemetery on June 15, 1848.

Four years later, Frederick Robbins finally persuaded his older brother, Chester Hamlin, to join him in Texas. At the time, Chester was engaged in the mercantile business with Abel Head, the uncle of Shanghai Pierce. After the brothers built a frame house on the Texas homeplace, Chester traveled to Rocky Hill, Connecticut, in 1854 and

---

mittee of health" charged with reporting the causes of sickness.

The George Burkhart store, a two-story structure, was one of the largest stores in Matagorda. On April 30, 1859, Burkhart ran the following advertisement in the Matagorda Gazette:

... I am now opening a full and complete stock of spring and summer goods selected under my own supervision in the cities of Philadelphia and New York.

On August 21, 1861, Burkhart was commissioned as captain of the 22nd Reserve Company of Matagorda County.

18. Galen Hodges died on May 10, 1884, in Victoria, Texas. His only heir was a daughter, Julia Amelia Wadsworth. The Colorado House was torn down in 1932 by Hodges's grandson, Albert H. Wadsworth. Today there is a Texas historical marker at the site of the hotel at the corner of Fisher and Market streets. The marker is located at the base of the post office flagpole.

married a distant cousin, Chloe Marie Theresa Robbins. The new-lyweds returned to Texas, only to find that their comfortable home had been destroyed by the hurricane of September 1854.

In 1855, Chester and Frederick laid the floor plan for "Tadmor," an octagon-shaped, two-story mansion with an observation tower on top. The biblical name for this "house in the wilderness" comes from I Kings 9:18: "Baalath, and Tadmor in the wilderness, in the land of Judah." Slaves hauled oyster shell up from Dog Island, burned it to make lime, then mixed that with water, sand, and oyster shell to mold a unique concrete house which measured sixty feet from outside to out-side. The outer walls were eighteen inches thick; the inner walls were twelve inches.

When it was completed in 1861, Tadmor had four large rooms separated by four small, triangular rooms on both floors. The first floor housed the parlor, dining area, closets, and a "museum." The bedrooms were on the second floor. The cypress lumber in the house was boated in from Louisiana. The kitchen and pantry were in a sepa-rate wooden structure attached to the northwest side by a short breeze-way. Above the kitchen was a tack room and quarters for the hired hands. On the west side of the house was a hen house and cistern; far-ther out on a prairie knoll was the family cemetery. Among the fea-tures of the house were ventilators in the walls for cooling each room, a circular stairway in the center, north and south chimneys, porches surrounding the first and second floors, and a cellar for keeping food-stuffs cool and dry.

For years people en route from Ashby and Deming's Bridge to Matagorda would ride as far as Tadmor, put their horses out to pasture there, then travel on to town by boat.

During the Civil War, a Union gunboat off to the south in Mat-agorda Bay mistook Tadmor for a Confederate fort, fired on it with cannon, and left gaping holes in the east wall of the Robbins home. (One such cannonball that did not explode was still in the possession of family descendant Mrs. Eva Robbins Savage when she was interviewed in 1971.)[19]

---

19. Chester H. Robbins died on January 22, 1869, and was the second to be buried in the Tadmor family cemetery. Frederick's wife, Mary, died in 1871 at the birth of their second child, Frederick McCully, who was raised by Chester's wife, Chloe. Frederick W. Robbins died on November 13, 1873.

After being sent East to attend college in Virginia, Fred McCully returned to Tad-mor, married Eva Eugenia Parker, and had four children. In 1908, Fred completely

Residents of Matagorda had courageously supported the Confederate cause. On July 26, 1860, a public meeting at the Matagorda courthouse authorized Dr. E. A. Peareson to organize a local military company. At that same meeting Robert H. Williams, John Rugeley, and John McCamley agreed to obtain funds to equip the company. As a result of these actions, Company D, Sixth Regiment, Texas Volunteers (the Matagorda Coast Guards) was mustered into the regular Confederate army at Victoria on October 4, 1861. Fourteen of the company's fifteen officers were from Matagorda, as were forty-nine of its seventy-one privates. Since forty-six-year-old Dr. Peareson was the only physician in Matagorda and was needed on the home front, he was persuaded to resign at Victoria, and 1st Lt. James Selkirk was elected to take his place.

Company D was ordered to report for duty at Arkansas Post and immediately engaged in battle. The greatly outnumbered Confederate force was ordered to surrender, but Lt. Col. T. S. Anderson of the Texas regiment defied the order, and the Texans fought on until Anderson realized that the order came from the Confederate commander, Gen. Thomas J. Churchill. At that point the Texans finally put handkerchiefs on the ends of their bayonets. After the battle, Union commander Gen. John A. McClernand was amazed to find that Captain Selkirk's Matagorda company did not have a single man dead or wounded.

Company D was sent by boat up the Mississippi River to the Federal prison at Springfield, Illinois. Several of the poorly clad Matagorda men froze to death on the journey. After being imprisoned for several months, the company was exchanged, assigned to General Churchill again, and participated in the battles of Chickamauga, Missionary

---

remodeled the stately old home, repapered the walls, and installed a carbide lighting system. Twice a year he made train trips to Houston to buy groceries at Henke and Pilot's. In 1938, Fred built his wife, Eva, a new ranch house a quarter mile north of the old place; it was vacated when Eva passed away in 1943.

Tadmore was thus left vacant for the first time in seventy-nine years. However, the mansion's fine furniture and antiques were safeguarded by Fred's daily visits until his death in 1959. After that time, vandals stripped the old place of its furnishings, even Fred's guns.

Today Tadmor lies in ruins, with only fragments of the outside wall still standing. It is visited only by an occasional hunter.

Jack Brannon, who worked on the Robbins ranch as a student, was allowed to take one of the interior doors of Tadmor in 1976 by the family of Benjamin Palmer Robbins, a son of Fred who died on August 3, 1973. As a tribute to his deceased and dearest friend, Brannon wrote a book titled *Mr. Robbins, I Miss You* in 1985.

Ridge, and Franklin. The Matagorda unit suffered heavy losses in each of these battles, and only a handful of these brave men lived to return to their homes after the war.

Matagorda County companies were also among the 4,000 to 6,000 Confederate troops gathered at Fort Caney at the mouth of Caney Creek. Fort Caney was completed in mid-March 1864, and its four garrisons faced repeated shellings from seven Federal gunboats of the West Gulf Blockading Squadron for two months prior to that time. As a result of this barrage, labor on the rifled thirty-pounder mounted in the main fort had to be performed after nightfall. One Confederate soldier's head was blown off by long-range Federal guns on January 10, 1864. Twelve days later, some 2,500 Union troops landed ten miles below Fort Caney but moved *down* Matagorda Peninsula. On March 13, these forces returned to their ships and left the Texas coast to join Maj. Gen. Nathaniel P. Banks at Alexandria, Louisiana, for his unsuccessful Red River campaign against East Texas.[20]

Matagorda's most heroic — and tragic — figure of the war years was Edward S. "Ned" Rugeley, Sr. Ned's father, John Rugeley, served in the Alabama state legislature before settling on Caney Creek in 1840. He became a very successful sugar and cotton planter and was elected to the Texas Congress in 1843. His sixth child, Ned, graduated from the University of South Carolina in 1841 and earned a law degree in 1845. After marrying Mary E. Smith of Alabama, Ned moved to Matagorda and practiced law there a few years before becoming a large-scale planter on Caney Creek. In 1861, he was elected captain of Company D, Texas Cavalry, Reuben Brown's Regiment. Known locally as the Caney Mounted Rifles, Captain Ned's company was assigned to guard the Texas coastline around Matagorda and to repel any invasion.

On November 30, 1863, Union forces occupied Pass Cavallo, only forty miles below Matagorda. One month later a Federal gunboat landed sixty men on the peninsula four miles below town. On the morning of December 30, 1863, Captain Rugeley learned that the Federals were building a fort and planning to attack Matagorda from across the bay. Leaving Sgt. George Burkhart in charge of fifteen men at Matagorda, Ned Rugeley called for volunteers to attack the fort at night, and the rest of Company D — some fifty-seven men — re-

---

20. Today the site of the main fort at Caney is several hundred yards out in the Gulf of Mexico. A Texas Historical Commission marker below Sargent on FM 457 at the mouth of Caney Creek tells the story of Fort Caney.

sponded to his call. Many of them were too young to join the Confederate army and one, Ned's half brother James, was only seventeen.

An hour before sunset on December 30, Captain Rugeley's attacking force left Matagorda on the steamer *Cora* and boarded the Confederate gunboat *John H. Carr,* which was anchored some 1,200 yards from the peninsula. At 10:00 P.M. all fifty-seven men and boys boarded a skiff and two lifeboats to commence the attack. Halfway to shore a fierce norther blew in, bringing winds of gale force and freezing rain. With the churning waves battering his three small vessels, Captain Rugeley ordered a return to the *Carr.* His skiff managed to reach the gunboat, and one of the lifeboats swamped near shore; the fifteen on board waded to safety on the eastern end of the bay. The second lifeboat, commanded by William Turner, sank in deep water with thirty-eight men on board. Brothers D. A. and Thomas E. McKinley drowned locked in each other's arms, but the rest managed to swim to shore. Since many of Rugeley's men were dressed only in short-sleeve shirts, nineteen of them died from cold or exposure in the dark hours that followed.

Rugeley later lamented that in another fifteen minutes his whole attacking party would have landed and captured the enemy force. When those who survived reached the entrenchment of the fleeing Yankees about midnight, their fires were still burning.

At daylight on December 31, twenty-one bodies were removed from the frozen beach and returned to the *Carr.* Several days later, the body of nineteen-year-old Henry Gibson washed up on the shore of his father's summer home just east of Matagorda.

At the time of this tragedy, preparations were being made for the traditional New Year's Eve Ball at the Colorado House. Instead of a festive dance, the bodies of Rugeley's men were "laid out" in the parlor of the hotel on the night of December 31. The men came as one to "sit up" with the corpses while the ladies gathered around the dining room fire or in Mrs. Hodges's room upstairs. Thirty years would pass before the ladies of Matagorda held the ball again.

On January 2 and 3, 1864, seventeen soldiers were buried from Christ Episcopal Church. The last funeral was held on January 4, and the bodies were buried in one large common grave in Matagorda Cemetery. Of the twenty-two who drowned or froze to death, nine were less than twenty years of age, including James Rugeley.[21] Two young ladies who lost their sweethearts never married: Miss Harriet Talbot and Miss Mollie Wadsworth. Some forty years later, Mollie ruefully noted that after wearing mourning clothes for two years, both she and Harriet were assigned the role of old maid for life.

The Union blockade of the Texas coast crippled the commerce of the port of Matagorda and brought financial ruin to its merchants and large planters. The city was also dealt a terrible blow by a yellow fever epidemic in the fall of 1862. From September 25 to November 27, the dread disease killed forty-five of the 150 white residents of Matagorda. Among the victims were Mrs. Catherine Burkhart and two daughters, Mrs. S. Rhoads (Ann) Fisher, and James H. Selkirk. At the time there were only three doctors in Matagorda County; the patient was often dead before a doctor could see him.

During the Reconstruction period, Matagorda was occupied for two years by a black company commanded by white Union officers. Although their presence enraged local residents, their actions gave little cause for complaint.

The end of the war found "Captain Ned" Rugeley's Caney Creek plantation in ruins. After being elected to the state legislature, he represented his district in the Constitutional Convention of 1875. A destructive hurricane that year caused him to resign and return home to rebuild his plantation. Rugeley later served as county judge of Matagorda County for eight years. The father of ten children, Judge Rugeley died in Wharton on December 21, 1897.

After the war, the port of Matagorda began to yield to her sister city of Indianola, which was much closer to Pass Cavallo and in deeper water. Matagorda's decline was hastened when the railroads reached the Brazos River and diverted more business there. The town was also severely damaged by hurricanes in 1875 and 1886, and left full of rattlesnakes after the latter storm.

---

21. The twenty-two victims were George M. Bowie, J. M. Connor, W. G. Copeland, E. Duggan, H. Gibson, A. D. Hines, J. N. Howell, A. C. Johnson, John H. Jones, N. M. Kenerly, E. Lake, D. A. McKinley, Thomas E. McKinley, Jesse Matthews, A. J. May, James Rugeley, J. A. Seaborn, J. G. Secrest, T. C. Secrest, Julius Shaw, Tom Wadsworth, and B. H. Walton.

Soon after the Civil War, William Wadsworth collected money to build a monument to these young men who gave their lives in the Matagorda Bay skirmish. Upon William's death, his son Albert kept these funds for forty years. On July 6, 1930, a monument called the Matagorda Memorial was unveiled in the Matagorda Cemetery.

A source of town pride during this period was the construction of the first school building in 1888. Built on the corner of Cedar and Lewis streets, the school was in service until 1914, later used as a grocery store, and razed in the early 1970s. In December 1914, a new brick, two-story school building was completed on the site of the Bay View Hotel on the corner of Wightman and Market streets.[22]

By the 1880s, old Matagorda retained its prestige largely as the seat of county government. Even that advantage was threatened when planters along Caney Creek and in the northern part of Matagorda County began to agitate to move the county seat to safer ground and a more central location. On September 18, 1894, an election was held for removal of the county seat from Matagorda. The new town of Bay City, a site formerly known as Bay Prairie, received 778 votes to 141 for Matagorda. As a result, Bay City was declared the county seat for Matagorda County. The new town boasted a population of 1,000 by 1900.

Historic old Matagorda received a much-needed economic boost in the late 1880s when Antonio B. Lorino established the first fish and oyster house in town. Morgan Smith and Edward Bell soon opened another such business, as did a Mr. Horn, who used fifty Chinese workers in his new oyster canning factory. When the Cane Belt Railroad Company (now the Santa Fe) reached Matagorda in 1902, the town became a commercial fish and oyster shipping center. W. G. Thornhill, the railroad depot agent, resigned his position and opened his own fish and oyster house. Lorino and Thornhill marketed 25,000 barrels of oysters and 242,350 pounds of fish in 1911. By that time seventy-one boats were engaged in the seafood industry. By 1912, Matagorda was the largest fish and oyster shipping point in Texas, and the famed Tiger Island oyster was being shipped to all parts of the United States.

On August 28, 1901, the *Matagorda County Tribune* included an article about Matagorda. Among its assets listed were a drug store, one physician, a good lumber yard, fleets of oyster and pleasure boats, three good churches, an Odd Fellows Hall, a splendid public school building, an oyster packery, a public warehouse, three grocery stores, three dry goods stores, a hardware store, a good hotel, many elegant

---

22. This structure was razed in 1970, and a new school building was completed on the site in January 1971. Since that time, all classes through grade six have attended this school (all other students go to school in Bay City).

bay front homes, and no lawyers or saloons.

Matagorda enjoyed one more economic boom in the 1920s after the Texas Gulf Sulphur Company discovered a major sulphur deposit at Big Hill, a domelike land surface about sixty feet high just east of Matagorda. The company began mining operations on March 19, 1919, and built a modern town called Gulf on the site for its employees. The community had company homes, stores, schools, a hospital, a community center, a theater, service station, dairy, and a dance pavilion on the bay. During the 1920s, many Matagorda residents worked at Gulf. The sulphur deposits depleted rapidly, however, and operations ceased there on September 19, 1932.

By that time the company had a new plant producing sulphur at Newgulf in Wharton County. Many of the Gulf employees were transferred there, the town of Gulf was closed, and Matagorda began to decline. Although the old Gulf plant reopened in January 1936, it shut down operations permanently that August. Soon only the 250-foot-tall twin smokestacks of the Gulf plant were left as landmarks to guide boats on the bay. After being severely damaged by Hurricane Carla in September 1961, they were dynamited in 1964. The Big Hill mine that was once a boon to the Matagorda economy is now a large, sunken lake, a home to area birds and wildlife.

It is ironic that Matagorda, once famed as a seaport, is now landlocked due to the rapid deltation of the Colorado River. The first river raft was located some twelve miles above Matagorda in 1838. A second and much larger logjam eventually built up at a point forty-six miles upriver between Bay City and Wharton. This obstruction caused the Colorado to periodically overflow its banks, and great floods in 1913, 1914, 1919, and 1924 partially submerged both towns along with large areas of cultivated, fertile lands.

In 1925 reclamation districts in Wharton and Matagorda County started to cut a deep, wide channel along the eastern bank of the Colorado and to remove the eastern edge of the raft. By 1928 this pilot channel extended the entire length of the raft. The following summer a flood swept through the channel with such force that it swept the entire raft and impounded sediments into Matagorda Bay, creating a delta covering 1,780 acres by 1930. This plain of alluvial deposit extended across the bay to Matagorda Peninsula by 1935 and covered 7,098 acres by 1941.

Between 1934 and 1936, the Matagorda County reclamation district dredged a new channel through the drift and delta to the Matagorda Peninsula. Thus the Colorado River could deposit its sediment directly into the Gulf of Mexico.

The land bridge from Matagorda to the peninsula created East Matagorda Bay, brought an end to the port of Matagorda, and left the old town surrounded by land. Once a major seaport and cultural and social center, Matagorda is in 1991 a sleepy village with a population of 600. It is best known as an excellent fishing area and weekend retreat for city dwellers. Now only the most dedicated history buff knows of the town's significance in early Texas history.

Albert Clinton Horton home.
— Photo by J. C. Hoke, Wharton, Texas

S. Rhoads Fisher home.
— Courtesy of J. C. and Babe Stanley

Christ Episcopal Church
— Photo by J. C. Hoke, Wharton, Texas

Methodist Church
— Photo by J. C. Hoke, Wharton, Texas

Matagorda Post Office, 1871–1964.
— Photo by J. C. Hoke, Wharton, Texas

Entrance to Matagorda Cemetery, founded in 1830.
— Photo by J. C. Hoke, Wharton, Texas

State marker and grave, Albert Clinton Horton, Matagorda Cemetery.
— Photo by J. C. Hoke, Wharton, Texas

State marker and grave, Benjamin and Esther Wightman, Matagorda Cemetery.

— Photo by J. C. Hoke, Wharton, Texas

State marker and grave, S. Rhoads Fisher, Matagorda Cemetery.

— Photo by J. C. Hoke, Wharton, Texas

State marker and grave, Ira Ingram, Matagorda Cemetery.

— Photo by J. C. Hoke, Wharton, Texas

State marker and grave, Richard Royster Royall, Matagorda Cemetery.

— Photo by J. C. Hoke, Wharton, Texas

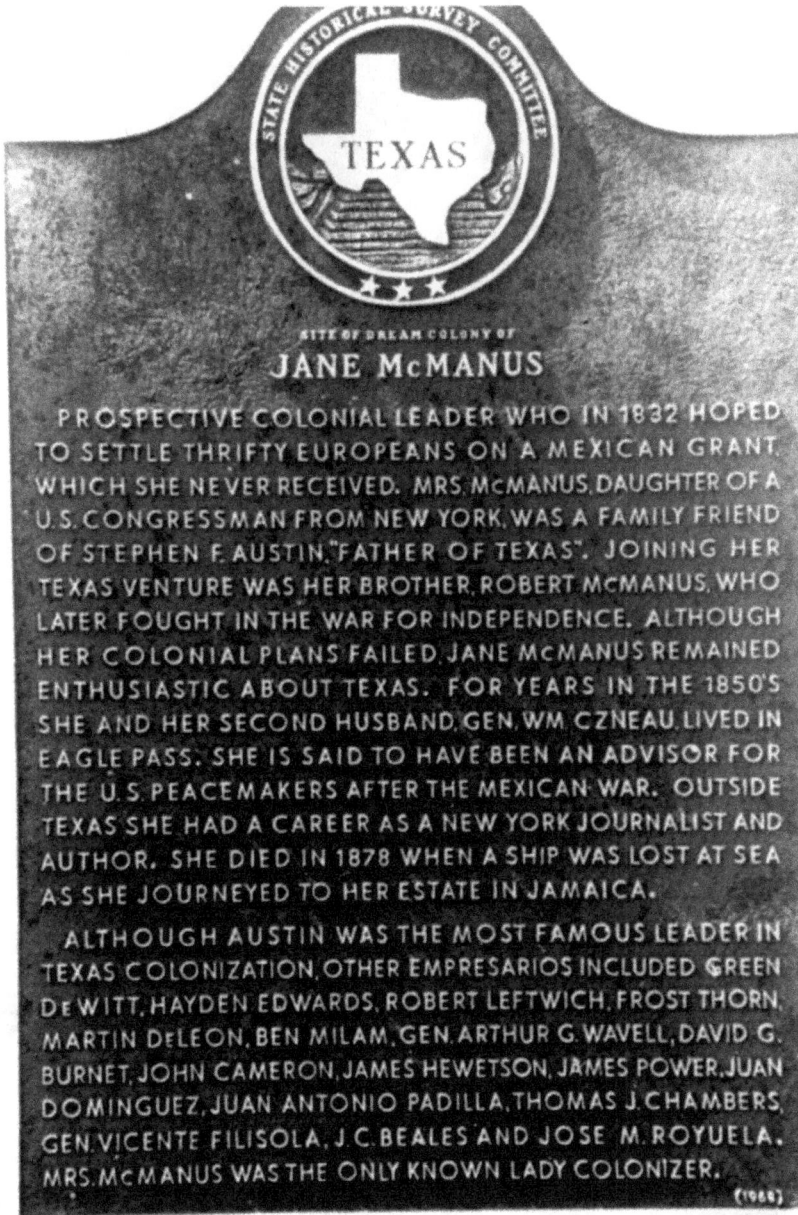

SITE OF DREAM COLONY OF

JANE McMANUS

PROSPECTIVE COLONIAL LEADER WHO IN 1832 HOPED TO SETTLE THRIFTY EUROPEANS ON A MEXICAN GRANT, WHICH SHE NEVER RECEIVED. MRS. McMANUS, DAUGHTER OF A U.S. CONGRESSMAN FROM NEW YORK, WAS A FAMILY FRIEND OF STEPHEN F. AUSTIN, "FATHER OF TEXAS". JOINING HER TEXAS VENTURE WAS HER BROTHER, ROBERT McMANUS, WHO LATER FOUGHT IN THE WAR FOR INDEPENDENCE. ALTHOUGH HER COLONIAL PLANS FAILED, JANE McMANUS REMAINED ENTHUSIASTIC ABOUT TEXAS. FOR YEARS IN THE 1850'S SHE AND HER SECOND HUSBAND, GEN. WM. CZNEAU, LIVED IN EAGLE PASS. SHE IS SAID TO HAVE BEEN AN ADVISOR FOR THE U.S. PEACEMAKERS AFTER THE MEXICAN WAR. OUTSIDE TEXAS SHE HAD A CAREER AS A NEW YORK JOURNALIST AND AUTHOR. SHE DIED IN 1878 WHEN A SHIP WAS LOST AT SEA AS SHE JOURNEYED TO HER ESTATE IN JAMAICA.

ALTHOUGH AUSTIN WAS THE MOST FAMOUS LEADER IN TEXAS COLONIZATION, OTHER EMPRESARIOS INCLUDED GREEN DeWITT, HAYDEN EDWARDS, ROBERT LEFTWICH, FROST THORN, MARTIN DeLEON, BEN MILAM, GEN. ARTHUR G. WAVELL, DAVID G. BURNET, JOHN CAMERON, JAMES HEWETSON, JAMES POWER, JUAN DOMINGUEZ, JUAN ANTONIO PADILLA, THOMAS J. CHAMBERS, GEN. VICENTE FILISOLA, J.C. BEALES AND JOSE M. ROYUELA. MRS. McMANUS WAS THE ONLY KNOWN LADY COLONIZER.

(1968)

Jane McManus state marker, Matagorda City Park.
— Photo by J. C. Hoke, Wharton, Texas

Albert Clinton Horton
— Courtesy Wharton County Historical Museum and
Thomas Abell, Wharton, Texas

Waterfront view of Matagorda, Texas, in 1860.
— Courtesy Geraldyne and Doug Havard

Norman Savage
— Courtesy Mrs. Ruby Baty, Wharton, Texas

"Tadmor"
— Courtesy Jack Brannon, Bay City, Texas

IV

Houston:
A Seaport Dream Come True

Allen's Landing Park, located at the foot of Houston's Main Street, is in the shadows of one of the most spectacular skylines in the world. The site was a muggy, mosquito-infested marshland in September 1836, when Augustus C. and John Kirby Allen climbed the slippery bayou bank in pursuit of a dream: the founding of an inland seaport on the Texas coast. What began as a dubious land promotion scheme of the Allen brothers was to evolve into the fourth largest city in the United States, and a world leader in oil, petrochemicals, architecture, space, and medicine.

Augustus Chapman Allen, the oldest of six sons, was born on July 4, 1806, in Canaseraga, a frontier village in Madison County, New York. The third oldest son, John Kirby, was born on March 31, 1810. A. C. Allen was five feet, six inches tall and weighed 140 pounds. He wore a mustache, was heavy-bearded, and had sharp, angular facial features. His smooth-faced younger brother, John Kirby, was taller, leaner, and wore long sideburns.

Poor health as a boy turned Augustus to daydreaming and a love of history books. At age seventeen he graduated from the Yates Polytechnic Institute at Chittenango, New York. A. C. then taught calculus and civil engineering there and utilized his expertise in helping to build the Erie Canal. After resigning his teaching position in 1827, A. C. became a bookkeeper for H.&H. Canfield Company in New York City.

On May 3, 1831, he married Charlotte Baldwin, the youngest of seven children. Charlotte was a tall woman with strong, commanding features. The newlyweds settled in a large, frame, towered house called "The Castle" in Baldwinsville, New York. Charlotte later admitted that the first year of marriage was difficult with this obsessed, driven man who expressed love only through sex. The frivolous, light-hearted John Kirby Allen was very fond of Charlotte, whom he regarded as an older sister.

While living with his maternal uncle, Col. Thomas Rose, in Orrville, New York, John Kirby operated a hotel and mercantile store. In 1830, he joined his mentor and tutor, A. C., in New York City, and the two brothers became commission import-export merchants and full partners in the Canfield business. In July of that year, the Allens met Don Lorenzo de Zavala when he lectured at the New York Institution's Lyceum while en route to Paris.

In March 1832, the brothers had a chance meeting with Sam Houston, who was then the ambassador of the Cherokee Nation, at the New York Institution Exhibit Hall. They all dined together at the new Delmonico's. At the time, a yellow fever quarantine had finished H.&H. Canfield Company and left the Allens in debt. Hearing talk of Texas from de Zavala and Houston inspired A. C. with a new business dream: his own port city in Texas. His brother's dream would fire John Kirby's sense of adventure. Despite Charlotte's opposition, A. C. was determined to come to Texas after reading Stephen F. Austin's contemporary account of the founding of his first Anglo-American settlement there.

Mid-December of 1832 found the Allen brothers on the *Lotus Eater,* a stern-wheeler bound for Natchitoches, Louisiana, the head of navigation on the Red River. After making friends with William Goyens, a free mulatto, mechanic, and teamster from Nacogdoches, the three managed to jump ship before the steamer's boiler blew, killing twenty-five passengers and leaving John Kirby with a severe blow to the head. He was cared for by Goyens's beautiful daughter, Teesha, at Natchitoches, and then the four made the four-day trip over El Camino Real to Nacogdoches.

On January 7, 1833, the Allens made their first Texas commercial contract with the widow of James Dill, buying the right to acquire her five leagues of land within a year. John Kirby soon took the five-league land option to Natchez, Mississippi, to test its marketability while A. C. made the eight-week trip upstream back to Baldwinsville, New York, in June. He departed for Texas that October with a promise from Charlotte to join him the following summer.

After acting as Sam Houston's campaign manager, John Kirby accompanied delegate Houston to the convention in San Felipe de Austin on April 1, 1833. Allen then returned to Nacogdoches, purchased the Dill House from Helena Dill, and renamed it La Casa de Allen. By the time A. C. returned in December, his brother had purchased options on five 11-league grants and was operating a general mercantile store. The two spent the winter in and around Nacogdoches, trading land and buying options and land outright. During this time, John Kirby became attached to Miss Anna Raguet after saving her life by pulling her from the path of a charging stallion. The blue-eyed, blonde-haired beauty brought him into the circle of friends of her prominent father, Henry Raguet.

In the spring of 1834, A. C. Allen first inspected Texana while exploring Matagorda and Lavaca bays inside the ten-league littoral limit. That July, A. C. met his wife, Charlotte, at Natchitoches and took her to Nacogdoches, where he enclosed a bedroom loft for their use at La Casa. In late November the Allens were rebuffed when they tried to buy Clopper's Point on the west bank and mouth of Buffalo Bayou. Nicholas Clopper chose instead to sell his 1,600 acres to Col. James Morgan.

In February 1835, Charlotte Allen's breech baby died at birth. After her extended bed rest, A. C. sent his wife back to New York in June. John Kirby Allen and William Goyens traveled to Monclova, the state capital of Coahuila-Texas, in April to help Samuel May Williams obtain a bank charter. The group was arrested at Del Rio upon their return and placed in the Presidio prison at San Antonio. Once Allen was released, he disguised himself as a priest and was poised to help prisoner Williams escape until he heard that Colonel Ugartechea was going to release Samuel May on his pledge to calm the Texas firebrands and agitators. John Kirby was back in Nacogdoches by mid-June 1835, just in time to help Frost Thorn organize a Committee of Vigilance and Safety. Allen also donated $500 in gold to the organization and agreed to store a bundle of captured Mexican army muskets at La Casa.

A. C. Allen sailed to New Orleans in early August 1835. Two weeks later, Stephen F. Austin arrived there after a long imprisonment in Mexico City. He stayed with Allen at Richardson's City Hotel. After accompanying the frail Austin to Texas on the schooner *San Felipe*, A. C. was back in New Orleans on October 13. There he helped arrange a $100,000 loan for Texas after reading a bulletin about the

Battle of Gonzales. As a member of the Texas Committee in New Orleans, A. C. helped to raise $7,000 and to send two well-equipped companies of 150 men to Texas, including the New Orleans Grays.

On October 17, 1835, he wrote an open letter to the president of the Consultation meeting at San Felipe. In the letter he and John Kirby offered to arm, man, and fit out at their own expense a privateer to cruise off the Texas coast. After the Consultation accepted the offer by acclamation and issued the Allens a letter of marque in early November, prominent commission merchant William Bryan found A. C. a 127-ton Baltimore schooner, the *Brutus*, for which Allen paid $5,500.

Five leading marine insurance companies and nineteen major merchants obtained a restraining order to keep the *Brutus* in port until January 4, 1836, when A. C. was ordered to appear in the United States District Court in New Orleans. The court order was based on the assertion that the ship intended to make war on Mexico, a country with whom the United States had friendly relations. After hearing numerous witnesses, Judge Gallien Preval ruled that there were insufficient grounds for issuing any criminal process against the defendant, A. C. Allen, thus clearing the way to launch the newly armed and manned *Brutus*.

At Banks' Arcade, Allen offered to donate the ship to the Texas commissioners — Austin, William H. Wharton, and Branch T. Archer — but Austin insisted that A. C. take a note from the Texas provisional government for its value. The Allen brothers and William M. Christy also put together a good loan for the Texas commissioners — $200,000 for five years at eight percent. When Captain Hurd sailed the *Brutus* for Texas in late January 1836, A. C. Allen was with him.

John Kirby Allen was in Nacogdoches on February 1, 1836, when an election was held to choose four delegates to the convention at Washington-on-the-Brazos. He was running a tight fourth in the balloting, with 200 votes, until Robert Potter displaced him by ramrodding through the votes of 120 angry volunteers from Kentucky. John Kirby would attend the historic convention, however, as Sam Houston's aide-de-camp.

After being reconfirmed as commander-in-chief of the Texas army on March 4, General Houston left for Gonzales two days later and sent John Kirby to Fort Jesup with the objective of persuading General Gaines to move his United States forces west of the Sabine River. During this period A. C. was busy preparing charts for the Texas naval squadron at Matagorda. In late March the two brothers met briefly at

Harrisburg before John Kirby returned to guard duty at Nacogdoches, then escorted fifty civilian refugees across the flooded Trinity River.

By mid-April 1836, A. C. was back in New Orleans working with the city's Texas Committee. He soon received some joyous news from Charlotte in New York: he was the father of a healthy baby boy, Samuel Augustus. After news reached New Orleans of General Houston's victory at San Jacinto, A. C. was among the members of the Texas Committee who officially greeted the wounded hero, Houston, on May 22, 1836.

When A. C. Allen returned to Texas with Commissioner Austin in late June, he brought a consignment of foodstuffs for the Texas government and army. He then traveled to army headquarters at Victoria, where he wrote John Kirby telling of his plans to develop a townsite to offer the Texas government as a capital.

The elder Allen then visited Texana, the county seat of newly organized Jackson County. The town met all of his requirements for an inland port city. Texana was the farthest point inland with no logjam obstruction; it also offered drainage, shelter, deep water, rich land, and natural beauty. A. C. was thus willing to offer Dr. F. F. Wells the huge sum of $100,000 in gold for the league of land on which Texana was located. The Wells league began at the forks of the Navidad and Lavaca rivers, covering two and one-half miles of land line and twelve miles of river front. After giving the offer careful consideration, Dr. Wells asked Allen to double his bid. This so angered A. C. that he was said to have jumped on a stump, pointed a damning finger down Texana's Broadway Street, and shouted: "Never will this town amount to anything, I curse it. You people listening within the sound of my voice will live to see rabbits and other animals inhabiting its streets."

After his failed mission to Texana, Allen made an offer for the ruins of Harrisburg, which had been burned by Santa Anna shortly before the Battle of San Jacinto. He was also stymied there, however, by litigation over a fouled title.

In mid-August 1836, A. C. had dinner with Robert Wilson at Columbia. Wilson, an engineer and steamboater from Harrisburg, convinced Augustus that a steamer could navigate Buffalo Bayou well past that burned-out town. Allen then made a quick trip to the bayou, rented a skiff, and took soundings all the way to White Oak Bayou. The short journey convinced him that the actual head of navigation was indeed well above Harrisburg.

At the same time, Dr. T. F. L. Parrott was advertising in Gail

Borden's *Telegraph and Texas Register* at Columbia the two leagues of the deceased John Austin for sale. The lower portion of the eastern half of this land grant included the point where White Oak Bayou joined Buffalo Bayou. On August 24 and August 26, 1836, respectively, A. C. Allen signed two deeds in buying one and a half of John Austin's two leagues in partnership with his brother, John Kirby. In the first transaction, they paid William T. Austin one dollar an acre for the western and upper league granted his brother John. In the second deed, the Allens paid Mrs. Elizabeth E. Parrott $5,000 ($1,000 in cash and the remainder in four notes) for the southern half of the lower league granted her late husband on July 20, 1824. This tract of 2,000 acres was in the bend along the south and west banks of Buffalo Bayou.

After purchasing this land, A. C. sent a message to Nacogdoches asking Representative John Kirby Allen to meet him at Harrisburg three weeks before the Texas Congress convened on October 1. The two met on a misty morning in early September and, with two of Wilson's men as guides, started upstream in a hollowed-out cypress log canoe. Taking soundings and rough field notes for the next eight miles, they found the water to vary in depth from eight to twelve feet in midchannel. That evening they reached their destination, the south bank of Buffalo Bayou opposite its confluence with White Oak Bayou.

A. C. suddenly pulled the oars inboard and stood up. Pulling out a hand-sketched map of the area, he marked an "X" and said, "It marks our site, gentlemen. On this spot, I, Augustus C. Allen, now place my destiny." The four men then disembarked and climbed up the slippery bank (known today as Allen's Landing) to survey the muggy marshland scene.

While the two roustabouts set up camp on the bank, A. C. kneeled on the ground and sketched a plat of a port city on the flat of John Kirby's black silk top hat. A. C. then gave his surprised brother a copy of the August 30 issue of the *Telegraph and Texas Register*. On page 3 was an advertisement for "The Town of Houston," which read as follows:

> Situated at the head of navigation, on the west bank of Buffalo Bayou, is now for the first time brought to public notice . . .
>
> The town of Houston is located at a point on the river which must ever command the trade of the largest and richest portion of Texas. By reference to the map, it will be seen that the trade of San Jacinto, Spring Creek, New Kentucky, and the Brazos, above and below Fort Bend, must necessarily come to this place, . . . making

it, beyond all doubt, the great interior commerical emporium of Texas.

. . . Tidewater runs to this place, and the lowest depth of water is about six feet. Vessels from New Orleans or New York can sail without obstacle to this place, and steamboats of the largest class can run down to Galveston Island in eight or ten hours, in all seasons . . .

The town of Houston must be the place where arms, ammunitions, and provisions for the government will be stored, because, situated in the very heart of the country, it combines security and the means of easy distribution . . .

There is no place in Texas more healthy, its having an abundance of excellent spring water, and enjoying the sea breeze in all its freshness. No place in Texas possesses so many advantages for building, having pine, ash, cedar, and oak in inexhaustible quantities; . . .

Nature appears to have designated this place for the future seat of government. It is handsome and beautifully elevated, salubrious, and well-watered, and now in the very heart or center of population, and will be so for a length of time to come. It combines two important advantages: a communication with the coast and foreign countries, and with the different portions of the republic. As the country shall improve, railroads will become in use, and will be extended from this point to the Brazos, and up the same, also from this up to the headwaters of San Jacinto, . . .

Preparations are now making to erect a water sawmill, and a large public house for accommodation will soon be opened. Steamboats now run in this river, and will in a short time commence running regularly to the island. The proprietors offer the lots for sale on moderate terms to those who desire to improve them, and invite the public to examine for themselves.

A. C. Allen, for
A. C. and J. K. Allen

This site for the town of Houston proved to be a very shrewd choice. Taken as a whole, Buffalo Bayou was an exceptional Texas stream. Most of it was comparatively deep and wide, fairly uniform in depth, and had clear waters and large banks. Above Harrisburg, however, it became narrow and winding with dangerous snags and overhanging tree. The bayou pointed toward the rich Brazos Valley and flowed into Galveston Bay, where an island at the bay's head offered promise of a fine sea harbor. Most important of all to speculators, the chosen site was at a break in transportation, a point where goods must be transferred from steamboat to ox-wagon.

The Allens hired Gail and Thomas H. Borden to survey and map Houston, a job which lasted from September until November 1836.

Employee Moses Lapham did most of the actual work and got a "bad case of chills" for his efforts. With commercial utilization foremost in mind, the site was platted in a gridiron pattern, and the sixty-two townsite blocks were located on a northeast-southwest axis to take advantage of the prevailing southeastern Gulf breeze. All of the seventeen wide downtown streets and the five public squares were south of Buffalo Bayou and ran parallel to that stream. There was a Water Street along the riverfront and a Congress Square (known today as Market Square).

The brothers advertised that the largest steamboats could reach Houston without obstacles. In proving their claim, however, they fudged by chartering the eighty-nine-foot *Laura,* the smallest steamer in Texas at the time, to make a demonstration voyage from Columbia to Houston in January 1837. To the utter embarrassment of the promoters, the *Laura* could not find the city and went three miles beyond the landing site and marking stakes before backing up. Among those on board with John Allen was Francis R. Lubbock, later to be the Confederate governor of Texas. His memoirs, *Six Decades in Texas,* and those of a later arrival, Dr. John Washington Lockhart, offer a revealing commentary on both the credibility of the promoters' claims and their town. Lubbock observed that "J. K. Allen was a very bright, quick man, with much magic about him, and well calculated to enthuse the young. A. C. was more taciturn and settled; he was a married man, with his family then in Nacogdoches . . ." Francis noted that there was easy navigation and plenty of water only until they reached Harrisburg; no boat had ever been beyond that point, and the *Laura* passengers had to rig Spanish windlasses on shore to heave various logs and snags out of the bayou narrows. Although it was only six miles by dirt road from Harrisburg to Houston, the torturous bayou trip took three days! In recalling the first time he ever saw the new city, Lubbock wrote:

> Just before reaching our destination a party of us, becoming weary of the steamer, took a yawl and concluded we would hunt for the city. So little evidence could we see of a landing that we passed by the site and ran into White Oak Bayou, realizing that we must have passed the city when we struck in the brush. We then backed down the bayou, and by close observation discovered a road or street laid off from the water's edge. Upon landing we found stakes and footprints, indicating that we were in the town tract.

When they finally arrived on January 22, 1837, Lubbock found only a few tents — the largest one being a saloon — and several small houses being built. He promptly closed one of the first deals with the Allens by paying $250 for a lot and the same price for a tiny house.

Houston was more of a breakdown than a break in transportation, according to the memoirs of Dr. John Washington Lockhart, who arrived there at age fifteen in 1839. He recalls a Buffalo Bayou that was a miserable stream for navigation. On an earlier trip his steamer lost half the cabin to an overhanging tree. Lockhart remembered that sometimes the steamer's bow was on one bank while the stern was on the other; deck hands then used long poles to push the prow off the bank into the bayou again. The closest thing to a wharf at Houston was a sandbar which gradually sloped into the bayou. Thus the steamer tied up to a large cypress tree near the foot of Main Street.

Young Lockhart found many barrooms but few houses, some very muddy principal streets, and foul water except for that hauled in by barrel. Ox-wagons bogged down on the impassable roads leading out of town, especially during the spring and winter, and the roads were lined with ox carcasses. The city trading season ran from September until April, with a steady stream of ox-wagons braving muddy, water-covered paths called roads to bring harvested crops to the city. There merchants purchased the goods and loaded them onto shallow-draft steamboats bound for Galveston and oceangoing ships.

The cleverest scheme of the Allen brothers for promoting the growth of Houston was a bid to have Congress select their city as capital of the Republic of Texas. At the time, the housing facilities at the temporary capital of Columbia were totally inadequate. In October 1836, John K. Allen, as an elected representative from Nacogdoches, placed a memorial before Congress, pledging what he would do if Houston was chosen as the capital:

> I offer to give all the lots necessary for the purposes of the government. I also offer to build a State House and the necessary offices for the various departments of the government, and to rent them to the government on a credit until such time as it may be convenient to make payment. Or, if the government sees proper to erect the buildings, I propose when the seat of government is removed, to purchase the said buildings at such price as they may be appraised at.

Evidently, John Kirby Allen was cutting quite a swath by this time.

Dr. Ashbel Smith, surgeon-general of the Republic of Texas Army, said of him:

> In regard to Major Allen, I have lived in the same house with him, . . . He is an astute financier, I believe his house and honesty can be safely depended upon. He is a leading member of Congress, and stands very high in the confidence of the Government. His private wealth is very great, his landed interest immense, as great perhaps or greater than that of any other man in this country.

On November 30, 1836, a cash-shy Congress on the fourth ballot accepted the Allen proposal over those of fifteen competitors, and the capital was moved from Columbia to Houston in early May 1837. When the Texas Congress met there for the first time on May 1, the unfinished capitol lacked both chairs and a roof! President Sam Houston arrived on April 26, described the site as being "far superior" to others for business or government, and observed:

> On the 20th of January, a small log cabin & 12 persons were all that distinguished it from the adjacent forests, and now there are upwards of 100 houses finished, and going up rapidly (some of them fine frame buildings) and 1500 people, all actively engaged in their respective pursuits.

Having the new capital as a namesake was not the only cause for Houston's enthusiasm: the Allens also gave him twelve lots in the new city.

The Executive Mansion on Caroline at Preston was a two-room shack with dirt floors and liquor kegs, barrels, boxes, and spare cots for furniture. A lean-to in the back was for President Houston's two black servants. In 1838, a shamed Texas government purchased a small store building at Main and Preston for the president's use; this first Texas White House was located where the Scanlan Building is today. The capitol at the corner of Texas and Main was on the site of the present Rice-Rittenhouse Hotel and was the only two-story building in town.

Soon after the successful voyage of the *Laura* up Buffalo Bayou, A. C. Allen returned to Baldwinsville, New York, for a long-awaited visit with Charlotte and their baby son. Little Samuel Augustus had died at eleven months, however, and his grief-stricken father had never seen him. Tortured by guilt feelings, A. C. spent much of his time in New York reestablishing the family unit. He and Charlotte returned to Houston in the fall of 1837. Their only surviving child, Martha Elizabeth Warner Allen, was born there in July 1838.

The city of Houston (or Mud Town, as some called it) was incorporated on June 5, 1837. On August 14, James S. Holman, clerk of the Eleventh District Court, was elected to a one-year term as mayor with twelve votes to eleven for F. R. Lubbock and ten for Thomas W. Ward. In 1838, Dr. Francis Moore, Jr., the one-armed editor of the *Telegraph and Texas Register,* was elected mayor.

A charter revision of 1840 divided the city into four wards, with two aldermen elected from each ward. The Fifth and Sixth wards were later added north of Buffalo Bayou.

The original city limits were Buffalo Bayou on the north, Walker Street on the south, Bagby on the west, and Caroline on the east. During the Moore administration, the city limits were extended to nine square miles, with the courthouse in the center. The city limits were extended to twenty-five square miles during the Reconstruction period, then again reduced to nine in 1874.

The Torrey brothers built the first frame house in Houston to serve as a trading post with the Indians. It was nestled in a grove of magnolia trees on the north side of Preston near the east end of the Preston Street bridge. The Torrey place was later purchased by H. D. Taylor.

In 1837, the first two-story houses in the city were built by N. Fuller and A. C. Briscoe. These homes were located at Preston and Smith and Main and Prairie, respectively.

Sam Houston's town became the county seat of Harrisburg (later Harris) County on December 22, 1836. The first public buildings in Houston — the county courthouse and county jail — were constructed by Harrisburg County in 1838. The courthouse was a double log cabin holding two rooms that were each sixteen feet square. The court met in one room, and the county clerk's office was located in the other. The county jail was a square log box with no doors or windows. A prisoner was lowered by ladder into the jail from a trap-door on the roof. Both buildings were on the Congress Avenue side of the courthouse square, where the Harris County Civil Courthouse is today.

The first permanent city public improvement came in 1840 during the administration of Mayor Charles Biglow when a contract was awarded for the construction of a market house and city hall on Market Square. The earthen-floored, one-story market house extended from Preston to Congress. Butchers and produce vendors operated on both sides of a broad aisle down the middle of the rat-infested structure. The Congress side of the building was two stories high; the city jail was on the lower floor and the city hall on the second level. The old market house was finally torn down in 1871.

In 1837, Thomas Elsberry built Houston's first large warehouse at the corner of Main and Commerce streets. For years the firm of Allen and Pool conducted their business in this structure, the only cotton warehouse in the city. The building fronted on Commerce and extended back to a crude wharf. Thus cotton bales could be tumbled out the back door and landed near a waiting steamboat.

Cotton was the major item of commerce before the Civil War. Cotton shipments down Buffalo Bayou increased from 1,000 bales in 1839 to 14,000 bales in 1844. That number jumped to 38,923 bales in 1854, 46,220 bales in 1857, and 115,854 bales in 1860.

Ox-teams brought cotton to Houston on rut-filled dirt pathways called roads. Five yoke of oxen carried five bales of cotton, six yoke carried six bales, and so on. In good weather a round trip from Washington County to Houston took fourteen days; bad weather required a month for such a trip. Since a teamster typically rode a Spanish pony when driving his oxen, he made towpaths along both sides of the road. While waiting to reload for the return trip, teamsters stayed at one of two wagon camps in Houston.

One of Houston's earliest residents was Col. Benjamin Fort Smith, a former Indian fighter and agent, slave trader, and veteran of San Jacinto. After moving there from Brazoria County in early 1837, he hauled in logs from the forest and built the city's first hotel on two lots at the northeast corner of Franklin and Travis streets (where the Southern Pacific building is today).

The first proprietor was George Wilson, who sold the establishment to Mrs. Pamelia Mann on June 8, 1837. After moving from burned-out Harrisburg, the new owner renamed the place the Mansion House. Pamelia quickly made this combination tavern and brothel the city's leading hotel. Strategically located only a short walking distance from both the executive mansion and capitol, this den of iniquity was often visited by President Houston and Surgeon General Ashbel Smith. One of Dr. Smith's duties was to hold a tight rein on Sam's drinking, but the two bachelors frequently walked to Mrs. Mann's place to unwind and sample its assorted pleasures.

The Mansion House was described as "a commodious, two-storied, plastered building with porches." The parlor was furnished with a sofa, a cherry center table, an eight-day clock, six chairs, and a pair of spittoons. The dining room contained two long tables set with china and German silver cutlery; diners could order coffee, tea, hard liquor, or wine from black serving girls. The second floor contained three rooms with each having washstands, mirrors, and beds. At least one of the rooms was furnished dormitory-style with double and single beds.

In writing about Pamelia Mann in the *Southwest Review* (Summer, 1935), William Ransom Hogan described her hotel thusly:

> The Mansion House was no shrine of gourmets, but sensitive palates were rare in that day of five-to-fifteen-minute meals. When it was desired, feminine companionship of a robust and none too virtuous nature must be provided. Boarding houses, often dignified with the name of hotels, were set up to care for this portion of the male population which had to exist without benefit of wifely solicitude. In this last respect, Mrs. Mann and her "girls" achieved a satisfying success.

It was, no doubt, the "satisfying success" of the Mansion House that inspired two Houston morals ordinances. A city law of 1840 invoked a fine of at least fifty dollars and a jail term of up to thirty days for any woman committing lewd acts or exhibiting herself in a public place in a style "not usual for respectable females." The law also decreed that brothels in the city limits could not be within two squares of a family residence. In order to insure good behavior, an 1841 ordinance required a twenty-dollar bond for a "female of ill fame" found in a public place after 8:00 P.M.

The capital was a wild, lawless town in the early years. Dr. Lockhart described Houston as a "rough place" where it was common to see men on the street with two to four pistols and a bowie knife belted around. The handful of criminals who were caught and convicted faced fines, jail terms, whippings, brandings, or hangings. According to John H. Herndon, as many as 3,000 spectators viewed the hanging of two convicted murderers in 1838.

The next year a mob of drunken gamblers and loafers armed with bowie knives and pistols stopped a play, roughed up the theater manager, then proceeded to terrorize the customers at the Exchange Hotel bar and break up a dance upstairs. It took a local military group, the Milam Guards, to quell this mini-riot.

Dueling was common in Houston until the oft-time mayor, Dr. Francis Moore, Jr., started a one-man campaign to end the practice. This strident editor of the *Telegraph and Texas Register* blasted those "blackguards and knaves" who carried weapons and insulted the peace-loving town; he said they should be "frowned down" by respectable townspeople. His efforts met with success: challenges began to be settled peacefully, dueling became ungentlemanly, a city ordinance of 1840 prohibited carrying deadly weapons, and his paper could report in 1842 that there had been no duels in four years.

One reason for the poor moral tone in Houston was the absence of churches. In 1839 the *Morning Star* lamented that there was not a single place of public worship or one resident minister in the city.

Even in such a seemingly hostile environment, numerous cultural activities were in progress in early Houston. In December 1837 the Philosophical Society of Texas was formed there for the "collection and diffusion of correct information regarding the moral and social condition of our country; its finances, statistics, etc." Mirabeau B. Lamar was elected president, with Dr. Ashbel Smith serving as vice-president and William Fairfax Gray as recording secretary. Other society members included Sam Houston, William H. and John A. Wharton, and Albert Clinton Horton.

Artist Thomas Jefferson Wright had a studio in the city in 1837, and his works were displayed in a portrait gallery in the capitol. Sam Houston commissioned Wright to paint an oil portrait of Deaf Smith, and the resulting original is the only life likeness of Smith known to exist. (In 1939 the San Jacinto Chapter of the Daughters of the Republic of Texas donated the painting to the Museum of History at the San Jacinto Monument, where it remains on display.)

Debates were sponsored by the Franklin Debating Society in 1837 and the Houston Young Men's Society in 1839.

Houston could boast of the first volunteer fire company in Texas, Protection No. 1, organized in 1836. This company, consisting of a line of men passing water buckets, functioned until 1850. In that year the first engine was purchased, a hand engine worked by beams on each side. Protection No. 1 covered the entire city until 1858, when Hook and Ladder Co. No. 1 was organized. In 1860, Liberty No. 2 was created. Two years later, Mayor T. W. House united the three companies when he organized the first Houston Fire Department.

Stagecoach service in Houston began in 1839 when the Texas Stage Line charged five dollars for a one-day trip to Richmond. The firm of Smith and Jones began a Houston-to-Austin line in 1841. R. T. Kane first offered stage service to Washington, Texas, in 1843.

Small-scale banking began in Houston in 1838, when cotton and mercantile merchants Thomas W. House, William Marsh Rice, and Benjamin A. Shepherd first advertised excess funds available for lending. By 1854, Shepherd was involved exclusively in independent banking operations. In 1866, Thomas M. Bagby started the First National Bank, the first to operate only as a bank. It failed within a year, but Shepherd assumed control and made the bank a success.

In 1840 the Texas Congress authorized the city of Houston to build and maintain wharves. The next year the city council established the Port of Houston, which included all wharves, landings, slips, and roads along Buffalo and White Oak bayous. Within a few months the bayou at the foot of Main Street was lined with docks for small, shallow-draft vessels.

On April 5, 1840, the Houston Chamber of Commerce was organized, with Mr. Perkins as president. The chamber's main function was prescribing standard rates for freight handling and storage in wholesale commerce. After several years, however, the first chamber ceased to exist.

Houston had one major drawback: an unhealthy location that one irate congressman described as "the most miserable place in the world." Poor drainage and fever-carrying mosquitoes combined with oppressively high temperatures and humidity to create a dangerous, uncomfortable environment. In 1838, Dr. Ashbel Smith wrote that "heat is so severe during the middle of the day that most of us lie in the shade and pant." A year later, the editor of the *Houston Morning Star* started his column with the lead, "Oh for a good cold norther!"

William Bollaert, the English writer who visited Texas between 1841 and 1844, observed that all Houstonians slept under mosquito bars in the summers. Yellow fever was the most dread disease in the city, with ten epidemics occurring between 1839 and 1867. During the 1839 epidemic, one-third of the population came down with "Yellow Jack"; the town sexton reported 229 deaths from it between July 24 and December 3. Although the cause of yellow fever was a mystery at the time, it was known that cold weather stopped the spread of the disease. There were probably more prayers offered for frost than rain in Houston.

The city was to play an ever-larger role as a hub of commerce, but its political significance was short-lived. As early as September 1837, Congressman Thomas J. Rusk introduced a resolution to appoint a committee to choose a desirable place for relocating the capital. His reason for the resolution was "the disagreeable weather, mud, mud,

mud and mostly . . . the expected dread yellow fever" of Houston.

In early 1839, a joint commission was appointed to locate a new site, and they selected Waterloo, a tiny village of only four families on the upper Colorado. The loss of the capital caused the editor of the *Morning Star* to comment:

> . . . We *will* have a great city, in spite of them, and if they don't be-have very well up there in Austin, we will *cut off their supplies,* and throw them upon corn bread and beef.

On October 12, 1839, the government abandoned Houston when thirty teams and wagons started the removal of archives and furniture from the capitol to Austin. President Mirabeau B. Lamar and his cabinet relocated there the same month.

Bachelor John Kirby Allen died of congestive (yellow) fever at age twenty-eight on August 15, 1838. The obituary appearing in the *Telegraph and Texas Register* was written by Sam Houston, who said:

> Major Allen was a warmhearted man, ardently attached to his fellow creatures; he was unbounded in his liberality to many who, it would be thought, had no claims upon his favor. His generous hospitality, his warm benevolence, his solicitude for the promotion of his adopted country, his urbanity as a gentleman, his remarkable enter-prise and practical good sense and his practical usefulness as a citi-zen, will be admitted by all who have cultivated his acquaintance.

John Kirby was buried in Founders Memorial Cemetery outside the city limits on the road to San Felipe. Today this cemetery on West Dallas Street is in the shadow of the downtown Houston skyline. An-other brother, George Allen, is also buried there.[1]

---

1. All of the family records were later destroyed in a warehouse fire at Allen's Land-ing. According to oral history and family legend, George Allen's second son, Samuel War-ner, threw the Allens into bankruptcy at the turn of the century, resulting in the loss of over 500,000 acres and some 200 businesses. Legend has it that Samuel Warner liquidated family holdings at ten cents on the dollar, then took the cash and moved to Washington state on his private train. As a result, nothing tangible has been left to hand down to to-day's Houston descendants of the original Allen brothers.

One of George Allen's great-great-great nephews, physician Ralph E. Dittman, now lives in Houston and has written a 718-page historical novel titled *Allen's Landing: The Au-thentic Story of the Founding of Houston.* A cousin of Dr. Dittman, John Kirby Allen IV, lives in Baytown and is a lab technician for Aristech Chemical Corporation. According to him, the closed U.S. Steel plant in Baytown is on land once owned by the Allen brothers. This 2,200-acre plan site on the western edge of Chambers County was reopened as Buffalo Steel Company in 1990.

After his brother's death, Augustus C. Allen guided the family in developing Houston. In 1842, he was among the first to volunteer for duty in the Texian army that drove Gen. Adrian Woll and his 1,200 Mexican troops from San Antonio. On the advice of his physician, Augustus moved south to Brownsville in hopes of improving his failing health in 1848. There he was appointed as deputy collector of customs.

Since John Kirby left no will, the three other living Allen brothers eventually demanded their shares of the estate from A. C. After Charlotte became unhappy with the way her husband was dividing the family assets, she separated from him in 1850. Although the estranged couple did not obtain a divorce, they were never reunited.

Augustus then began a new life in Mexico as the United States consul to Minatitlan, a port on the Pacific Ocean. He became a close friend of President Juarez and promoted an ambitious project to cut a canal across the isthmus of Mexico. Realizing that his days were numbered, A. C. returned to Washington, D.C., to surrender his consulship in the winter of 1863. Evidently, the sudden change from a tropical climate to frigid weather was too much for his frail condition. He was stricken with pneumonia and died in Washington on January 11, 1864. With the Civil War raging, a Union blockade of Southern ports prevented the family from getting Allen's body to Houston. On August 29, 1864, he was buried in Greenwood Cemetery in Brooklyn, New York. (To commemorate the city of Houston's 150th birthday, on Founders Day, August 30, 1986, Dr. Ralph Dittman, a family descendant, tried unsuccessfully to have A. C. Allen's remains exhumed and reburied in Houston's Founders Cemetery. Dr. Dittman said the effort was a lost cause without a formal resolution passed by the City Council, which would be used in a court case in New York seeking permission for the exhumation.)

Charlotte Allen raised their only daughter, Martha Elizabeth, who preceded her mother in death in 1886.[2] For forty-five years, Charlotte remained a pillar of Houston society. She was renowned for both her lavish hospitality to friends and for extending a charitable hand to the sick, hungry, and destitute. Charlotte also enjoyed the respect of her business peers in Houston. Mrs. Allen lived into her nineties and died on August 4, 1895. She was buried under an imposing monument in Houston's Glenwood Cemetery.

---

2. Martha Elizabeth later married Maj. James Converse, and they had one child, Thomas Pierce Converse. When Thomas died in Houston in 1939, he was the last of A. C. Allen's issue.

The importance of organized religion was recognized by the Allen brothers, who set aside a quarter block on the northwest corner of Capitol and Main streets "for church purposes." The small building erected there was used by all denominations.

In 1836 Rev. Z. N. Morrell, an itinerant Baptist preacher, held the first evangelical service in Houston. After the Allens donated half a block on the north side of Texas Avenue (the site of the present Houston Chronicle Building), the Methodists began the first permanent church in the city in 1837. This church resulted from the labors of Charles Shearn, who brought a minister from New Orleans at his own expense and provided the preacher with a room in his own home. After the Civil War, Shearn paid for the church building on Texas Avenue. This Shearn Church eventually became the First Methodist Church on Main Street.

The First Presbyterian Church was organized in the Senate chamber of the capitol in 1838. Five years later, the members erected a church building on Main Street near the corner of Capitol Street, but the structure burned down in 1859.

Thirty-nine people attended the organizational meeting of the Episcopal church in 1839. The congregation took the name of Christ Church in 1845 and consecrated their first building on May 9, 1847. Three churches were built and torn down on this site at Texas and Fannin before the cornerstone of the present Christ Church Cathedral was laid in 1893. This imposing structure was badly damaged by fire in 1938.

On April 10, 1841, the First Baptist Church was organized due to the fund-raising efforts of two women, Mrs. C. M. Fuller and Mrs. Piety L. Hadley. These women started a building fund after being given a raw-boned mule, which they fattened and sold. Proceeds from the mule and the sale of homemade articles at a fair brought in $450. A second fair resulted in sales of $900. These funds were used to purchase lots on the southeast corner of Texas and Travis, later the site of the Milby Hotel.

The two women then wrote Rev. William M. Tryon, who had been the missionary pastor of the Independence Baptist Church for almost five years after coming to Texas in March 1841. Reverend Tryon agreed to take charge of the Houston church and its seventeen members in 1847. As mission pastor of the First Baptist Church of Houston, Tryon led a fund drive to build a new brick structure on the church property. Under his leadership, sixty-seven additions were made to the church before the thirty-nine-year-old pastor succumbed to yellow fever on November 16, 1847, shortly after making visits to the sick and needy. He was buried in Houston's Glenwood Cemetery.

Tryon's successor was twenty-four-year-old Rufus C. Burleson, the choice of both the church and the Domestic Mission Board of the Southern Baptist Convention. Reverend Burleson took charge of the church in January 1848.

Among those who attended his Houston services was Susanna Dickinson, the only Anglo adult survivor of the Alamo assault. When Mrs. Dickinson first moved to Houston, she stayed at the Mansion House for a time. It was said that she ran with a fast crowd in town and that Pamelia Mann was a girlfriend.

After preaching on the mission of the church one Sunday night in 1849, Pastor Burleson asked the packed congregation to join him in a prayer asking God to save the worst sinners in Houston. Mrs. Dickinson, nominally a member of the Episcopal church, was one of five to come forward weeping and asking to be saved the next Wednesday night during prayer meeting. She told the pastor she was aware of her lost condition, accepted Jesus Christ as her personal Savior, and was joyfully converted. A crowd of 1,500 lined the banks of Buffalo Bayou to see her baptized, after which she became a zealous church worker. In July 1851, Susanna's daughter, Angelina, the "Babe of the Alamo," was married to John Maynard Griffith by Burleson.

On June 18, 1851, Reverend Burleson's highly successful pastorate ended at Houston when he replaced the retiring Henry L. Graves as president of Baylor University at Independence.

A new Baptist church erected in 1883 was destroyed by the 1900 hurricane. Three years later, another structure was built at the corner of Fannin and Walker streets.

The Catholic church in Houston dates from 1841, when Father Querat purchased a quarter block on the south side of Franklin and Caroline streets. A small wooden building, a schoolhouse, and the priest's home in the back were used until 1869, when the block at Crawford and Texas was purchased. The handsome brick Annunciation Catholic Church was completed in 1874. The steeple added in 1881 was designed by famed Galveston architect Nicholas Clayton.

In 1851, the first German Lutheran church was organized in Houston. Two years later, the congregation purchased the northwest corner of the block at Texas and Milam and erected a large frame building.

A Jewish synagogue was organized on Franklin Avenue in 1854.

In the 1870s it was led by the sons of Rabbi Samuel Raphael, Benjamin and Mose.

The government of the Republic moved back to Houston briefly in 1842 after two Mexican forays into San Antonio. During this time the Senate met in the Odd Fellows' Hall and the House of Representatives met in the new First Presbyterian Church at Main and Capitol. Soon the Texas government moved on to Washington-on-the-Brazos, where it remained until the Republic joined the Union in 1845.

The first bridge over Buffalo Bayou was constructed at the foot of Preston Avenue in 1843. After it was swept away by a flood ten years later, the "Long Bridge" was built at the same location, then remodeled in 1878. This bridge was very important in opening the entire trade area north of Houston.

Elim Stockbridge opened a cornmeal mill at the foot of Texas Avenue in 1844. Early that spring, N. T. Davis erected the first compress in Houston. His machine required only two workers to compress a 500-pound cotton bale.

In 1851, Alex McGowan started the first iron foundry in the city on the banks of White Oak Bayou. The foundry first made sugar kettles and light farm machinery, then did repair work on the Houston and Texas Central road. Cushman's Foundry began operations in 1858 on the west end of the Preston Avenue bridge. When the Civil War erupted, all the work force for the pattern-making machinery volunteered for the Confederate army. The expensive plant was then converted to an arsenal to produce cannons and shells, and skilled mechanics were detailed to the project.

In 1840, German immigrants formed a "verein" which was supplanted by the Houston Turnverein in 1854. This organization sponsored social events and promoted music and gymnastics. In 1857, the Houston Brass Band was formed.

The Houston Lyceum, started in 1854, had a major objective of supporting a library. The lyceum owned 382 books and sponsored lectures, debates, and musical programs before dying in the Civil War period.

In the early years there were at least four small private schools in the city. In late 1858, a $20,000 fund drive resulted in the opening of a two-story brick Academy Building. Dr. Ashbel Smith served as superintendent, with five teachers offering instruction to 140 students.

Among the early newspapers in Houston were the *Telegraph and Texas Register* (1835–1853), the *National Intelligencer* (1838–1840), the *Morning Star* (1839–1846), the *Weekly Telegraph* (1852–1873), the *Tri-Weekly Telegraph* (1855–1864), the *Daily Telegraph* (1864–1877), and the *Houston Union* (1868–1869). These papers were four to eight pages in length.

Two of the most successful early merchants in Houston were Thomas W. House and William Marsh Rice. House was born in Somersetshire, England, ran away from home as a youth to go to sea, and jumped ship in New York at age twenty-one. After taking charge of the bakery at the St. Charles Hotel in New Orleans, he moved to Houston in 1838, became a partner in a confectioner business, and produced and sold the first ice cream in the city. One side of his store was devoted to confections, while the other half was stocked with dry goods for the wholesale interior trade. After buying out a rival for $40,000 in 1853, his T. W. House and Company became the largest wholesale business in the state. House once remarked that a keg of his nails had gone into every church in Texas. The company was so busy that ox-wagons waited half a day for their turn at his loading docks.

House took cotton in payment for goods, and a large private bank grew out of his cotton factoring. He helped organize the Houston and Galveston Navigation Company, the Houston and Texas Central Railroad, the Board of Trade and Cotton Exchange, and founded the city's first public utility, the Houston Gas Company, in 1866. During the Civil War, he served as mayor, provided blockade runners at Galveston, and sent cotton wagons to Mexico; on the return trip they brought vital supplies. House left an estate of $1 million when he died in 1880 and one of his sons, Edward Mandell, became Houston's most famous native son during the presidency of Woodrow Wilson.[3]

---

3. Edward M. House, the youngest of eight children, was born on July 26, 1858, and grew up in the family home at Smith and Capitol streets in Houston. When Thomas House suffered a stroke in 1879, Edward dropped out of Cornell University and was back home when his father died a few months later.

In the next decade, Edward married, moved to Austin, and took over the family businesses. After retiring from active business, House managed Governor Jim Hogg's difficult reelection campaign victory in 1892 and was commissioned an honorary lieutenant colonel on the Hogg staff. The quiet, mild-mannered "Colonel" House also worked behind the scenes in stage-managing the election of three other Texas governors.

After joining the Progressive movement at the turn of the century, Edward in 1912 wrote the novel *Philip Dru: Administrator,* in which he detailed how an enlightened, reform-minded chief executive could mold a more just American society.

That same year, House played a key role in the nomination and election of Democrat Woodrow Wilson to the presidency. Although he held no formal office, Edward became Wilson's closest adviser and confidant; the president once said of him, "Col. House is my

William Marsh Rice, the namesake of a Methodist circuit rider, was born in Springfield, Massachusetts, in 1816. After leaving school to clerk in a grocery store for five years, Rice used his savings to buy his own store at age twenty-one. Business losses in the Panic of 1837 resulted in his decision to start anew in Texas. When his shipment of merchandise bound for Galveston was lost at sea, Rice relocated at Houston, where he received a headright certificate to 320 acres on February 12, 1839. Two months later, he contracted to furnish liquors for the bar of the Milam Hotel. By June of that year he was furnishing cash against mortgages on property.

Rice's first Houston business partner was Barnabas Haskill, who left Texas in the winter of 1841–1842. William and his new partner, Ebenezer B. Nichols, were commission and forwarding merchants, bringing in a full supply of groceries from New Orleans and New York by December 1844. The firm of Rice and Nichols operated out of a three-story building on Main Street.

In 1850, Rice was an incorporator of the Buffalo Bayou, Brazos and Colorado Railway. On June 29 of that year, he married Margaret Bremond, the eighteen-year-old daughter of Paul Bremond, founder of the Houston and Texas Central Railway. The ceremony was held in Christ Episcopal Church, where William was a member of the vestry and had helped pay off the church debt. Their wedding reception at the Capitol Hotel was described as "the most splendid affair ever given in the city."

When partner Nichols moved to Galveston in 1851, Rice purchased the new home Ebenezer had just started. Legend has it that the materials were intended for a warship and were sold to Nichols by mistake. Rice moved this four-columned Greek Revival home to face on

second personality. He is my independent self. His thoughts and mine are one." After the death of Wilson's first wife, Ellen, in August 1914, Edward helped to maintain the president's emotional health and stability.

During World War I, Colonel House gained international fame in carrying out key diplomatic assignments. He also helped President Wilson draft his war aims — the "Fourteen Points" — and the covenant for the League of Nations. There was a bitter break between the two, however, at the Paris Peace Conference in 1919, and they never met again.

Edward House died at his New York home in 1938 and was buried in the family plot at Glenwood Cemetery in Houston.

On November 30, 1989, a Texas historical marker honoring Colonel House was dedicated in the lobby of the Federal Building in downtown Houston. This block is the site of the old House family home. The ceremony was sponsored by the Harris County Historical Commission and the Texas Historical Commission.

the Courthouse Square, then spent another $8,000 to finish it. Each New Year's Day, Margaret Rice would throw back the folding doors between the downstairs parlors and personally pour coffee for guests at a long reception table.

In 1851, Rice became a limited partner of the Houston and Galveston Navigation Company. By 1858 he owned the brig *William M. Rice,* which made ice runs from Galveston to Boston during the hot Texas summer months. The new firm of William M. Rice and Company brought him to prominence in buying and developing land in 1856. Four years later, he was an incorporator of the Houston Cotton Compress Company.

During the 1850s, Rice was a director of the Houston Academy, a trustee of both the Second Ward Free School and the Texas Medical College, an alderman from the Second Ward on the city council, and served one year with both the slave patrol and the Liberty Fire Co. No. 2138.

The census of 1860 listed Rice as being worth $750,000 in real and personal property, making him the second richest man in Texas; only John Hunter Herndon, a sugar planter and slave owner from Brazoria County, was worth more than Rice, whose fifteen slaves were utilized as house servants and in his warehouse and wharf operations.

During the Civil War, Margaret Rice worked tirelessly in war relief, and her husband gave to Confederate causes, including $200 to help build a home for the widow and children of Albert Sidney Johnston. On August 13, 1863, Margaret died of possibly yellow fever or cholera and was buried in the Episcopal Cemetery. The following December, William crossed the Mexican border en route to Monterrey. He also spent time in Matamoros and Havana after selling the entire stock of Rice and Company in April 1864. When Rice returned to Houston in August 1865, he was richer than ever.

Texas railroads began in the Houston area in the 1840s. In an effort to revive burned-out Harrisburg, Andrew Briscoe surveyed a rail route westward from there to the Brazos River in the spring of 1840. With the financial backing of Galvestonians, he completed two miles of graded roadbed, purchased crossties, and received a charter for the Harrisburg Railroad and Trading Company in 1841. The company could not afford the iron rails required, however, and the project stopped with no track laid.

In May 1850, the Houston Plank Road Company was organized by Paul Bremond, William J. Hutchins, William Marsh Rice, B. A.

Shepherd, Thomas M. Bagby, A. S. Ruthven, Thomas W. House, and others. The company possessed eminent domain for a fifty-yard-wide roadbed to the Brazos River and was empowered to charge a toll to users. By September, $50,000 had been collected in subscriptions and loans. The project was canceled that month due to growing interest in railroad construction.

Gen. Sidney Sherman and some Boston investors acquired and re-organized the moribund Harrisburg company in 1851 under a new charter. Sherman's Buffalo Bayou, Brazos and Colorado Railway began construction along Briscoe's surveyed route, with the project con-tracted to W. J. Kyle and B. F. Terry, who was to win fame as the commander of Terry's Texas Rangers during the Civil War. Built at a cost of $18,400 per mile, the line extended thirty-two miles from Har-risburg to Richmond on the Brazos by 1856.

At that time, northern newspapers began to advertise that Harris-burg was the head of navigation on Buffalo Bayou and that the new railroad would lead to the decline of Houston. Alarmed by this new threat, the voters of Houston quickly approved the building of a short railway to tap the new line and thus divert traffic. Using slave labor, Kyle and Terry started work on the seven-mile line on April 7, 1856. Houston spent $130,000 building the Tap Road, and it connected with Sherman's railroad at Pierce's Junction that October. In 1858, the Tap Road was sold to Brazoria County planters for $172,000 and renamed the Houston Tap and Brazoria. Within a year, shipments of sugar and molasses were arriving in Houston over this so-called "Sugar Road."

By September 1861, the Buffalo Bayou, Brazos and Colorado Railway extended seventy-five miles west to Alleyton on the Colorado River. The line was sold in 1870 for $25,000 and renamed the Galves-ton, Harrisburg and San Antonio Railway, which later became a part of the Southern Pacific system.

Paul Bremond, a Houston merchant, was one of the promoters of the Galveston and Red River Railroad incorporated in 1848. After some charter amendments, the line became the Houston and Texas Central Railroad and began construction on January 1, 1853. Bre-mond first intended to build to Austin, but concern over possible com-petition caused him to veer to the north. He quickly exhausted his own funds but managed to keep going with cash infusions from Thomas W. House and William J. Hutchins. The hundreds of Irishmen who built the line were promised that they would be paid upon reaching Hempstead.

In 1856, the Houston and Texas Central passed the twenty-five-mile mark at Cypress Creek and began to haul freight, enabling the line to earn almost $18,000 by February 1857. When the road reached the fifty-mile mark at Hempstead in 1858, some 800 Houstonians boarded a special train and went there to celebrate the end of ox-team freighting.

By September 1861, the line extended eighty-one miles northwest to Millican at a building cost of $22,650 per mile. Its tracks reached Bryan in June 1868 and Corsicana in November 1871. When the system connected with the Missouri, Kansas and Texas Railway at Denison in March 1873, Houston joined the national railroad network with rail connections to St. Louis.

The Galveston, Houston and Henderson Railroad was chartered in 1853 and completed fifty miles of track from Galveston to Houston in September 1861. This was the only Texas railroad that was maintained during the Civil War. In 1865 the GH&H completed a drawbridge over Buffalo Bayou and lined with the Houston and Texas Central.

In 1857 the Texas and New Orleans Railroad broke ground at Houston and completed 100 miles of track east to Beaumont by September 1861. Construction stopped during the Civil War, but linkage with other lines allowed the first train to leave Houston for New Orleans on August 29, 1880. The next year the T&NO became a part of the Southern Pacific system.

French immigrant Eugene Pillot built the Pillot Building at 106 Congress in 1857. It housed a dry goods store and legal offices above. The oldest cast iron-front building west of the Mississippi River, it remained in Pillot family hands until 1944. (The Pillot Building is owned by Harris County today [1991]. After the interior was demolished in 1983, the exterior collapsed the next year. On October 11, 1989, City Partnership Ltd. started reconstruction using ironwork, bricks, and other architectural details salvaged from the rubble.)

On March 10, 1859, a terrible fire broke out at midnight at the corner of Main and Congress. Raging for eight hours, the fire destroyed all of the block on the west side of Main Street between Preston and Congress, resulting in $300,000 in property losses. Many of the structures lost were uninsured wooden shanties. Within the year, much of the vacant space was filled with fine, substantial buildings. This new construction included William Van Alstyne's three-story building — the first in town — at the corner of Main and Congress. Then came the first four-story iron-front building in the state, constructed by J. R. Morris on the east side of Main Street between Preston and Congress. That same year William J. Hutchins began the famed Hutchins House, a four-story brick hotel completed after the Civil War on the site of the old Mansion House. Soon after the Hutchins House burned down, the vacant lot was purchased in 1911 by the Southern Pacific Railroad for an office building.

According to the *Tri-Weekly Telegraph*, Houston in 1860 had twenty-five dry goods houses, thirty retail groceries, five hardware stores, ten warehouses, fifteen commission merchants, five drug stores, twenty mixed wholesale and retail merchandise houses, and three bookstores. Trade was obviously much more important than manufacturing; there were only twenty-one such concerns in all of Harris County, employing 158 workers.

Houston's most famous saloon, the Bank of Bacchus, was opened in 1860 by Richard W. (Dick) Dowling, a native of County Galway, Ireland. His new drink, "Kiss me quick and go," soon became the talk of the town. This handsome, muscular redhead was a devout Roman Catholic who operated two other saloons in the city.

During the Civil War, Dowling closed the Bank of Bacchus and recruited a 100% Irish outfit called the Davis Guards. This forty-seven-man unit was mainly composed of Houston and Galveston dockworkers, railroad section hands, and barkeeps. After helping Gen. John Magruder recapture Galveston from Union forces on January 1, 1863, Lieutenant Dowling became an instant Confederate hero that September by repelling a Union attempt to invade Texas at the Battle of Sabine Pass.[4]

---

4. Sabine Pass, a narrow, six-mile strait, was the Gulf outlet for both the Sabine and Neches rivers. In January 1863, it was occupied by Confederate forces. Adm. David Farragut and Gen. Nathaniel P. Banks then made plans for a major Union campaign against southeast Texas — the only section with any railroads — beginning with the retaking of Sabine Pass.

On September 1, 1863, four Federal gunboats and seventeen transports carrying some 5,000 Federal troops sailed from New Orleans. To meet this formidable invasion force, Lieutenant Dowling's Davis Guard had only six small cannon in Fort Griffin, an unfinished timber-and-mud earthwork with twelve-foot-thick walls. Oyster reefs and mud flats left the Federals with only one dry landing area just south of Dowling's position. Dick also had buoy markers and stakes at three-hundred-yard intervals in Sabine Pass.

At 3:00 P.M. on September 8, the Union armada entered the pass led by two gunboats, the *Clifton* and the *Sachem*. In only forty-five minutes, Dowling's men fired their

The Bank of Bacchus reopened after the war, but Dick Dowling died in the yellow fever epidemic of 1867. Dowling and Tuam streets in central Houston are named in honor of the man and his birthplace in Ireland, respectively. In 1892, the Dick Dowling Camp was formed by local Confederate veterans. The Ancient Order of Hibernians later commissioned Frank Teich to sculpt Dowling in a Confederate uniform with sword in hand. This statue was first placed in Market Square in 1905. (It was moved to Sam Houston Park in 1940, then to Hermann Park in 1958, where it stands today without the stolen sword.)

Other Civil War volunteer units from Houston included the Turner Rifles, Bayou City Guards, Gentry Volunteers, Houston Artillery, Texas Grays, and the Rough and Ready Guards. By April 1862, an estimated twelve percent of all Harris County men had joined the Confederate service.

In the early 1850s, two rival military companies existed in Houston, the Washington Light Guards and the Milam Rifles. They drilled mainly to impress the ladies until the Civil War, when the two units disbanded and individual members joined new companies. Most of the Washington Light Guards joined the Bayou City Guards, which became Company A, 5th Texas Regiment, Hood's Brigade, in Robert E. Lee's Army of Northern Virginia. The Bayou City Guards were jokingly referred to as "the kid glove gentry." While encamped at Camp Van Dorn below Harrisburg, Mayor Thomas W. House sent them a large box of white kid gloves. The men proudly put the gloves on their bayonets for the send-off parade up Main Street en route to Virginia.

Some of the Milam Rifles joined Capt. Ed Riordan to form a new infantry company. Others from the two old "show" companies joined a cavalry company which saw service on the Rio Grande under Maj. Ike Stafford.

In 1861, a Fort Bend County sugar planter, B. F. (Frank) Terry, was authorized to recruit a regiment of mounted volunteers, a unit named the Eighth Texas Cavalry but more commonly called the famed Terry's Texas Rangers. That September ten companies of 100 men each met at Houston. All the young men in this regiment were skilled

---

cannon 137 times and suffered no injuries. During that brief time they disabled and captured the two lead gunboats, killed nineteen, took about 350 prisoners, and turned back the entire expedition. In their hasty retreat, two of the Federal transports threw 200 mules and 200,000 rations overboard to lighten the ships and get over the sandbar entrance. Confederate President Jefferson Davis called Dowling's remarkable triumph "the greatest military victory in the world."

marksmen and splendid horsemen. Their ranks included sons of leading families, college graduates, professional men, merchants, stockmen, and farmers.

After Colonel Terry was mortally wounded in the Battle of Woodsonville (Kentucky) on December 17, 1861, Capt. John Austin Wharton was elected to take his place and promoted to colonel. Twenty-four-year-old Wharton, the only son of William H. and Sarah Groce Wharton, was the captain of Company B from Brazoria and Matagorda counties. By early 1864, he had risen to major general and was placed in command of all cavalry forces in the Department of the Trans-Mississippi.

At war's end, General Wharton renewed his law practice at Brazoria and made a fateful business trip to Houston in April 1865. George W. Baylor, one of his subordinate officers during the war, was also in town. Wharton had earlier delayed Baylor's promotion to brigadier, causing the two to have "unpleasant misunderstandings" growing out of "military matters." On April 6, 1865, Wharton and Baylor exchanged "hot words" on a Houston street; both were still fuming minutes later when they met at Maj. Gen. John Magruder's headquarters in the Fannin Hotel. When they renewed their argument, Wharton called his critic a liar and slapped his face. The enraged Baylor instinctively pulled his revolver and fired, killing his antagonist.

Wharton's body was eventually reinterred in the State Cemetery at Austin. His portrait now hangs in the Texas Senate Chamber, presented by surviving comrades of Terry's Texas Rangers. George Baylor never stood trial since there were no credible witnesses to the tragic incident; the only other person in the room at the time was a near-deaf officer. Baylor went on to serve as a Texas Ranger officer for twenty years and grew repentant in old age, admitting before his death that the Wharton shooting had been a "lifelong sorrow."

The reality of defeat and military occupation hit Houston on the morning of June 20, 1865, when part of the 114th Ohio Regiment along with the 34th Iowa Regiment arrived by special train from Galveston. Some of the Union troops left as early as August, and the office of provost marshal closed that November.

The end of the Civil War brought renewed business activity to Houston. By 1868, the Houston Gas Light Company was supplying churches, hotels, and private homes with gas produced from oyster shells and coal. In 1869, the Houston City Mills, a textile factory, was employing eighty workers in a three-story building on Buffalo Bayou near the east end of town. Powered by an eighty-horsepower engine, the plant had fifty looms on the first floor and 2,200 spindles on the second level. In 1872, the City Cotton Mills was established in the Second Ward, but the uninsured plant was destroyed by fire in August 1875, with losses of $200,000. Dr. Pearl built an ice-making plant and meat packery on Buffalo Bayou below the city in 1869. That same year the first Planters' Fire Insurance Company was organized in Houston.

When Union forces took over his Houston warehouses as barracks and storage depots in the late summer of 1865, William Marsh Rice traveled to Palmer, Massachusetts, to visit his parents. There he announced that New York would be his new residence. The following January he was back in Texas as a director of the Houston Insurance Company. On June 26, 1867, he married widow Julia Elizabeth Baldwin Brown at Christ Church, and the newlyweds fled East to escape the worst outbreak of yellow fever in Houston's history.

In 1869, Rice, Thomas W. House, William J. Hutchins, and others founded the Buffalo Bayou Ship Channel Company with the objective of dredging a nine-foot channel from Houston to Bolivar Roads, the opening into the Gulf of Mexico, within three years. The federal government declared Houston a port of entry in 1870 and authorized a customshouse there.

Rice sold his Courthouse Square home to the Houston Savings Bank in 1871 and began an annual routine of spending the winter months in Houston. That October he purchased 100 acres in the little town of Dunellen, New Jersey. His three-story "country place" at Green Brook was only thirty miles by train from his Manhattan offices, where William served as agent of the Houston and Texas Central Railroad. The Rices lived in the country until February 1883, when they rented an apartment at the Grenoble in Manhattan.

In 1881, Rice's former partner, Abraham Groesbeeck, purchased the old Capitol Hotel at the corner of Main and Texas. After demolishing the frame boardinghouse, Groesbeeck built a four-story, eighty-room brick hotel. His new Capitol Hotel cost $25,000 and had a marble ground floor, electric bells, and a passenger elevator. On January 23, 1886, the hotel passed to Rice at a tax sale.

During Reconstruction, the most notorious Radical in Houston was Thomas H. Scanlan, an Irish merchant who had moved to the city in 1853 and spent the Civil War years in Mexico. Scanlan was appointed mayor of Houston by Radical Republican Governor Edmund

J. Davis in August 1870. When Scanlan took office, the city debt was less than $300,000; when he was removed four years later, the debt had grown to $1,414,000.

The mayor was best known for tearing down the old market house and building an extravagant new facility. After touring New York, Philadelphia, New Orleans, Chicago, and Louisville, Scanlan built the finest market house in the South. Begun in 1872, the brick structure was changed in progress and completed at a cost of $400,000 in city bonds. The twin-towered, three-story building was 250 feet by 125 feet, supplied with water and gas, and included a thousand-seat theater, city government offices, and stalls for vendors.

After the market house burned down on July 8, 1876, the city took an insurance settlement of $82,500. A new building constructed on the old foundation cost only $100,000, leading political critics to cite the replacement cost as proof of Mayor Scanlan's wastefulness. (The new Scanlan Building burned in 1901.) Corruption was never proved against his administration, however, and Scanlan was reelected in 1872 along with a complete slate of Radicals. According to the *Weekly Telegraph*, the fraudulent election was decided when nonresident black voters poured in from the countryside to register and vote. In January 1874, Democratic Governor Richard Coke turned out the Scanlan crowd and appointed James T. D. Wilson as mayor of Houston.

T. H. Scanlan built an elegant mansion for himself and his spinster daughters on Main Street. He left them a considerable fortune when he died, and the Scanlan sisters spent part of that legacy for an office building in his memory. When the Scanlan Building was completed in 1909 at the corner of Main and Preston, it was the finest building in town. (The structure was renovated and modernized in 1981.)

In 1874, the Houston Board of Trade and Cotton Exchange was established. Three years later, it was reorganized as the Houston Cotton Exchange and Board of Trade. The first building at the corner of Franklin and Travis was completed in 1884. (It was restored in 1973 and is still in use.)

The first free public schools in Houston opened in 1877. The first telephone exchange was installed in 1880 to provide service for fifty telephone users. And in 1882 the Houston Electric Light and Power Company received a franchise. Two years later, five 2,000-candlepower electric arc lights were strung along Main Street at the intersection of Franklin, Preston, Texas, Rusk, and Lamar. The company and its successors formed the Houston Lighting and Power Company in 1922.

In 1887, the Sisters of Charity of the Incarnate Word opened the first general hospital in Houston, the forty-bed St. Joseph's Infirmary at Franklin and Caroline.

Electric streetcars came into operation in the city in 1891. By that time Houston was the most important rail center in the state, with twelve railroads operating in and out of town.

Jacob Binz built the city's first skyscraper at the corner of Main and Texas in 1894. Located across from the Capitol Hotel, the six-story Binz Building served as an office building. (It was torn down about 1950, and an eleven-story glass building now occupies the site.)

The Houston Business League was formed in 1895 and had 1,200 members by late 1910 when the organization adopted the new name, "Chamber of Commerce."

In 1899 sixteen acres were purchased for the first city park. Located behind city hall in downtown Houston, Sam Houston Park is bounded by Bagby, Walker, and Dallas streets. It initially included a small zoo. Over the years the park became increasingly isolated and inaccessible because of freeway construction, Buffalo Bayou, downtown office expansion, and lack of parking space. Empty much of the time, Sam Houston Park has become the preserve of the Harris County Heritage Society, which maintains several restored historic buildings on the grounds. (One of these is the former home of William M. Rice and his first wife, Margaret. The couple lived there until Margaret's death in 1863.)

In 1886, Cesar Maurice Lombardi, president of the Houston School Board, first approached William M. Rice about donating a large, well-equipped high school building to the city. In May 1891, Rice finally rejected the proposal, but announced his intention to endow an institute separate from the public school system.

On May 19, 1891, the William M. Rice Institute was incorporated in Austin. Seven trustees agreed to hold Rice's $200,000 note with interest as an endowment fund. The school was dedicated to the advancement of art, literature, and science and was to provide free education to white students of the city of Houston and state of Texas. Plans for the Rice Institute, including the buildings, were to be put into effect after Rice's death.

Shortly after suffering a severe stroke, Mrs. Elizabeth Rice drew up a new will in Houston on June 1, 1896. Under the community property law of Texas, she claimed half of the assets acquired by her husband during their marriage but left nothing to Rice's institute in the new document. After Elizabeth died of a third stroke in Waukesha, Wisconsin, on July 24, 1896, William claimed to know nothing of the new will and contested it on the grounds that he was a resident of New York state, and thus his property was not subject to disposal by his wife.

When Rice moved to New York City permanently on May 7, 1897, he was worth an estimated $3 million. Taking twenty-one-year-old Charles F. Jones as his valet, he moved into an apartment at 500 Madison Avenue. On September 23, 1900, Rice was murdered in his sleep by valet Jones, who performed the deed under the direction of lawyer Albert T. Patrick.[5]

After Rice's death, the Capitol Hotel was renamed the Rice Hotel. William left no children, and Mrs. Rice's executor, Orren Holt, settled out of court with Rice's executors for the sum of $200,000. Claims by other family members brought the total charges against the Rice estate to over $1 million.

On April 29, 1904, the Rice Institute trustees were left with assets of $4,631,259.08, including the Rice Hotel. The Rice trustees secured 300 acres of empty prairie near Hermann Park off South Main Street and named Dr. Edgar Odell Lovett, a faculty member at Princeton University, as president in 1907. In preparing for his new post, Dr. Lovett spent twelve months visiting other great centers of learn-

---

5. In November 1899, Charlie Jones first met lawyer Patrick, who had been hired by Mrs. Rice's executor, Orren Holt, to take testimony and interview witnesses. Once he became aware of Rice's wealth and the terms of his will, Patrick drew up and forged the signature on a new Rice will on June 30, 1900. In this "Patrick will" he was designated as residuary legatee, and Rice Institute was not to get a cent.

Patrick then persuaded valet Jones to systematically give Rice mercury pills in hopes of weakening his heart. Acting on orders from Patrick, Jones carried the weakened Rice to bed on Sunday, September 23, 1900. He then placed a small, chloroform-soaked sponge in a cone-shaped towel over the sleeping Rice's face. Jones returned thirty minutes later to find the eighty-four-year-old Rice dead.

During a sensational trial, Jones confessed and implicated Patrick in a conspiracy to steal Rice's fortune earmarked for his Houston school through the forged will. Jones went free since he testified as a witness against Patrick, who was found guilty of murder on March 26, 1902, and was sentenced to die in the electric chair. The sentence was commuted to life imprisonment on December 20, 1906. After a New York City organization, the Medico-Legal Society, took up Patrick's cause and concluded that chloroform was not the cause of Rice's death, the New York governor granted Patrick a full pardon on November 27, 1912.

Valet Jones was allowed to return to Texas with his brother William. In 1954, Charlie shot himself in his Baytown home. Lawyer Patrick moved to Oklahoma, where he was counsel to an oil company and sold cars and air-conditioners before his death in 1940.

ing, traveling as far as Edinburgh and Tokyo.

The cornerstone of the Administration Building was laid by the trustees in 1911, and Rice Institute opened its doors to seventy-seven students on September 23, 1912. Today the ashes of William Marsh Rice are contained in a granite pedestal under his statue on the Rice campus. The statue is in the Academic Quadrangle facing Lovett Hall, the university's administration building.

The dream of the Allen brothers — an inland, deepwater port city — finally came to pass with the dredging of the Houston Ship Channel. The project began when Charles Morgan, owner of the Morgan Steamship Line, purchased the Buffalo Bayou Ship Channel Company in 1874, took over dredging across Morgan's Point, and promised to complete a twelve-foot channel to the Gulf. After the Port of Galveston began to charge wharf fees of his steamships, the angry Morgan dredged a channel up Buffalo Bayou to Sims Bayou, built a turning basin and docks there, and developed the new terminal of Clinton. In April 1876, the side-wheeler *Clinton* became the first vessel to navigate Morgan's new channel and reach Clinton, where Morgan's ships linked with Southern Pacific rail service to Houston. (In 1991, only a dilapidated dock on the north bank of the channel was left of old Clinton.)

Charles Morgan died in 1878, but he and his successors placed a heavy chain across the channel to force payment of a toll for using his cut across Morgan's Point. Responding to local complaints, the federal government purchased Morgan's improvements in 1892, removed the chain, and freed the channel to all ships.

In 1896, retiring Congressman Joseph C. Hutcheson pushed through a bill authorizing the survey of a twenty-five-foot channel up Buffalo Bayou to Houston. Hutcheson's replacement, Thomas H. Ball, received an appointment to the Committee on Rivers and Harbors, and the committee paid a tugboat visit to the proposed channel in late January 1897. There were still two obstacles to overcome: army engineers did not think Buffalo Bayou could be made navigable above Harrisburg; and some questioned the need for the project since Galveston was already serving as a Gulf port.

Once the great hurricane of 1900 raised doubts about Galveston's shipping future, Congressman Ball obtained a $1 million appropriation for Buffalo Bayou in 1902, and work on the channel began. Two years later, engineers located a turning basin at the head of Long Reach, a straight stretch of the bayou just above Harrisburg. The turning basin was over four miles from the foot of Houston's original Main

Street docks, but the city annexed the area in 1926. An eighteen-and-one-half-foot channel to the turning basin was completed by August 1908.

At the time, no federal funds were available to dredge the channel to twenty-five feet, the depth required for vessels then in use along the Gulf Coast. To remedy this problem, H. Baldwin Rice and Congressman Ball suggested the creation of a navigation district to control the channel, sell bonds, and offer matching funds to the federal government. When Congress approved the plan in 1910, county voters approved the creation of the Harris County Houston Ship Channel Navigation District and a $1.25 million bond issue for channel improvements. Investors were not forthcoming, so Jesse H. Jones persuaded other Houston leading bankers to join him in purchasing the port bonds in proportion to their capital and surplus.

The voters approved $3 million in bonds for port facilities in 1913, and the city council established a city harbor board, which merged with the navigation district board in 1922 to create a five-member Port Commission empowered to acquire wharves and warehouses.

On November 10, 1914, a twenty-five-foot channel to the turning basin was officially opened when President Woodrow Wilson pressed a button in Washington setting off a cannon at the port of Houston. On August 22, 1915, the Southern Steamship Company began regularly scheduled service between Houston and New York when the steamer *Satilla* made her first visit to the port. By then the first oil refinery had been built on the Houston Ship Channel.

By 1930, Houston ranked as the eighth port in the United States, and eight oil refineries were in operation along the ship channel. The channel was thirty feet deep, with 7,400 feet of public docks, seventeen berths, and seventy-two miles of service railroads around the port. (Today Houston is the third largest port in the United States, and the ship channel has the greatest concentration of refineries and petrochemical plants in the world.)

During World War I, Houston was the scene of a bloody race riot involving black soldiers and city policemen. When Camp Logan, a training camp for National Guard units, was set up west of town at the present site of Memorial Park, a black unit from Illinois was assigned to guard the property during construction. Racial tension soon surfaced when the Illinois troops were called "nigger" and encountered segregation and police harassment. To minimize contact with the white community, the white officers of the unit invited black visitors to the camp, sparking rumors of lewd women and liquor abuse.

On August 23, 1917, policemen Lee Sparks and Rufe Daniels raided a dice game at San Felipe and Wilson. When they arrested a black woman, a partially drunk private, Alonzo Edwards, came to her defense and was struck four times. After the two were jailed, Cpl. Charles Baltimore, a black military policeman, confronted the two policemen about the arrest that afternoon. When angry words were exchanged, Sparks hit Baltimore, who fled to a nearby house and was found hiding under a bed. After being struck several times, Baltimore was also taken to jail.

Shortly thereafter, a rumor spread that a black soldier had been killed by Houston police. Even after Maj. Kneeland Snow, the white commander of Camp Logan, secured the release of Baltimore, there was talk of trouble in camp that evening. Major Snow then revoked all passes, increased the guard, and ordered all rifles and ammunition secured. A racial riot was triggered, however, when a black private shouted "Get your guns, men! The white mob is coming!" Although the statement was untrue, the black troopers panicked, armed themselves, and began firing random shots about the camp. At this point Sgt. Vida Henry led a mob of 75 to 100 men intent on punishing the Houston police. Firing as they marched, the black soldiers moved out toward the San Felipe district at 9:00 P.M. The riot continued through the night and resulted in the death of twenty-five policemen, two white soldiers, eight white civilians, one Hispanic, and four black soldiers, including Sergeant Henry, who killed himself to avoid capture.

The insurrection ended after acting Mayor D. M. Moody requested martial law, and 350 Coast Guard troops from Galveston and 602 infantry soldiers from San Antonio were brought in to maintain peace.

The Camp Logan riot (or mutiny) resulted in the largest court-martial in American military history. The United States Army executed thirteen soldiers by hanging and sentenced forty-one other participants to life in prison. Two additional trials resulted in life terms for twelve soldiers and the death sentence for sixteen others. Responding to pressure from black America, President Woodrow Wilson commuted ten of the latter to life in prison.

After the war, the Hogg family acquired the old Camp Logan grounds. In 1924, William C. (Will) Hogg sold the property to the city of Houston to be used as park land. Hogg, a champion of zoning and city beautification, won a major battle by insisting that if the land was used for anything other than a park, it would revert to the Hogg estate. This restrictive clause has kept both the Astrodome and oil wells out of Memorial Park, the largest in the city.

The advent of the twentieth century brought an extraordinary group of builders, promoters, and philanthropists to Houston. Such men as Jesse H. Jones, Joseph S. Cullinan, Ross S. Sterling, John Henry Kirby, George H. Hermann, Monroe D. Anderson, and Hugh Roy Cullen truly left their mark on the city.

Jesse H. Jones was born in Robertson County, Tennessee, on April 5, 1874. His father moved the family in 1883 to Dallas, Texas, where Jesse began his business career in the lumber company of his uncle, M. T. Jones. While serving as general manager of the company, Jesse moved to Houston in 1899 to manage a branch of the firm. He soon began his own South Texas Lumber Company and made his first fortune in the lumber trade before expanding into banking, real estate, and commercial building. He purchased the *Houston Chronicle* from Marcellus Elliot Foster for $2.5 million in 1926.

His only experience in the infant oil business came when Jones invested $20,000 in the Humble Company. Pleased that he doubled his money by selling his stock a year later, Jesse thus missed out on the vast fortunes that other early Humble stockholders were to amass as Humble evolved into Exxon, U.S.A.

Using borrowed capital to buy land in south Houston, Jones erected some thirty commercial buildings along Main Street by the mid-1920s. His new Rice Hotel, opened in 1913, was built partly because Jesse needed a nice place to live downtown. He personally favored limiting downtown buildings to ten stories and went above that ceiling only after his competitors did so. Jesse owned or controlled forty-nine buildings when he died.

In 1927, Jones built the Lamar Hotel on the corner of Main and Lamar on the site of his old lumberyard. He lived on the top floor of the hotel and held court for years in Suite 8-F. Starting in the early 1930s, this is where Houston's bankers, financiers, and oil millionaires met informally to plan the future needs and expansion of the city. One of the founding members of the 8-F group was George R. Brown of the Brown and Root Company. (Today an asphalt parking lot marks the site of the demolished Lamar Hotel.)

In January 1928, Jones donated $200,000 to the Democratic National Committee and said he wanted the national convention held in Houston, which had an estimated population of 275,000 and had barely risen into the top thirty cities in the country. The Democratic

party also wanted the convention in the South to alleviate hostility toward the eventual nominee, Governor Alfred Smith of New York, a
Roman Catholic and opponent of national prohibition. These circumstances allowed Jones to beat out rival San Francisco in securing the
Democratic National Convention for Houston.

In only sixty-four working days, Jesse built the block-long,
20,000-seat Sam Houston Hall from Texas yellow pine at the corner of
Walker and Bagby and within walking distance of his Rice Hotel.
(Today the Sam Houston Coliseum and the Music Hall stand on the
site of this long-gone convention hall.) The Democratic delegates
spent a steamy week deliberating in an un-air-conditioned hall,
prompting convention reporter Will Rogers to write that "if perspira-
tion was a marketable commodity, the party could pay off the national
debt." On June 28, 1928, Franklin D. Roosevelt stood without
crutches in Sam Houston Hall and nominated the "Happy Warrior,"
Al Smith, for president of the United States. It is noteworthy that
Houston was the first Southern city selected as the site for the Democratic convention since the Civil War.

By the late 1920s, Jesse Jones owned controlling interest in the
National Bank of Commerce and wanted impressive new quarters for
the bank. When he contracted to build a new office building for Gulf
Oil on Main Street, Jones reserved space on the lower floors for his
bank. The banking lobby he built in 1929 is still the grandest one in
the city, although the bank is now called Texas Commerce Bank. At
thirty-five stories, Jones's Gulf Building was the tallest in Houston
until after his death.

The New Deal took Jesse Jones to Washington as a public servant
in the 1930s. He served as chairman of the Reconstruction Finance
Corporation (1933–1939), administrator of the Federal Loan Agency
(1939–1945), and secretary of commerce (1940–1945). The experience of supervising the basic New Deal lending programs resulted in
Jones writing the book *Fifty Billion Dollars* in 1951. He was also in-
strumental in obtaining federal funds for such local building projects as
the San Jacinto Monument and the Sam Houston Coliseum.

After an unsuccessful bid for the Democratic vice-presidential
nomination in 1940, the conservative Jones gradually became more
identified with the anti-Roosevelt political faction and resigned his
federal positions in 1945.

Jesse Jones died on June 1, 1956. In 1937 he and his wife, Mary
Gibbs Jones, created a charitable foundation, Houston Endowment,

Inc. Jesse had once publicly stated that "we still need a better opera house." That dream became a reality when Houston Endowment offered to build a replacement on the downtown site of the old city auditorium, and the $7.4 million Jesse H. Jones Hall for the Performing Arts opened in October 1966.[6]

John Henry Kirby was born in Tyler County in 1860. After briefly attending Southwestern University, Kirby clerked in the law office of Texas Senator Samuel Bronson Cooper at Woodville. Kirby was admitted to the bar in 1885 after reading law under Cooper. The next year he successfully represented some Eastern forest owners in a case involving title to three leagues of land. Impressed by Kirby's ability, the Easterners formed the Texas and Louisiana Land and Lumber Company, as well as the Texas Pine Land Association, and made Kirby general manager of both timber companies.

In 1890, Kirby moved to Houston to join the law firm of Hobby and Lanier. To improve the logging of his timber holdings, he began construction of the Gulf, Beaumont, and Kansas City Railroad between the Neches and Sabine rivers in August 1893. The line reached the new town of Kirbyville in 1895, and Kirby built his first sawmill at Silsbee in 1896. He went into the timber business for himself with the chartering of the Kirby Lumber Company in July 1901. At the

---

6. Most of the properties Jesse Jones gave to Houston Endowment, Inc. were income-producing, improved real estate. The endowment was named as principal beneficiary in his will. When Mrs. Jones died in 1962, she joined him in the bequest.

As of 1990, Houston Endowment had assets of $700 million and was the largest foundation in Texas and one of the twenty largest in the United States. One of the endowment's assets, the *Houston Chronicle,* was sold to the Hearst Corporation for $415 million in 1987.

Since 1937, the foundation has given more than $200 million for educational and cultural purposes; $42 million of such grants were donated in 1989.

The Mary Gibbs Jones Scholarship program was started in 1958 for Houston-area high school graduates. Kathryn J. Whitmire, later the mayor of Houston, received such a scholarship in 1964, and it covered her costs for four years at the University of Houston.

The Alley Theater, the Wortham Center, and Rice University have been major beneficiaries of the foundation.

Houston Endowment donated $3 million to help build the Jesse H. and Mary Gibbs Jones Gulf of Mexico Exhibit Building, the first phase of the Texas State Aquarium which opened in Corpus Christi in July 1990.

Other grants have included $4 million to the Rotary Club of Houston Foundation for construction of a facility for cancer patients and their families in the Texas Medical Center; $3 million to the Greater Houston Area Red Cross to build a new headquarters; and $1 million to help establish the Mickey Leland Center on World Hunger and Peace at Texas Southern University.

peak of activity (1910–1920), the giant company had twelve operating mills, five logging camps, and some 16,500 employees.

The richest man in Houston at the turn of the century, Kirby lived in a Victorian brick and stone mansion on Smith and Gray. He was president of the Southwestern Oil Company of Houston and organized the Kirby Petroleum Company in 1920. As president of the National Lumber Manufacturers' Association (1917–1921), Kirby had a part in developing American lumber standards.

John Henry Kirby also served two terms in the Texas House of Representatives and was a member of the War Industries Board during World War I. This "father of industrial Texas" died on November 9, 1940.

George Henry Hermann was born in a log cabin on the site of the present City Hall Reflection Pool on August 6, 1843. Four years earlier, his parents had come to Houston with five dollars, pawned the family jewelry, and started a bakery.

During the Civil War, Hermann served in Company A, 26th Texas Cavalry, and saw action in both Texas and Louisiana. After the war, he operated a sawmill in present Hermann Park, sold cordwood, and was a cattleman. He inherited substantial land when his parents died, and he went into the real estate business in 1885. The discovery of oil at Humble in 1905 made him a millionaire. The eccentric bachelor then devoted his time to travel, visiting physicians and hospitals in America and Europe.

Before his death, Hermann gave the city 285 acres of land off South Main Street. This gift became the nucleus of Hermann Park, the most important one in the city after the park received the city zoo in 1922. In the 1920s, Hermann Park provided a free campground for tourists. A statue of George Hermann facing his hospital now stands on the southeast corner of his park.

Hermann died at Johns Hopkins Hospital in Baltimore on October 21, 1914, and was buried in Glenwood Cemetery. Since there were no close relatives, the bulk of his $2.6 million estate was left to a foundation for the erection and maintenance of the Hermann Hospital, which opened in 1925. George wanted his hospital to provide free medical care to the indigent, and some such treatment is still provided annually. Hermann Hospital is also a teaching hospital for the University of Texas Medical School and is a pioneer in helicopter ambulance service.

The land where George was born (the block between the present

City Hall and Smith Street) was donated to the city with an odd stipulation that the police not disturb anyone taking a nap or wanting to sleep there at night. Legend has it that Hermann wanted to insure that his sawmill workers would have a place to sleep off hangovers after their Saturday night binges. This policy is still observed in the park and reflection pool area.

Another rich bachelor, Monroe D. Anderson, was to build on George Hermann's medical legacy. Anderson was one of four founders of Anderson, Clayton and Company, a cotton firm organized in Oklahoma City in 1904. After moving headquarters to Houston in 1916, this business became one of the largest cotton brokerage firms in the world. Anderson and Clayton bought cotton, operated gins and oil mills, built warehouses and compresses, and produced its own bagging material.

Monroe Anderson headed the company until his death on August 6, 1939. Three years earlier, the M. D. Anderson Foundation was established to benefit the public, advance knowledge, and alleviate human suffering. This trust received the bulk of his estimated $20 million estate.

The three trustees gave some money to the University of Houston and Rice Institute, but their major project was the creation of the world-renowned Texas Medical Center. In 1942, the foundation purchased 134 acres from the city adjacent to Hermann Hospital to provide a site for a state cancer hospital to be operated by the University of Texas. The M. D. Anderson Hospital and Tumor Institute began in the old home of Capt. James A. Baker on the near southwest side and is housed today in a huge, pink, marble-fronted modern building.

Soon the Texas Dental School moved into the area. The Baylor College of Medicine agreed to relocate there from Dallas in 1943, after being given a twenty-acre site and a $1 million building. While awaiting the new building, Baylor medical students attended classes in a warehouse building on Allen Parkway for four years.

Eventually, the center included the Arabia Temple Crippled Children's Clinic, New Hermann Hospital, Methodist Hospital, Texas Children's Hospital, St. Luke's Episcopal Hospital, Jesse H. Jones Medical Library, Ben Taub Hospital, and the University of Houston College of Nursing.[7]

---

7. The Texas Medical Center has evolved into the world's largest medical complex. As of 1990, it sprawled over 600 acres and fifty buildings, including fourteen hospitals and one hospice. Each year there are 2.5 million inpatient and outpatient visits, including

Will Clayton was also a founder of Anderson, Clayton and Company. In 1916, Will and his wife, Susan, built a stately brick home in the 5300 block of Caroline. After World War II, Clayton helped to devise the Marshall Plan as undersecretary of state for economic affairs. Upon the death of Will and Susan, the family donated the Clayton home to the Houston Public Library in 1958. The Clayton Library is now a branch library where all books and documents deal only with genealogy.

Houston owes its beginning as the executive headquarters of the oil industry in the Southwest to Joseph S. Cullinan. Born in Sharon, Pennsylvania, on December 31, 1860, Cullinan rose through the ranks of a Standard Oil affiliate to become owner of the Petroleum Iron Works in his hometown of Washington, Pennsylvania.

In response to an invitation from the mayor of the city, Cullinan visited Texas to explore the commercial possibilities of the new Corsicana oil field in October 1897. In partnership with investors Calvin N. Payne and Henry Clay Folger, he organized J. S. Cullinan and Company. By December 1898, he had storage tanks, pipelines, and an operating refinery at Corsicana. To stimulate demand for petroleum, Cullinan introduced two new uses for oil: a dust-settling agent for city streets and a fuel for locomotives.

After selling his Corsicana refinery to the Magnolia Petroleum

---

those by world leaders, kings, princesses, and African chieftains.

The center's forty-one institutions employ over 50,000 people — the largest work force in Houston — and make use of 8,000 volunteers. Six universities conduct major programs in the center, and 10,000 students study and train there daily. At last count there were 1,533 medical research projects under way there. In the 1980s, more than $1.6 billion of construction projects were in progress in the center.

Several physicians have become famous through their work at the Texas Medical Center. In 1948, Dr. Michael DeBakey was named head of surgery at Baylor College of Medicine. Six years later, surgeons on six continents watched as he performed heart surgery on public television. Since that time, Dr. DeBakey has become world-renowned as an innovator and educator in heart surgery. He now performs his surgery at The Methodist Hospital, where a bronze bust of him adorns an adjoining chamber of the elegant hospital lobby.

Dr. Denton Cooley has brought fame to the Texas Heart Institute based at St. Luke's Hospital. Dr. Cooley and his "team" (the heart surgeons trained by him) have performed more than 75,000 heart surgical procedures. In 1968, he completed America's first successful heart transplant. The next year, Dr. Cooley implanted the world's first artificial heart.

Dr. James "Red" Duke of The University of Texas Health Science Center provides health information segments carried by seventy commercial television stations in the United States.

Company — the forerunner of Mobil Oil — Cullinan moved to Beaumont and incorporated the Texas Fuel Company in March 1901. This company purchased, stored, and transported oil from the Spindletop oil field. Reorganized as the $3 million Texas Company in April 1902, the new firm acquired barges and tank cars, leased the new Sour Lake and Humble oil fields, and linked these fields by pipelines to Port Arthur, where the Texas Company built the first refinery in early 1905.

Joseph Cullinan served as president of the Texas Company from 1902 until 1914. Convinced that Houston was the logical regional headquarters for the budding petroleum industry, Cullinan moved the company general offices there from Beaumont in 1908. Five years later, the Texas Company main offices were moved to New York City.

After resigning from the company in 1914, Cullinan formed the American Republics Oil Company and built the Petroleum Building on Texas Avenue to house it. In 1917 he purchased from the George Hermann Estate a triangular tract of land at the junction of South Main and Montrose, then donated it to the Houston Art League for a museum. The Museum of Fine Arts was built on the property in 1924. He purchased the land between the museum site and the Rice campus in 1917 and developed Shadyside, the most exclusive subdivision in the city. Lots were sold only to his relatives, friends, and business associates — not to the general public.

Cullinan was a major supporter of the Symphony Society, formed in Houston in 1913. He and his wife, Lucie, had four children. The founder of Texaco died in Palo Alto, California, on March 11, 1937.

Ross S. Sterling, one of Houston's early oil millionaires, was born in Anahuac, Texas, on February 11, 1875. He had been an oil operator for two years when the first great strike was made at Humble in northeastern Harris County in January 1905. Five years later, Sterling purchased two wells in the Humble Oil Field, which developed into the Humble Oil Company in February 1911. The original company resulted from a combination of Sterling and W. W. Fondren with R. L. Blaffer and W. S. Farish. After being reorganized, the $1 million company received a new charter as the Humble Oil and Refining Company, a merger of five oil and refining companies, in June 1917. Two years later, Humble started construction of the huge Baytown refinery, doubled the number of shares, and sold fifty percent of its stock to the Standard Oil Company of New Jersey.

Ross Sterling served as president of Humble from 1917 to 1922. During this time the Humble Company Building on Main was finished. (In 1960 Humble moved to a new forty-four-story building on Bell, now called the Exxon building.) In 1925 Ross sold his Humble interests and began to develop real estate in the Houston area. In 1925 and 1926 he purchased two newspapers and combined them as the Houston *Post-Dispatch,* which later became the Houston *Post.* Sterling sold the paper to J. E. Josey in the 1930s. (William P. Hobby purchased controlling interest in 1939, and the *Post* is still owned by the family today.)

Sterling served one term as governor of Texas, 1931–1933. When rulings of the Texas Railroad Commission regulating oil proration were ignored in East Texas, Governor Sterling placed four counties under martial law and temporarily shut down all oil production. In 1933 he was defeated by Miriam A. Ferguson in his bid for a second term as governor.

After returning to private life in Houston, Sterling built another fortune as president of the Sterling Oil and Refining Company from 1933 until 1946. He also served as chairman of the Houston National Bank and the Houston-Harris County Channel Navigation Board.

He and his wife, Maud Abbie Gage Sterling, had five children. The couple established a boys' camp in memory of Ross Sterling, Jr., who died in 1924. The family summer house on Galveston Bay at LaPorte was an extravagant, scaled-down replica of the White House. This mansion was left to the Houston Optimist Club to be used as a home for boys. (Years later it was purchased and restored by banker Paul Barkley.)

Ross Sterling died in Fort Worth on March 25, 1949, and was buried in Houston.

Houston oilman and philanthropist Hugh Roy Cullen was born on July 3, 1881, in Denton County. His formal education was limited to a few years in the San Antonio public schools. After marrying Lillie Cranz in 1903, the couple had four daughters and one son, Roy Gustav, who was killed in an oil field accident in 1936.

As a young man, Hugh Roy Cullen was a cotton broker in Oklahoma before moving to Houston in 1911. He became an oil contractor in 1918 and pioneered in deep drilling and the penetration of the heaving shale in the Humble field. The most successful wildcatter of his day, Cullen made major oil discoveries in the Houston area at Pierce Junction, Blue Ridge, Rabb's Ridge, Humble, and the O'Connor field. He owned half of the South Texas Petroleum Company, orga-

nized the Quintana Petroleum Company, and amassed a fortune of
$250 million.

Cullen began a new career as a philanthropist in 1937–1938
when he chaired a $1 million building-fund for the private University
of Houston, which started as a junior college in 1927. At that time he
donated $260,000 to the university for the construction of the Roy
Gustav Cullen Memorial Building in memory of his son. This structure was located on a new 110-acre campus southeast of downtown. It
was the first of many buildings on the present campus named for members of the Cullen family. The street the campus fronts is also named
Cullen.

In 1946, Cullen and the M. D. Anderson Foundation gave
enough land to double the size of the University of Houston campus.
The next year he and Lillie established the $160 million Cullen Foun-
dation to provide continual aid to education, medicine, and charitable
institutions in the state of Texas.

Hugh Roy gave over $11 million each to his favorite projects, the
University of Houston and Houston hospitals. In addition to being the
school's greatest benefactor, Cullen served as chairman of the board of
regents of the University of Houston.

He announced in 1955 that after providing for his family, he had
given away ninety-three percent of his wealth. This oilman-philan-
thropist who so enjoyed giving money and getting attention died in
Houston on July 4, 1957.

Another of the Houston tycoons of this period was Gus Wortham, who founded the American General Insurance Company in
1926. At that time he began to acquire the property on Allen Parkway
between Montrose and Waugh Drive. The American General Center
has been developed on this land.

Wortham also purchased part of the adjacent old Magnolia Cemetery and ordered that a family mausoleum be built there so he could
keep an eye on things. Both Gus and his wife, Lyndall, were interred
there when they died in 1976 and 1980, respectively. In accordance
with Wortham's wishes, all the buildings in the American General
Center are visible from his resting place.

In keeping with the great tradition of philanthropy among Hous-
ton's rich, the Wortham Foundation has funded the construction of the
Wortham Center, home of the Houston Grand Opera and the Houston
Ballet.

Houston's foremost subdivision, River Oaks, was started by Will and Mike Hogg and Hugh Potter in 1923. This wooded tract on the western edge of the city would be home to many of Houston's super-rich. The tightly restricted residential area has curvilinear streets, deed restrictions, and a maintenance fund to aid in upkeep. The simple, elegant, well-proportioned homes designed by architect John F. Staub attracted the quiet wealth of Houston's "best oil money." In 1933, Staub designed one of the finest River Oaks mansions for Hugh Roy and Lillie Cullen (owned in 1991 by Oscar and Lynn Wyatt).

The focal point of the subdivision is the River Oaks Country Club. Just outside the subdivision entrance is the River Oaks Shopping Center on West Gray, the first neighborhood shopping center in Houston.

One of the original River Oaks mansions, Bayou Bend, was built for Ima Hogg. Miss Ima was the co-founder of the Symphony Society formed in 1913. She and her brothers were the children of James S. Hogg, the first native-born governor of Texas (1891–1895), who made a fortune in oil and real estate after leaving office. Having lived there for years, Ima Hogg in 1966 donated Bayou Bend and her priceless collection of early American furniture, porcelain, brass, silver, and art to the Houston Art Museum (formerly the Museum of Fine Arts).

Will Hogg, a critic of uncontrolled city growth, agreed to head a revived planning commission in 1927. Two years later, he submitted a city plan which included proposals for parks and zoning. To ensure orderly growth, his zoning plan provided specific areas for residences, apartments, business, and light and heavy industry. The plan encountered stiff oppositions from real estate agents and contractors, however, and the city council rejected the idea of zoning after 350 protestors disrupted a council meeting.

On March 17, 1949, Houston basked in the national spotlight with the opening of Glenn McCarthy's Shamrock Hotel. Located five miles from downtown on South Main, the $21 million, eighteen-story hotel featured a large portrait of McCarthy in the lobby, sixty-three shades of green in the interior, a 1,000-car garage, and a fifty-meter, fan-shaped swimming pool. Hotel rooms ranged in price from $6 to $45 per night, with penthouses available for $2,100 per month. After viewing the prosaic design of the hotel, fame architect Frank Lloyd Wright remarked, "I always wondered what the inside of a juke box looked like."

McCarthy, a millionaire wildcat oilman, chose St. Patrick's Day for his grand opening and brought in 175 movie stars by special plane and train for a $42 dinner and weeklong party. Many of the 50,000 curious onlookers so crowded the hotel lobby that Jesse Jones became stuck in the entrance, and Mayor Oscar Holcombe had to wait outside for two hours. McCarthy even arranged for Dorothy Lamour's NBC network radio show to be broadcast from the Shamrock's glittering Emerald Room. So many crashed the show that the actors resorted to shouting their lines above the crowd noise. The more rowdy types even seized the microphone and hooted Texas crudities into it. At that point NBC cut the Lamour show off the air, and the star fled to her room for a good cry.

The grand opening of the Shamrock Hotel was the wildest such affair in Houston's history. Legend has it that the event gave Edna Ferber the idea for her novel, *Giant.* (The Hilton Hotels gained complete ownership of the Shamrock in 1955, and the green-roofed structure was demolished in 1989 to provide for an addition to the Texas Medical Center, Texas A&M University's Institute of Biosciences and Technology.)

The most active homebuilder and developer in the post-World War II era was Frank W. Sharp. In 1954, he started developing Sharpstown, the largest subdivision in America at the time. Much of this 6,500-acre tract on the southwest side of Houston had been a dairy. Sharp projected 25,000 mostly three-bedroom brick houses in a $400 million planned community where "contented people's . . . needs are being met on three levels — physical, mental, and spiritual."

While the Texas Highway Department was deciding on a new route for U.S. Highway 59 South, Sharp led a group of investors that gave a 300-foot-wide, 10.5-mile right-of-way to the state to bring the Southwest Freeway through his subdivision in 1957. This $2 million land donation gave Sharp valuable freeway frontage. In 1961 he completed the first fully air-conditioned shopping center in Houston alongside the new freeway. This huge mall included a heliport and the Sharpstown State Bank.

When Houston welcomed the first seven astronauts on July 4, 1962, promoter Sharp offered each of them a $60,000 home in his Sharpstown subdivision, an offer the space agency rejected. In 1963, he donated a valuable tract of land to entice the Baptist General Convention to establish Houston Baptist College in Sharpstown.

Sharp ran afoul of the law in 1971 after he and several high state political figures, including House Speaker Gus Mutscher, Jr., were implicated in a scheme involving stock fraud and bribery. The scandal resulted in the failure of the Sharpstown State Bank, and Sharp lost control of his subdivision.

Today one would most likely associate Houston with the Johnson Manned Spacecraft Center (1962), the Astrodome (1965), and the world-renowned Texas Medical Center. Surprisingly, though, a recent poll of Houstonians revealed that of all the aspects of their city, they are most proud of the downtown skyline.

Largely through the efforts of developer Gerald D. Hines and such innovative architects as Philip Johnson and I. M. Pei, the central business district has exploded skyward since the 1970s to create a major tourist attraction. Today such awesome buildings as the seventy-five-story Texas Commerce Tower, the seventy-one-story First Interstate Bank building, the twin trapezoid towers called Pennzoil Place, the tiered Gothic NCNB Center, the fifty-story Texaco Heritage Plaza, the fifty-story First City Tower, and the fifty-story Number One Shell Plaza are linked by a 6.2-mile public tunnel system.

Ada Louise Huxtable, the former architecture critic of *The New York Times,* said, "Houston is the place that scholars flock to for the purpose of seeing what modern civilization has wrought. It is the city of the second half of the 20th Century."

Today the Main Street-Market Square Historic District includes all or part of eighteen city blocks south of Buffalo Bayou between Milam and San Jacinto. Although this area was named to the National Register of Historic Places in 1984, seven architecturally significant buildings have been torn down since that time. Lack of zoning is one reason that Houston has done little to preserve its historic commercial district.[8] Houston is the only major metropolitan city that has no ordinance protecting historic buildings.

---

8. Until January 9, 1991, Houston was the only major city in the United States without zoning and land-use controls. On that date, the fifteen-member city council unanimously approved a proposal by Councilman Jim Greenwood to change the city's Planning Commission to the Planning and Zoning Commission and to charge it with drawing up a comprehensive land-use plan to be enforced with zoning regulations. The city council also adopted a timetable aimed at having a final zoning plan for all property by early 1993. "It is an historic occasion," said Mayor Kathy Whitmire, who predicted that "a unique Houston-style zoning" would be developed.

Problems with Houston's lack of zoning were magnified when the city experienced an incredible growth between 1970 and 1982. During this period, developers and businesspeople were allowed to operate wherever they wanted. Parking garages and office buildings soon abutted residential neighborhoods. Councilman Greenwood's proposal is intended to direct growth through land-use planning so as to keep such residential areas free from encroachment by commercial and industrial businesses.

It is a sad eventuality that the wrecking ball which brought development and growth has also destroyed many Houston landmarks over the years. A city created by promoters and developers is sure to be left with many more historical markers than structures. Glimpses of nineteenth-century Houston can still be seen, however, in such out-of-the-way places as Allen's Landing Park, Old Market Square, and Sam Houston Park.

One must conclude that if the Allen brothers came back as tourists today, they would feel vindicated after seeing the skyscrapers of the "great interior commercial emporium" they touted in 1836.

The original plan of the City of Houston.
— Courtesy Houston Metropolitan Research Center,
Houston Public Library

Jesse H. Jones
— Courtesy Houston Metropolitan Research Center,
Houston Public Library

Ross Sterling
— Courtesy Houston Metropolitan Research Center,
Houston Public Library

M. D. Anderson
— Courtesy Houston Metropolitan Research Center,
Houston Public Library

Joseph S. Cullinan
— Courtesy Houston Metropolitan Research Center,
Houston Public Library

George H. Hermann
— Courtesy Houston Metropolitan Research Center,
Houston Public Library

William Marsh Rice portrait.
— Courtesy Office of the President, Rice University

Hugh Roy Cullen
— Courtesy Houston Metropolitan Research Center,
Houston Public Library

A. C. Allen
— Courtesy Houston Metropolitan Research Center,
Houston Public Library

John K. Allen
— Courtesy Houston Metropolitan Research Center,
Houston Public Library

Capitol Hotel, Houston, 1837.
— Courtesy Harris County Heritage Society

V

Texana:
A Tale of Lost Opportunities

If the Allen brothers could have had their druthers in 1836, the city of Houston would sprawl today some 100 miles southwest of its present location. Decisions made at Texana, Texas, in 1836 and 1881 led to the death of that town and life for Houston and Edna. This is the story of old Texana, the ghost of an intended metropolis.

In 1685, the site of Texana was an Indian village when it was visited by the French explorer LaSalle, who went there to recover boats and blankets the Indians had stolen from his wrecked ship in the Lavaca River. The village was northeast of Fort St. Louis, the stockade he had built on the west bank of Garcitas Creek in present Victoria County. In 1821, Stephen F. Austin visited the Texana area in present Jackson County, which became the extreme western boundary of his original land grant. Six of Austin's "Old Three Hundred" colonists received their league of land in the county. Robert Guthrie, William B. Bridge, Elizabeth McNutt, and Francis F. Wells received title to their land in July 1824; Maj. James Kerr and John Allen followed in May 1827. A colony of thirty families lived between the Lavaca and Navidad rivers by 1832; most were relatives and friends from Decatur and Tuscumbia, Alabama, so the region was called the "Alabama Settlement." Among these newcomers were Judge William Menefee, a signer of the Texas Declaration of Independence, and William J. E. Heard, a company commander at San Jacinto. John Henry Brown, the noted early Texas historian, later paid this tribute to the Alabama Settlement:

Sixty years have been added to the scroll of time since their arrival in the wilderness. In all the bloody struggle afterwards they were sterling patriots. As citizens they were intelligent, moral and upright. Among them . . . there has never been a stain or a law breaker. Their influence has ever been potential for good . . . And yet these people were but fair samples of a large majority of the people resident on the Lavaca and Navidad in the colonial days of Texas, the cheeks of whose surviving children often burn . . . at the still occasionally repeated slander that — Texas was originally settled by outlaws and desperadoes.

Initially, this settled area was part of the Austin municipality and was called the Lavaca District.

Texana, the first town in present Jackson County, was founded in 1832 by Dr. Francis F. Wells and his sister-in-law, Mrs. Pamelia McNutt Porter. It was located two miles north of the junction of the Lavaca and Navidad and was first called Santa Anna. Dr. Wells, a native of Virginia, came to Texas from Louisiana as one of the "Old Three Hundred" and on July 21, 1824, received the league of land (4,428 acres) on which Santa Anna took root. He was listed as a doctor in a census of March 1826, and the *ayuntamiento* (governing council) of San Felipe de Austin granted him a license to practice medicine in November 1829.

Maj. George Sutherland, an area pioneer who stood six feet, four inches tall and weighed almost 300 pounds, started a large general merchandise store at Santa Anna in June 1834. He sold out the following April, and the firm was renamed John S. Menefee and Company. For two years the town of Santa Anna comprised only a general store and the home of Mrs. Sarah Royster, prompting Mr. Menefee to later recall, "A traveler rode up one day and inquired how far it was to Santa Anna. I told him he was in the heart of the town!"

By 1835 it was apparent that General Santa Anna had become a tyrant and dictator, so an election was held at the general store to change the town's name. James Kerr suggested the name "Pulaski," while John Menefee proposed "Texana." The latter name was chosen by a vote of 84 to 19.[1]

---

1. John Sutherland Menefee was born in Tennessee on June 24, 1813. When he was seventeen his father, Thomas, brought the family from Alabama to the Texana area. While John was in the mercantile business at Texana, he furnished the Texas army with ten kegs of powder. Both he and George Sutherland fought in the Battle of San Jacinto, serving as privates in Company D, First Regiment Texian Volunteers, commanded by Capt. Moseley

Jim Bowie and a sick companion named Desplaines visited Texana on June 14, 1835. Bowie had recently been at Matamoros, Mexico, where he barely escaped arrest after hearing that Gen. Martín Perfecto de Cos had embargoed all foreign vessels in port, intending to use
them for transporting Mexican troops and supplies to Texas. Since
Desplaines was running a high fever and was unable to travel, he and
Jim Bowie rested for several days at Texana. During this time Bowie
courted a local belle, Miss Clara Lisle, and was the house guest of Capt.
Sylvanus Hatch, an original settler and close friend who lived on the
Lavaca River.[2] On June 19, Bowie sent an historic letter from the

---

Baker. John was elected county clerk of Jackson County in 1837 and county judge in
1846. He also served in the House of Representatives of the Fourth Congress in
1839–1840.

When Mexican armies twice invaded Texas in 1842, Menefee volunteered for scouting duty. During one such mission to Arenosa Creek in Jackson County, he was attacked
by an Indian warrior and had seven arrows shot into his body. In a final act of desperation,
John threw his empty pistol at the brave and hit him right between the eyes. After pulling
out the arrows, the bleeding scout hid under the creek bank for a day before crawling to
the safety of a nearby ranch. For years Menefee kept those arrows in his home as souvenirs
of a close brush with death.

He was also an active member of the Texas Veterans Association and kept a remarkable diary, excerpts of which were published in the *Texana Clarion* in 1880. John S. Menefee died on November 4, 1884, and was buried in the old family cemetery on the Navidad River five miles east of Edna. In 1936, the Texas Centennial Commission placed a
monument at his grave.

2. There is a fascinating Texana legend about Jim Bowie's last romance. In September 1833 his beautiful Castilian wife, Maria Ursula, and their two children died when a
cholera epidemic swept through Monclova, their summer home. The despondent husband
began to drink heavily after losing his family. As his broken heart began to heal, Jim
began to escort Clara Lisle of Texana two years later. Although Miss Lisle was smitten by
this dashing colonel, Bowie did not seem to return her affection at first. During his weeks
of preparation at San Antonio before the siege and fall of the Alamo, Jim was invited to
attend a grand ball at Texana. Dressed in his best Spanish suit, he arrived late and immediately sought out the beautiful Clara. While the handsome couple were dancing a waltz,
Bowie whispered in her ear, "You are divine!" When they walked out on the veranda later
in the evening, he placed a silver chain around the ecstatic Clara's neck and bade her a
tender farewell. Just before galloping off in the darkness toward San Antonio, Jim promised to see her again when he could.

Later, as the siege of the Alamo tightened, there were feelings of terror and suspense
among the people of Texana. On the night of March 6, 1836 — the day the Alamo fell
before Santa Anna's onslaught — the anguished Clara stayed with her best friend, Isabella
Wilson. In the middle of the stormy night, Miss Lisle suddenly screamed, sat upright in
bed, and told Isabella she had dreamed of Bowie coming to see her that night. In her
dream Clara had heard the tramping of his horse's hooves, then the sound of Jim's footsteps
on the gallery and a knocking on the door. When she threw open the door and exclaimed,

Hatch house to the citizens of San Felipe in which he warned of war preparations being made by General Cos at Matamoros.

On July 17, 1835, the Lavaca-Navidad meeting was held at William Millican's gin house three miles northeast of present Edna. The oldest resident, Maj. James Kerr, was elected president of the gathering while Rev. Samuel C. A. Rogers was chosen as secretary by forty pioneers who lived near the two rivers. One of these men, nineteen-year-old William Sutherland, would die at the Alamo; another delegate, Elijah Stapp, later signed the Texas Declaration of Independence while George Sutherland and John S. Menefee fought at San Jacinto. Although these men could have been shot for treason, they unanimously declared their belief that Santa Anna was hostile to state sovereignty and the state constitution and resolved to oppose any force that might be introduced into Texas for other than constitutional purposes. The delegates also called for a general consultation of representatives from all of the municipalities of Texas. At the conclusion of the meeting, these audacious pioneers called on the militia "to hold themselves in readiness to march at a moment's warning." The signers of this protest document planned to keep its contents a secret until it could be passed on for signatures in as many settlements as possible. Major McNutt was commissioned to first take it to Provisional Governor Henry Smith at San Felipe. Before reaching his destination, the courier destroyed the document just before being captured by Mexican troops. This Lavaca-Navidad meeting, the first revolutionary protest against the Mexican government, is considered the forerunner of the Texas Declaration of Independence.

On December 5, 1835, the General Council of the provisional state government created the municipality of Jackson, with Texana as the "capital." During the Texas Revolution, Texana was a major port of entry, receiving station, and training camp for United States volunteers. The majority of James Walker Fannin's army who died in the Goliad Massacre first drilled for two weeks at Texana. One such company, the "Red Rovers," were young sons of planters from Lauderdale

"Jim, have you come at last?," all she could see was a huge, shrouded form which neither moved nor spoke. When Clara whispered, "Who are you?," the apparition threw open its arms and thundered in reply, "Death!" After describing the dream to her friend, Clara said she feared it was an omen of some awful evil.

A short time thereafter, the terrible news reached Texana that the Alamo had fallen and that all of its defenders, including her beloved Bowie, were dead. Clara Lisle died only a few weeks later, thus ending the tale of Jim Bowie's last romance.

and Franklin counties in Alabama, the same locality as the original Texana settlers, so they were entertained in a "royal fashion." Military leaders such as Houston, Travis, Bowie, and Crockett visited the town to observe training exercises and enjoyed the hospitality of Captain Hatch's home on the Lavaca.

During the Runaway Scrape, Texana was abandoned, but a raft was left there in the Navidad River as a means of escape for women and children. When Mrs. Francis F. Wells tied the family silver around her waist under her skirt, she stepped too close to the raft's edge and almost capsized it. Mrs. Wells had good reason to flee: Gen. Jose Urrea's army camped there on April 2, 1836, and he was ordered to destroy Santa Anna's former namesake.

Uncle Jeff, a slave of Maj. George Sutherland, was told to bury his master's mahogany desk along with wash tubs, pots, kettles, and cooking utensils. When the family returned to Texana after the war, they found only wild animals; the Mexicans had stripped the area of all poultry, sheep, hogs, and horses. The Sutherlands had to wait another three months before George returned on a ship loaded with flour, pickled pork, rice, sugar, and coffee. Mrs. Sutherland had more to lament than property losses. Writing to a sister in Alabama on June 5, 1836, she said:

> . . . Yes, sister, I must say it to you, I have lost my William. O, yes he is gone. My poor boy is gone, gone from me. The sixth of March in the morning, he was slain in the Alamo in San Antonio. Then his poor body committed to the flames . . . He was there, a volunteer, when the Mexican army came there . . . Poor fellows . . . The Mexicans kept nearly continual firing on them for thirteen days. Then scaled the walls and killed every man in the fort but two black men . . .

After the Battle of San Jacinto, the Republic of Texas Army headquartered at Camp Independence from December 1836 until May 1837. Located only a few miles from Texana, this camp was on Captain Hatch's land on the east bank of the Lavaca and was the site of a famous duel in February 1837. Felix Huston, a fiery adventurer and lawyer from Natchez, Mississippi, had been voted commander-in-chief by these troops the previous summer. He wanted to continue the war against Mexico, lead an expedition against Matamoros, and head up a military colony along the Rio Grande. President Houston sought to block the risky scheme by replacing Huston with Albert Sidney Johnston, a West Point graduate who had arrived in Texas in July 1836. After being appointed to the rank of senior brigadier general, Johnston arrived at Camp Independence on February 4, 1837. This demotion was a blow to the pride, ambition, and honor of Huston, who felt disgraced as an officer; besides, he knew that the majority of the unruly volunteer army preferred him as their commander. That very night he sent a letter to Johnston accusing him of treachery and an attempt to ruin his reputation, then challenged him to a duel.

Johnston felt pressed by circumstance to accept the challenge. He chose pistols as weapons, although he was more skilled with rifle and rapier. The duel took place at 7:00 A.M. on February 5 in Hatch's cowpen. Both men fired, missed, and reloaded several times; finally, on the fifth exchange, Johnston fell with a ball through his right hip. Critically wounded, he was taken to Hatch's house, where he was bedridden for a month. Johnston was left with partial lameness from an injured sciatic nerve.

Although Huston thus retained his camp command, feelings of remorse led him to accept Johnston as commanding general by the end of the month. He later returned to the practice of law and became a fast friend of Johnston, who was destined to become the only full Confederate general that Texas contributed to the Civil War effort.

Jackson County was organized by the Republic of Texas Congress on March 17, 1836, with Texana as the county seat. Early that summer, Augustus C. Allen came visiting in pursuit of a business dream: his own inland port city in Texas. The town of Texana met all of his requirements. It was the farthest point inland with no logjam obstruction, and the site also offered drainage, shelter, deep water, rich land, and natural beauty.

Allen was thus willing to offer Dr. F. F. Wells the huge sum of $100,000 in gold for the league of land on which Texana was located. The Wells league began at the forks of the Navidad and Lavaca rivers, covering two and one-half miles of land line and twelve miles of river front. After giving the offer careful consideration, Dr. Wells asked Allen to double his bid. This so angered Augustus that he was said to have jumped on a stump, pointed a damning finger down Texana's Broadway Street, and shouted: "Never will this town amount to anything, I curse it. You people listening within the sound of my voice will live to see rabbits and other animals inhabiting its streets."

As the angry Allen rode away, the future of Texana still looked bright. On April 25, 1837, Dr. Wells laid off a new town map and filed it with the Jackson County clerk. In this revived Texana, the backs of the business houses were toward the Navidad, with five streets paralleling the river (Commerce, Broadway, Duval, Lamar, and Bonham) and ten streets running east and west from it (Crockett, Bowie, Fannin, Travis, Lavaca, Milam, Austin, Ward, King, and Common). Many of the streets in Dr. Wells's 1834 plan for Texana were renamed for Texas revolutionary heroes.[3] The public sale of town lots included a total of fifty blocks.

A touch of civility was added in 1838 with the organization of the Texana Methodist Church, the oldest church in Jackson County. Rev. S. C. A. Rogers was the first pastor. That same year the Mississippi Conference created the Houston Circuit, with Texana the extreme western appointment for the "circuit rider." Robert H. Hill received this assignment and on May 21, 1840, married Sarah Royster and Benjamin White at Texana. This was the first Protestant marriage ceremony ever performed in the county. The dangers and hardships endured by pioneer Methodist circuit preachers such as Reverend Hill inspired the following tribute from an early traveler:

When I heard a rustling in the bushes, I knew it meant one of three

---

3. One San Jacinto hero, James A. Sylvester, became a resident of Texana. On December 18, 1835, Sylvester enlisted as second sergeant and color bearer in Capt. Sidney Sherman's volunteer company at Newport, Kentucky. James carried the only battle flag at the Battle of San Jacinto, a banner given to the company by the ladies of Newport. In the center of this beautiful blue and gold silk flag is a female figure, the Goddess of Liberty, with the phrase, "Liberty or Death," above her head. This prized relic is mounted today behind the Speaker's desk in the Texas House of Representatives chamber.

On the morning of April 22, 1836, the day after the historic battle, it was James Sylvester who found and captured General Santa Anna while out on a volunteer search patrol. At San Augustine on August 3, 1836, Gen. Sam Houston appointed James a captain and gave him a printed pamphlet listing those who fought at San Jacinto. On the back was this personal note:

Presented to James A. Sylvester by General Sam Houston as a tribute of regard for his gallant and vigilant conduct first in the battle of San Jacinto and subsequently in the capture of Santa Anna, whose thanks were tendered by Santa Anna, in my presence to Captain Sylvester, for his generous conduct towards him, when captured.

Sylvester was honorably discharged from the Texas army in June 1837 and settled at Texana, where he was elected assessor and treasurer of Jackson County that February. After enlisting in the Somervell Expedition of 1842, he left Texana the next year and moved to New Orleans to work as a printer for the New Orleans Picayune. The lifelong bachelor died in that city on April 9, 1882, and was buried in the Odd Fellows Cemetery there. On November 5, 1936, Sylvester's remains were reinterred in the State Cemetery at Austin.

things, an Indian, a bear, or a Methodist Circuit Rider, for while the first two mentioned were the far more numerous, the latter was far more active.

On September 15, 1851, Dr. Wells donated one town lot to the trustees of the Texana Methodist Church, and a forty-by-sixty-foot building was completed soon thereafter.

In May 1838, the Texas Congress authorized a mail route from Galveston to Matagorda and Texana with deliveries every two weeks. After September 1840, weekly steamboat service on the *Swan* connected Texana and Indianola via Matagorda Bay. Starting in 1847, a stagecoach left Houston each Tuesday and arrived at Victoria on Friday after stops at Richmond, Egypt, and Texana. A school called the Texana Academy was chartered on January 2, 1850, and a courthouse was built in 1858. The town's emergence as a port was signaled in 1850, when the New Orleans stern-wheeler *Envoy* docked at the Texana wharves. This steamboat was 122 feet long, fifteen feet at the beam, and could carry a load of 600 cotton bales.

During the 1850s, Texana was a thriving trade center with fifteen to twenty ships calling weekly, bringing settlers and cargo for the interior and picking up cotton, hides, and tallow for the market. People were coming too; the population of Jackson County increased from 996 in 1850 to 2,612 in 1860.

The Brackenridge family was among the most prominent of Texana newcomers during this period. John Brackenridge was a Presbyterian minister who helped organize the First Presbyterian Church in Washington, D.C., before serving as chaplain to both the United States Senate and House of Representatives. All three of his sons were named for presidents of the United States who attended his services. One of the boys, John Adams Brackenridge, was born in 1800 and studied at the College of New Jersey, the forerunner of Princeton, before starting a law practice near Boonville in Warrick County, Indiana. In April 1827, he married Isabella Helena McCullough, the daughter of a well-to-do Kentucky planter. John Adams was a founder of the local Presbyterian church and was considered "perhaps the ablest local attorney" to ever practice in Warrick County; his law library was said to be the best in southern Indiana. Among those who heard him present a defense in a murder trial at Boonville was eighteen-year-old Abraham Lincoln, who complimented Brackenridge and later said that this "best speech he ever heard" inspired him to study the law. Lincoln was given access to John Adams's law library and permission to borrow his books, and the two became lifelong friends.

By 1850, Brackenridge's income was not keeping up with his growing family of eight children. Thinking that the mild, balmy Texas climate might improve his poor health, he bought a league of land between the Navidad and Lavaca rivers and near Texana in late 1851. John Adams started a mercantile business at Texana and also served as supplier for his two oldest sons, Tom and George W., who, along with James H. Bates, engaged in mercantile operations in the interior. In 1855 the four men formed the partnership of Brackenridge and Bates with their main warehouse at Texana and a branch in Seguin; they also offered basic banking services to their mercantile customers. On a knoll overlooking the Navidad, the senior Brackenridge was soon able to build a fine two-and-one-half-story house with a gallery across the front and a library for his books. The yards of lace and ribbon charged by the women in his family attest to the active social life they led. It was said that Mary Eleanor Brackenridge outshone all the other local belles. She thought nothing of riding a horse sidesaddle for thirty miles to a ball, dancing all night, then riding home with James Bates as her escort.[4] When eight-year-old Elizabeth Ann Brackenridge died

---

4. Mary Eleanor Brackenridge was born in Warrick County, Indiana, on March 7, 1837. After she and her mother moved to San Antonio to live with brother George in 1866, Eleanor served as his hostess and championed many causes. She pioneered in the women's club movement by organizing the San Antonio Mutual Admiration and Improvement Society. In September 1901, the Eleanor Brackenridge Literary Club was founded and named in her honor in Edna. This is the second oldest women's study club in Texas in terms of continuous existence. A popular street in Edna is also named for her. On her birthday on March 7, 1919, "Friendship Day" was established in Texas and has been observed by women's clubs since that time.

Eleanor was also a tireless ally of the Woman's Christian Temperance Union and played a key role in bringing about state and national prohibition. In recognition of her contribution, the WCTU and local club women dedicated a giant live oak tree to her in Brackenridge Park.

A leader in the women's suffrage movement, Eleanor served as lifetime honorary president of the Women's Voters League and was the first woman voter to register in Bexar County in June 1918.

Like her brother George, she was a staunch supporter of education. In 1903, she was one of three women appointed to the first board of regents of the new College of Industrial Arts (now Texas Woman's University) at Denton and served in that post until her death. Eleanor was also responsible for the introduction of home economics courses in the San Antonio public schools and had a school named for her in the city.

Eleanor Brackenridge also founded the Bexar Chapter of the Daughters of the American Revolution, was an active worker in the Order of the Eastern Star and the Presbyterian

on July 16, 1856, her grieving father chose a site near the house for a family cemetery while his wife, Isabella, and son George planted a double row of cedars along the path to the burial plot; two of those original cedars still stand today.

Among the best friends of the family was Clark L. Owen, who had married Laura Wells, a daughter of the founder of Texana. Owen, a native of Shelby County, Kentucky, had served six months in the Texas army in 1836. After becoming a planter and stock raiser on Carancahua Creek, he took part in the Battle of Plum Creek and the Mier Expedition before President Houston appointed him commander of Texas troops in the southwest in 1843. Clark also served as a senator in the Sixth Texas Congress and by 1860 was the second richest man in Jackson County, with assets of $125,967. He and John Adams agreed to jointly educate their children by bringing a governess from New York, Sarah Agnes Pinney, who conducted classes for both families at the Owen plantation.

On Sunday morning, September 30, 1855, the Texana Presbyterian Church was organized with Brackenridge and his daughter, Mary Eleanor, among the twelve charter members. At 7:00 that evening, John Adams was ordained as one of three ruling elders of the church, then chosen as its representative at the meeting of the Seguin Presbytery and the La Grange Synod. In 1859, the Texana congregation built a frame church at the corner of Broadway and Ward streets. Built in the Greek Revival style, the church had a bell tower with spire, a slave gallery above the vestibule, and was lighted by ornate oil lamps. To their father's sorrow, neither of the two oldest Brackenridge sons was ever converted to Christianity or joined a church, although George W. did keep a promise to read the Bible daily.

By 1860, the senior Brackenridge owned over 10,000 acres of land, 200 cattle, and had a net worth of $58,625, making him the seventh richest man in Jackson County. John Adams was a Unionist whose last public speech was an impassioned plea against secession. It is noteworthy that his last case in court involved the defense of slaves charged with killing their master. During the Civil War, he refused to

church, and served as a director of the San Antonio National Bank.

Miss Brackenridge died at her home, Fernridge, on February 14, 1924, and was the last family member to be buried in the old Brackenridge cemetery four and a half miles southeast of Edna off State Highway 111. In accordance with her beloved brother's wishes, nature has been allowed to reclaim the burial plot, and the cemetery is hidden today by a motte of trees and underbrush.

accept Confederate money at his Texana store, bartering for cotton instead; however, three of his sons did join the Confederate army. Using his father's money, George Brackenridge bought cotton from Lavaca Bay planters for as little as .075 cents per pound, enabling the family to corner several thousand bales of the suddenly-precious commodity by war's end.

A lingering illness during his last year forced the suffering John Adams Brackenridge to resort to opium and other pain-killing drugs; realizing that the end was near, he divided his estate among his wife and children in September 1862 but totally ignored Tom and George in the property division. He died that December and was buried in the family cemetery.

Company D, First Texas Cavalry, had headquarters at Texana during the war and included many Jackson County men. Among the 114 privates in the company were two brothers, Abel Head and Jonathan Edward Pierce. A. H. "Shanghai" Pierce already had a reputation for "finding" cattle, so Capt. John C. Borden, the company commander, appointed him to the special rank of "Regimental Butcher." Company D did two years of garrison and picket duty in the Texana area before being sent to Louisiana to participate in the successful Red River campaign of April 1864. Although Clark Owen opposed secession, he organized the first Confederate unit at Texana, Company K, Second Texas Infantry. He was elected captain of this eighty-two-man company, which fought in fourteen Civil War battles, including Shiloh, Corinth, and Vicksburg. Captain Owen was killed on April 6, 1862, the first day at the Battle of Shiloh. To honor his memory, the Clark L. Owen Camp No. 666 of United Confederate Veterans was organized at the Edna courthouse in 1896. Forty-nine Confederate veterans are buried in the Edna cemetery.

The Civil War also produced a famous Texana expatriate and philanthropist. George Washington Brackenridge was born near Boonville, Indiana, on January 14, 1832. After the family moved to Texana, losses in land speculation in the Seguin area brought the broke George back home an "unqualified failure" in 1857. For the next three years, he lived an aimless but agreeable life as Jackson County surveyor. In October 1860, George studied briefly at Harvard Law School, but the Civil War dashed his hopes for a college degree. A Unionist like his father, this handsome bachelor refused to join the Confederate army. While buying powder at Brownsville in the fall of 1861, young Brackenridge met Charles Stillman, who convinced him of the fortune to be made in the wartime cotton trade. During the war, Stillman used neutral Matamoros, Mexico, as a shipping point to evade the Union blockade and sell Texas cotton in New York. Using his father's funds, George began to purchase dirt-cheap cotton in South Texas and ship it to Stillman's Santa Rosa Ranch north of Brownsville; in a two-month period in the late fall of 1862, the firm of Brackenridge and Bates received more than $30,000 in gold from cotton sales to Stillman. After being denounced as a war profiteer, George hurriedly left Jackson County in July 1863 to avoid being hanged. By the end of the month, he was in Washington, D.C., calling on President Lincoln, who reminisced about George's father and secured an appointment for George as a first-class clerk in the Treasury Department.

In mid-October 1863, the clerk was appointed a special treasury agent charged with receiving captured and abandoned Confederate property and cotton. That December, Agent Brackenridge was sent from New Orleans to Brownsville, where he continued his dealings with Charles Stillman. George was ordered back to New Orleans in May 1864 and remained there except for a brief stint at Galveston, where he received the first permit to ship his father's cotton at war's end. Many special agents were later found guilty of gross irregularities in handling Confederate property, but George was never examined. One fact is certain: The war years made him rich with assets of at least $100,000 by 1866.

Considered a "turncoat" and "Damn Scalawag" in Jackson County, Brackenridge moved to San Antonio in the spring of 1866, taking his mother, Isabella, and sister, Eleanor, with him. With financial backing from Charles Stillman, he founded the San Antonio National Bank (now the First National) that July and served as president until 1912. Only the fourth nationally chartered bank in the state, it became a highly profitable livestock bank by financing cattle drives to Kansas. George was the banker for such famous cowmen as Mifflin Kenedy, Richard King, Charles Goodnight, and Shanghai Pierce, who referred to Brackenridge as "the Old Cock Roach" and called himself "Old Eight Percent" in George's presence. The bank also underwrote the financial needs of the city government through loans.

In 1869, the affluent newcomer purchased a cottage and 108 scenic acres at the head of the San Antonio River and renamed it "Fernridge" or "Head-of-the-River." After hosting ex-President Grant there in 1880, George was inspired to build a more elegant place of entertainment for his mother. This three-story Victorian mansion joined the old cottage, had a $39,000 dining room, and a hand-carved mahogany spiral stairway. Soon after it was completed in 1886, Isabella Brackenridge died there that fall and her son lost interest in the showplace. In 1897, the Sisters of Charity of the Incarnate Word purchased the entire estate for a college campus; they have preserved the mansion as a guesthouse and call it Brackenridge Villa today. George donated his riverfront land and one-time front lawn as a city park in 1899. This Brackenridge Park, one of the most beautiful municipal parks in the nation, was dubbed "Prohibition Park" after Eleanor insisted that alcoholic beverages could not be sold or consumed there.

George was known as a reserved, secretive millionaire who shunned public praise. Nevertheless, he delighted in promoting such controversial causes as Republicanism, prohibition, women's suffrage, equality for women, and equality for blacks. As owner of the *San Antonio Express,* he offered large rewards in 1918 for information leading to the conviction of those who lynched blacks. George also gave money to build three black schools in San Antonio and was the major financial supporter of Guadalupe Colored College at Seguin. He served as president of the San Antonio School Board, funded the vocational program in the city public schools, donated small libraries to some fifty South Texas high schools, and in 1916 gave $40,000 for a new high school named in his honor. In addition to his education philanthropies, Brackenridge provided the city with running water as president and owner of the San Antonio Water Works Company from 1878 until 1906.

Governor John Ireland appointed George a regent of the infant University of Texas in 1886. Calling the post his most valued title, he served twenty-seven years in this capacity, setting a record for longevity and quality of service. As the foremost defender of the university's intellectual integrity, Brackenridge was guided by four principles: no political interference in school affairs, academic freedom, hiring the best faculty available, and complete equality for women. He also gave money where it was most needed. In 1890, George gave a men's dining hall and dormitory, the four-story Brackenridge (or "B") Hall; this was the first major gift to the university from an individual and provided on-campus, low-cost housing for students of limited means. (John Lang Sinclair wrote "The Eyes of Texas" while living there.) The regent also helped hundreds of university students through generous loans. The recipients signed the statement, "I agree to repay when circumstances permit," and all but a handful kept their pledge. When the university medical branch opened at Galveston in 1891, Brackenridge gave $41,000 to build a women's residence there along with generous scholarships to entice women into the medical profession. He also established the Brackenridge Loan Fund for Women in Architecture, Law, and Medicine at Austin. In 1917, George even offered to underwrite the university budget for two years (some $1.5 million) when Governor James E. Ferguson vetoed the school's appropriation bill.

Perhaps his greatest contribution as regent was a farsighted stewardship of the two-million-acre land endowment to the university. When Brackenridge took office, these arid frontier lands had not even been surveyed and were under the control of the state land commissioner. What little income these lands generated came from haphazard leases to local ranchers. Due to George's insistence, these university lands were placed under the regents' control in 1895. At his own expense he then hired a land agent and compiled abstracts of the seemingly worthless lands, a service that proved to be enormously profitable after the Santa Rita oil well blew in on the university lands in 1923. (Today Santa Rita No. 1, the first drilling rig to strike oil, sits on the southern edge of the campus as a symbol of the university's great wealth.)

Brackenridge's ultimate goal as regent — the creation of a Big Campus — went unfulfilled. Convinced that the original forty-acre campus was too small, George in 1910 gave the university an undeveloped, wooded, 500-acre tract of land on the Colorado near Austin to be used as a new campus. Although university president Robert E. Vinson ardently pushed the proposal for years, it failed after a Brackenridge critic and rival benefactor, George W. Littlefield, died in November 1920, with a will leaving the university some $1.25 million in assets *provided* the campus was *not* relocated.

In a will written in 1913, the George W. Brackenridge Foundation was established, the first of its kind in Texas. In this will, George left the bulk of his estate in trust to be used for educational purposes but not for buildings. Initially, the foundation funds went into a revolving student loan program. Then, in 1963, the trustees authorized annual four-year scholarships for Bexar County High School graduates to attend the college of their choice.

Brackenridge maintained a lifelong sentimental attachment to his Jackson County roots. He kept his yacht, the *Navidad*, anchored on Lavaca Bay for coastal cruises. Each Thanksgiving Day, he made pilgrimages from San Antonio to the old homeplace, traveling either on the *Navidad* or his private Pullman car. A team from the Edna livery

stable would take George to the family cemetery, where he spent the
entire day alone in meditation before returning to his yacht or railcar at
sunset.

In 1916, Brackenridge placed a massive monument, a pink granite marker ten feet high and four feet square, in the center of the family
burial plot. The monument inscription includes a brief history of the
family — father, mother, four sons, four daughters, and a grandson.
At the same time, George enclosed the entire 150-foot-square cemetery with a solid stone wall that had no gate. The wall is four feet high
and one and a half feet thick. When asked why he wanted the cemetery
completely enclosed, George replied, "I don't want cattle grazing over
the graves." He also ordered that no care was to be given to the cemetery, that nature was to have a free reign there.

San Antonio's leading citizen died at his new "Fernridge" mansion on December 28, 1920. A special train carried the funeral party to
the old Brackenridge cemetery, where Dr. Vinson gave the eulogy.
Stairs were built over the wall, in order for the bereaved to enter the
cemetery for the funeral services.[5]

In his book *The Cavalcade of Jackson County* (1938), I. T. Taylor
describes the Texana of 1880 as being a "good size little town" and
lists the following business concerns:

> The Lone Star House — Hotel, proprietress, Mrs. Lucy M. Flour-
> noy; F. Jaschke — Boots and Shoemaker; W. Wood — Drug Store;
> Gideon Egg — Mercantile Business, dealer in Groceries, Hardware
> and Lumber; J. W. Allen — General Merchandise; Louis Dittmer —
> Manufacturer of Saddles and Harness; Benj. Milby and Company —
> Manufacturer of Excelsior Bee Hives; S. A. Arceneaux — Black-
> smith, wheelwright; City Meat Market — J. A. Sitterle, proprietor;
> Sanford and Kleas Drugs, medicine and groceries; Cheap Cash Store
> — D. H. Regan, proprietor; Cotton Gin and Mill — N. Strauss,
> proprietor; Coleman House — Hotel, W. H. Coleman, proprietor.

---

5. On May 7, 1989, the Brackenridge Plantation Historical Nature Trail was formally dedicated at the Brackenridge Plantation Campground on Lake Texana. The event
was a joint effort of the Lavaca-Navidad River Authority, the Jackson County Historical
Commission, and the Eleanor Brackenridge Literary Club.

The nature trail begins at the campground on the lake shore and passes the site of the
Brackenridge plantation home built in the 1850s. Only a huge underground concrete cistern is left to mark the site of the old house. The easy-to-walk nature trail ends at the
walled Brackenridge Cemetery.

Mr. Taylor also mentions the following professional men of Texana in 1880:

> Wells and Rowlett — General Land Agents, L. F. Wells and J. O. Rowlett, proprietors; T. R. Stewart — Attorney-At-Law; J. D. Owen — Attorney-At-Law; Dr. J. M. Bronaugh — physician and surgeon; F. B. Owen — Dentist; A. Owen — Physician and surgeon; Francis M. White — Attorney-At-Law; Wm. Wood — Postmaster.

The town had the only newspaper in the county, the *Jackson County Clarion,* which came off the press each Thursday and was sold in seven neighboring counties. In May, June, and July of 1880, an old pioneer, John S. Menefee, wrote an invaluable series of articles on "Early Jackson County History" in the *Clarion.*

Evidently, the countryside around Texana was among the most scenic to be found along the Gulf Coast. A pioneer Texana lady once wrote a friend and told of her most pleasant recollection:

> . . . the beautiful winding roads through the Texana Bottom, especially when the elders were in bloom and the old Virginia Creepers made dashes of color among the green trees; when the palmettos just rustled in the breeze and every now and then one caught the silver gleam of the Navidad as it leisurely winded its way to the bay.

Events were to prove, however, that the town and an idyllic way of life were living on borrowed time.

In 1881, Count Joseph Telfener, an Italian founder of the New York, Texas and Mexican Railway Company, asked Texana businessmen to pay a bonus of $30,000 for building the line through their town.[6] They refused since the railroad wasn't needed and would hurt

---

6. The count had already built a 350-mile rail line in Argentina when he married Ada Hungerford, one of two daughters of Col. Daniel E. Hungerford, a colorful New Yorker who had moved to California. In 1867, Ada's widowed sister, Louise Bryant, married John W. Mackay, the "Bonanza King" and wealthiest of the Nevada silver barons. At age twenty-eight, this Irish immigrant trudged from California to Nevada Territory with only a backpack and miner's pick, and camped at what became Virginia City in 1859. After forming the Consolidated Virginia Mining Company, Mackay and his three partners discovered the richest of the Comstock silver deposits in 1873. Three years later, Mackay purchased a lavish mansion in Paris, France, for Louise. The couple had two sons, John and Clarence, and moved to London in 1886. Clarence Mackay's socialite daughter Ellin married Irving Berlin, America's favorite composer, in 1926.

Ada Hungerford first met Count Telfener while visiting her sister Louise in Paris.

their lucrative shipping trade; besides, Texana was still the only town in the county. Why should they put money on a bluff? Their decision was to doom Texana. When he was rebuffed, Count Telfener chose a route six miles to the north. This land was the southeastern part of the original Robert Guthrie league, and his granddaughter, Mrs. Lucy M. Flournoy, conveyed the right-of-way for the railroad to the count. At

---

When Ada married Joseph in Rome on March 15, 1879, a representative of the Pope was present, and the Italian monarch was their guest at the wedding races. Soon thereafter, Telfener and his father-in-law, Colonel Hungerford, visited Texas with the grandiose goal of connecting New York and Mexico City by rail. The two chose Texas as their starting point because of the state's generous formula of land grants for railroad construction — sixteen sections of land for each mile of track.

The charter for this Texas railroad corporation was filed in Austin on November 17, 1880, with Count Telfener on the board of directors and Victoria as home to the company's principal offices. The rail line was to begin at Richmond on the Galveston, Harrisburg, and San Antonio Railway, to follow the most practical route through eleven South Texas counties, and to terminate at Brownsville on the Rio Grande. On June 16, 1881, the New York, Texas and Mexican Railway contracted to build, equip, and complete the 350 miles of track from Richmond to Brownsville by December 15, 1882. The first real construction headway came in January 1882. Two crews worked, one building west from Rosenberg Junction and the other moving east from Victoria. The count's work force consisted of some 1,200 laborers imported from Italy; he paid their passage to Texas and supplied them with food, clothing and shelter, hoping that they would buy land along the route, send for their families, and remain as residents. The road was quickly dubbed the "Macaroni Line" for the workers' favorite menu item. During the construction project, County Telfener spent little time in Texas, preferring instead to live a life of pampered ease at the Victoria Hotel in New York City.

The line was completed on schedule as far west as Wharton, but delays beyond that point were encountered when rains caused the heavy black soil roadbed to wash away. Sickness also took its toll among the workers, with only half of the original 1,200 remaining on the job. They were also idled for several weeks due to a dispute over back wages. Another problem was crude, primitive tools: the work crews had to resort to makeshift, human-powered pile drivers. Nevertheless, by the end of May 1882, the first train from the East crossed the Navidad River. The next month the angry count announced that his line would go no further west than Victoria after the state refused to grant his land certificates. He was due 940,000 acres of land for the ninety-one miles of track laid between Rosenberg Junction and Victoria, but a state law of April 22, 1882, had repealed all laws authorizing land grants for railroad construction. Since he had depended on land sales to recover his costs and turn a profit, Count Telfener said he must abandon the venture.

On July 4, 1882, the first through train left Rosenberg Junction at 10:00 A.M. and reached Victoria at 6:00 that evening. The train was made up of Engine Number Four, one coach, and two baggage cars. Passengers on board included the Telfeners and Colonel Hungerford. The construction cost for the ninety-one-mile line was $2,036,150, with an additional rolling stock cost of $156,270 for 101 pieces of equipment. Count Telfener operated the line until July 23, 1884, when he was "bailed out" by John W. Mackay, who

first a storing ground and feeding station along the line was called "The Big Motte" due to a large stand of nearby trees. Since Count Telfener fed his Italian workers a steady diet of macaroni, the place was renamed "The Macaroni Station." Finally, the count chose to call the site "Edna" in honor of his daughter.

On the morning of July 2, 1882, a curious throng from all over Jackson County descended on Edna to witness a phenomenon: the first trains many had ever seen! Two were scheduled to reach town between 11:30 A.M. and noontime; the train from Rosenberg, the eastern terminal, arrived first with the "iron horse" from Victoria chugging into Edna a few minutes later. To celebrate this historic occasion, the awed crowd adjourned to Mrs. Flournoy's Lone Star Hotel to hear a speech by Judge F. M. White and have a basket lunch. A large map of the Edna townsite was then hung on the wall and town lots were sold on the hotel front porch. Among the refreshments consumed on Edna's birthday was the first ice cream served in Jackson County; a black hackman from Victoria set up a stand and sold the delicacy for twenty-five cents a saucer.

Lucy Flournoy deserves to be called the "Mother of Edna." After operating a Texana boardinghouse for years, she conveyed the new railroad right-of-way, then became the first to actively promote Edna by surveying and laying off the new townsite. A devout Methodist, she also donated land for both a church and parsonage.

Edna's train killed Texana. On December 18, 1882, the county judge received a petition requesting an election to move the county seat from Texana to Edna. When the election was held on January 22, 1883, the proposition carried by a vote of 273 to 17. The county seat was moved to Edna on February 1, 1883, the old Texana courthouse was sold in May, and the county jail was moved to the new town that September. A general exodus of Texana settlers followed, using log

---

in turn sold out to the Southern Pacific Railroad on September 3, 1885.

Joseph Telfener died in Rome on New Year's Day, 1898, but the memory of his aborted railroad dream is perpetuated today by a series of place name towns along the Southern Pacific line from Victoria to Rosenberg. A traveler will pass through Telfener, Inez (named for his unmarried daughter), Edna (named for a daughter who married Don Giacomo de Martino, one-time Italian ambassador to the United States), Louise (named for Colonel Hungerford's daughter), Mackay (named for her husband, the "Bonanza King"), and Hungerford (named for the colonel, a railroad official).

rollers and ox-teams to move homes, stores, churches, and public buildings to Edna.[7]

By 1886, Edna had a post office, four grocery stores, four churches, two hotels, two dry goods stores, two drug stores, two saloons, a "private bank," a school, and a population of 400. Texana, on the other hand, had become a ghost town. In 1936, a state historical marker was dedicated on the Navidad River at the site of the old town. In a very real sense, the curse of A. C. Allen in 1836 became a reality when a dam project, the Palmetto Bend Reservoir, inundated much of the old Texana site in 1980. Appropriately, the 11,300-acre reservoir was named "Lake Texana" to honor the historic lost town.

---

7. Simon Young moved the old Brackenridge house from Texana to Edna in 1883 and converted it into the Emerald Hotel. On January 15, 1899, it burned in a fire that destroyed several blocks in town. As of 1990, three other old Texana homes still stood in Edna; as Texas Historic Landmarks, they bear the designation of Medallion Homes.

In 1883, a large, two-story frame building was moved from Texana to Edna and placed at the corner of Houston and Menefee streets. Six years later, it became home to an historic Edna business, the Westhoff Mercantile Company.

William Westhoff's company began to sell lumber and general merchandise at Indianola in 1866. After losing both his home and business in the hurricane of September 1875, Westhoff rebuilt and also opened lumber yards in Victoria and Cuero. When Indianola was destroyed by an even larger hurricane in August 1886, Westhoff transferred his operations to the Cuero lumber yard.

In 1889, he relocated at the budding new town of Edna, purchased the Texana frame building, and began to sell lumber, hardware, tools, wagons, and coffins there. Upon graduation from the Eastman Business College in New York, William's son, A. E. (Gus) Westhoff, came home to operate the family business in 1894. The firm was reorganized as the Westhoff Mercantile Company in 1911. (The company celebrated 100 years in business at the same location in Edna in 1989.)

The Westhoffs built a new brick structure on the original site in 1958. At that time the old Texana building was purchased for $750 by Bill Limberg and moved a short distance to the site of the present First Bank of Edna. The historic building was demolished one year later.

The only Texana public building left in Edna is the 1859 Presbyterian Church. It was moved there in 1884, used by the congregation until 1909, then sold and used as a commercial warehouse for seventy years. On December 28, 1978, the Texana Presbyterian Church Restoration Association was chartered with the objective of restoring the structure to its original condition. Actual work started in 1980, and the newly restored Texana Presbyterian Church was dedicated on Sunday, October 28, 1984. Bowen David Rose, the great-great-grandson of John McAmy and Lucinda Millican White, two of the twelve charter members of the church, rang the church bell to open dedication services.

This beautiful structure will be used for historical and club meetings and for informal wedding ceremonies. It is one of the oldest frame churches still standing in Texas and has been listed with the National Register of Historic Places, the only such listing in Jackson County.

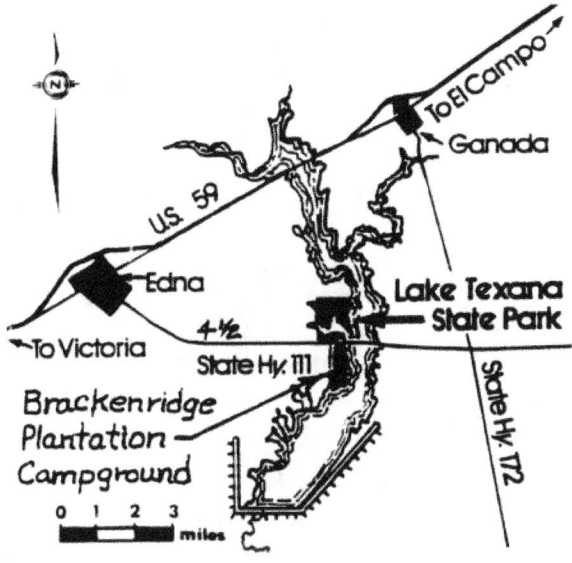

— Courtesy *Texas Parks and Wildlife*

Francis Flournoy Wells
— Courtesy Texas State Library, Archives Division, Austin, Texas

WHARTON
COUNTY

NAVIDAD RIVER

LAVACA RIVER

O EDNA

GARCITAS CREEK

O TEXANA

JACKSON
COUNTY

VICTORIA
COUNTY

LAVACA BAY

CALHOUN
COUNTY

MATAGORDA BAY

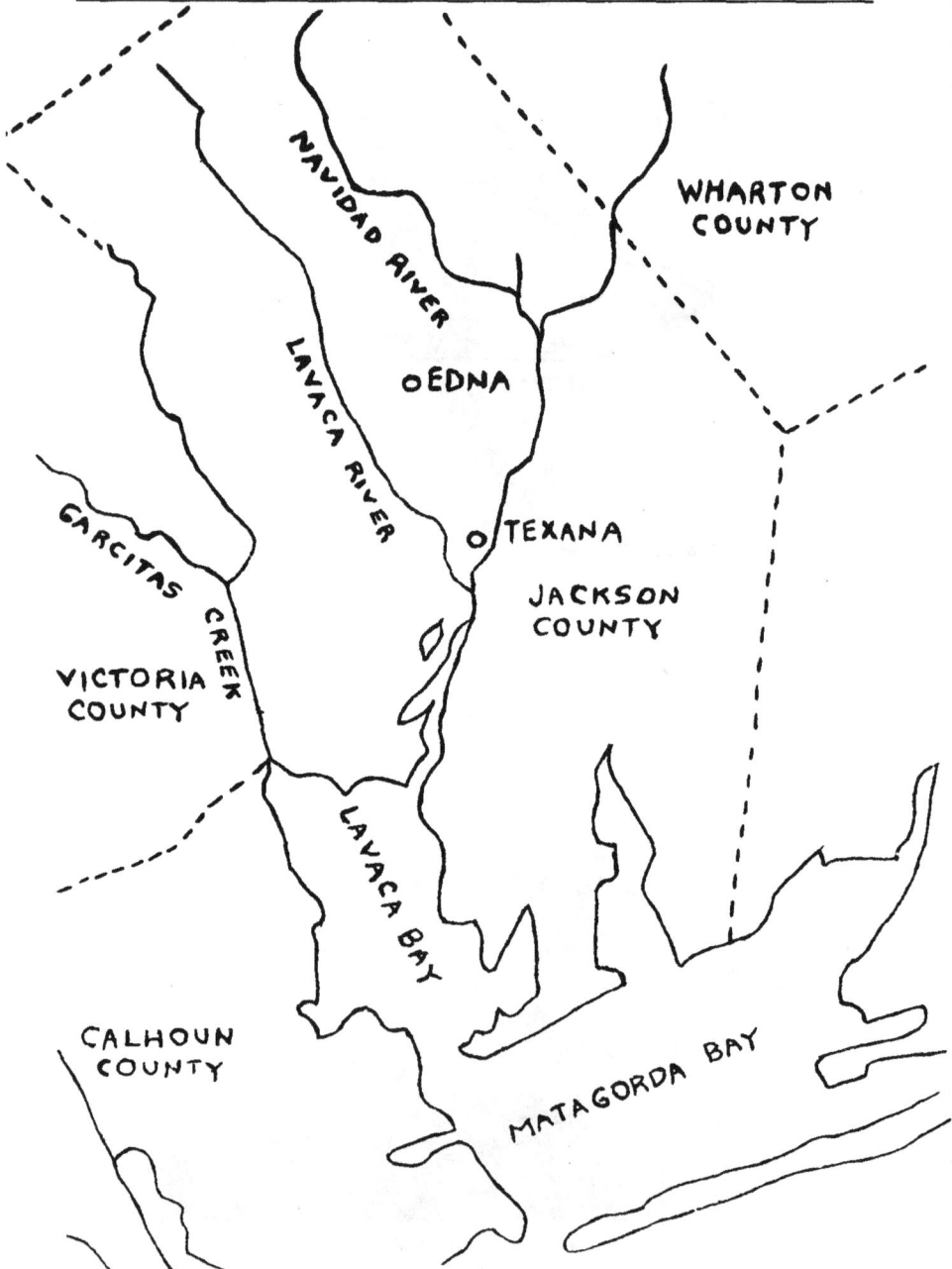

Map of Texana, Edna, and Jackson County.

— By Joe Tom Davis

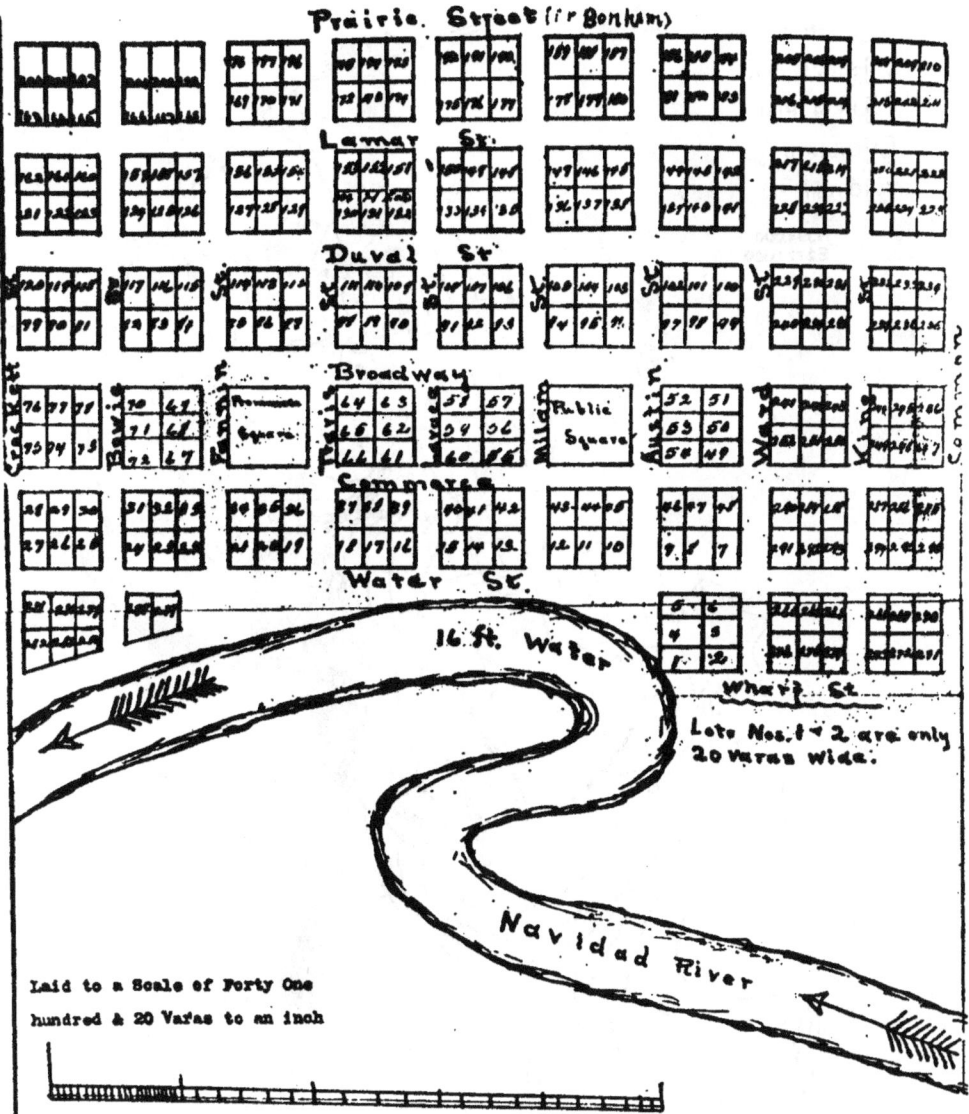

Francis F. Wells's plan of Texana, 1834.
— From Jackson County Clerk's Office, Edna, Texas

.Extant house

Control line

Stock pen

1834 Plat

Cistern

Datum

N394,000
E2,773,000

F.M. 1822

wharf area

old bend of river

NAVIDAD

RIVER

MN GN

FEET 800

VARAS 180

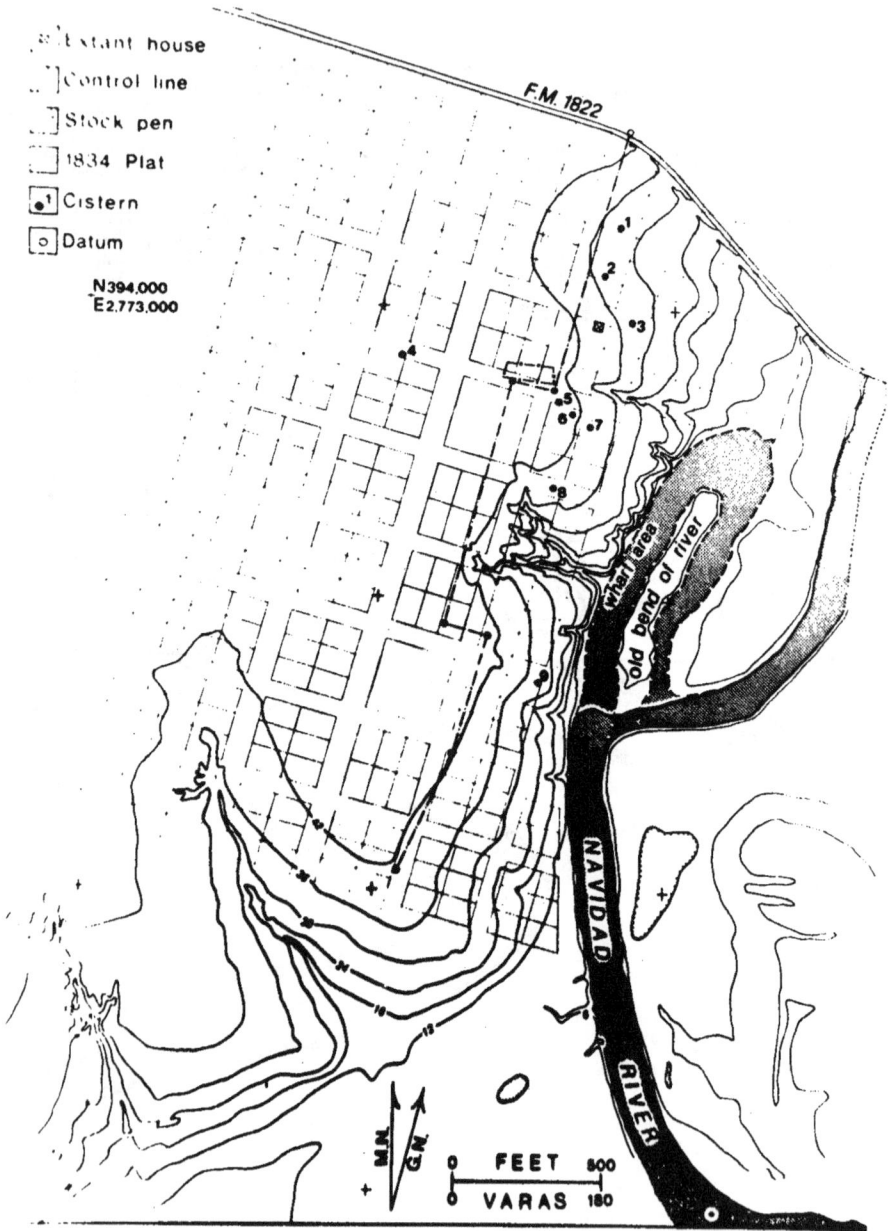

Texana, topographic map/1834 plat.

Courtesy State Archaeological Survey,
The University of Texas at Austin

Texana street scene.
— Courtesy Perry-Castañeda Library,
The University of Texas at Austin

Docking on the Navidad.
— Courtesy Texana Museum, Edna, Texas

George W. Brackenridge
— Courtesy *San Antonio Express-News,*
San Antonio, Texas

Mary Eleanor Brackenridge
— Courtesy Austin History Center,
Austin (Texas) Public Library

Texana state marker with portion of old townsite and Lake Texana in background.
— Photo by J. C. Hoke, Wharton, Texas

Brackenridge home built near Texana in 1850s; was moved to Edna in 1880s and became the Emerald Hotel.

— Courtesy Mrs. O. H. Staples, Edna, Texas

Texana Presbyterian Church, 1859. Now located in Edna, Texas.

— Photo by J. C. Hoke, Wharton, Texas

Bronaugh-Hasdorff home built in Texana in 1866 and moved to Edna in 1883. It is now owned by Luther and Alice Hamilton (203 E. Brackenridge Street).

— Photo by J. C. Hoke, Wharton, Texas

Horton-Black home built in Texana in 1876 and moved to Edna in 1882. It is now owned by David Seligman (404 S. Hanover Street).

— Photo by J. C. Hoke, Wharton, Texas

Westhoff Mercantile Co. Building moved from Texana to Edna in 1883.
— Courtesy Westhoff Mercantile Co., Edna, Texas

Map of Lake Texana State Park and Brackenridge Plantation Campground.
— Courtesy Lavaca-Navidad River Authority

VI

Helena:
A Wild Town Killed by a Bullet

Present-day Helena stands forlorn and forgotten some seven miles northeast of Karnes City on State Highway 80. For forty years, however, the town had a reputation for shooting, fighting, stealing, and drinking far out of proportion to its peak population of 600. It was the wildest Texas town during a particularly turbulent period. Helena's brief glory days were tinged with irony: it was founded by a man trained for the ministry; a sedate academy flourished amid its many saloons and gambling halls; it prospered in a setting of outlaws and rustlers; but it died because of a stray bullet. This is the story of the rise and fall of the "Toughest Town on Earth."

A Mexican settlement named Alamita ("Little Cottonwood") was founded in 1830 at a little spring in a clump of cottonwood trees a few miles south of the Cibolo confluence with the San Antonio River. This settlement, in present Karnes County, was located at the intersection of the Chihuahua Trail, a trade route connecting coastal Texas and Mexico, and the Ox-Cart Road, the travel and freight route from San Antonio to the coast opened by the Alarcon Expedition in 1718. In time the Ox-Cart Road was traveled by Spanish *conquistadores* and priests, the Gutierrez-Magee filibustering expedition, Alamo hero James Butler Bonham on his two futile rides to Goliad seeking help from James Walker Fannin, Santa Anna's messenger ordering the death of Fannin's men at Goliad, the earliest German and Polish settlers of Texas, and the famed United States Second Cavalry as it moved men and supplies over the road to protect the Texas frontier. This freight route from Indianola to San Antonio was also trod by pack animals, two-wheeled ox-carts, prairie schooners, and Wells-Fargo wagons drawn by sixteen mules. In the late 1840s, stagecoach service started on the Ox-Cart Road, with the only stop between Goliad and San Antonio being the halfway station of Alamita.

In 1852, Thomas Ruckman discovered old Alamita by accident while traveling to Goliad. He saw the potential of a roadside trading post near the site. Ruckman was of Dutch descent and a native of Northumberland County, Pennsylvania. After training for the ministry and graduating from the College of New Jersey (later renamed Princeton University) in 1848, Ruckman taught school for a year in South Carolina before coming to Texas at age twenty-two, arriving at San Antonio on Christmas Day of 1850. For two years he worked as a bookkeeper for several firms, then made a fateful trip of which he later gave the following account:

> In the summer of 1852 on my way from San Antonio to Goliad, I found a little store and blacksmith shop on the road about ten miles after I crossed the Cibolo. This little storehouse was mostly built of rough boards that had been split in the woods out of postoak trees.
>
> The proprietor . . . had a little while before that time purchased of Antonio Navarra agent Ramon Musquez a two hundred acre tract out of his four league grant, for which he paid one dollar per acre.
>
> On this tract where the cartroad from San Antonio to the Gulf crossed it, he built his store, home dwelling, and shop. Soon afterwards we laid out the town . . . and named it Helena . . .
>
> It is a beautiful location. A mile from the river on dry elevated ground — soil partly sand so that it is never muddy about the streets, always dry underfoot . . . And no place in the state surpasses it for health. Eighty-five miles in a straight line from the bay, the Gulf breeze strikes it fresh.

Ruckman envisioned his town as a night stop for freighters on the Ox-Cart Road and named the trading post Helena in honor of Helen Swisher Owings, the wife of his business partner, Dr. Lewis S. Owings. The two entrepreneurs hired Charles A. Russell, Goliad County surveyor, to survey and plat the new site, and Helena was officially established as a town on November 7, 1853, the date its post office opened.[1] The partners also initiated a campaign to create a new county

---

1. The Helena post office was originally a part of the John Ruckman General Merchandise Store. After both were blown down by a storm in 1942, the post office was re-

from parts of Bexar, Gonzales, DeWitt, Goliad, and San Patricio counties. Their efforts resulted in the state legislature creating Karnes County on February 4, 1854, named in honor of the late Texas revolutionary hero, Henry Wax Karnes, with Helena as the county seat.[2] On February 27 the first election for county officials was held on the porch of the Ruckman-Owings Store, which provided the tables, paper, pens, and ink for the voters. The two-story county courthouse built at Helena in 1856 was of frame clapboard construction; the lower floor was used as a courtroom and for church services while the upper level served as a Masonic lodge room for the Alamita Lodge No. 200. A tornado leveled that structure in 1863, and the two-story stone courthouse that replaced it in 1873 still stands today (1991).[3]

The pioneer storeowners evidently had some early "cash flow" problems, as is indicated by the following notice in *The Western Texan* of San Antonio, dated November 25, 1854:

> All persons indebted to the undersigned are respectfully informed that they will do well to call and settle, or their accounts will be left in the hands of a proper officer for collection, as we are very much in need of money.
>
> Our terms hereafter are NO CREDIT — Goods Cheap for Cash.
> DEER SKINS, BEEF HIDES AND PECANS WANTED!!
>
> Owings & Ruckman
> Helena, Texas   November 9, 1854

---

built three years later using the same lumber. Postal service was discontinued in 1951, and the old post office building is now on the Courthouse Square.

2. Henry Wax Karnes, a native of Tennessee, was sixteen when his family moved to Arkansas. One of his friends and neighbors there was Lewis Owings. In 1835, Karnes came to Texas and was serving as overseer on Jared Groce's Bernardo plantation on the Brazos River when the Texas Revolution began. He joined the Texas army at age twenty-three and saw duty as both a scout and spy for General Houston. After taking part in the Battle of Gonzales and the Siege of Bexar, Karnes led an infantry company at the Battle of San Jacinto. He then served as an Indian agent for the Republic of Texas before joining the Texas Rangers in 1838.

Karnes saw considerable action as an Indian fighter; many Indian enemies regarded him as being supernatural due to his flaming red hair. In August 1839 he was severely wounded in hand-to-hand combat with a Comanche chief and was not fully recovered when he contracted yellow fever and died at San Antonio on August 16, 1840. His heroic exploits in Texas inspired his old friend, Dr. Owings, to suggest in 1854 that this new county be named after Karnes.

3. After the decline of Helena, the courthouse was used as a county schoolhouse from 1896 until 1946. A bell and belfry were added for school purposes. The historic structure now serves as the Karnes County Museum.

That same day, *The Western Texan* carried an advertisement of Owings and Ruckman telling of new fall and winter goods just received from New York and Boston. This assortment of merchandise was not to leave the store unless *paid for* and included such items as fancy and staple dry goods, ready-made clothing, boots, shoes, hats, caps, hardware and cutlery, crockery and glassware, stationery and perfumery, family groceries, oils and paints, umbrellas, clocks, violins, Yankee notions, and all of Dr. Janes's patent medicines.

The Ruckman-Owings partnership proved to be short-lived. In November 1854, Dr. Owings started a new venture, a stageline of four-horse mail coaches from San Antonio to Victoria via Helena and Goliad. After being appointed the first governor of Arizona Territory, he left Helena for good in 1857. Thomas Ruckman, on the other hand, was just beginning to lay down roots in his new town. Soon after marrying Miss Jeanie Long, he was visited by an itinerant brickmaker from Kentucky in the spring of 1856. Once the craftsman determined that the soil along the banks of the San Antonio River contained the right proportion of clay and sand for high-quality bricks, the two men struck a deal: Ruckman would set up a hand mill and kiln along the river; the brickmaker, in return, would provide the material for Ruckman's new home. About 90,000 of these new bricks went into the galleried, two-story, brick-and-cottonwood house that Ruckman built along the river in 1857. This double-walled structure was modeled after Ashley Hall at Princeton University. Within six months, a work force of twenty Polanders, hired from nearby Panna Maria, turned out some 300,000 bricks from the Ruckman kiln. Ruckman also built a large gristmill for mealing corn and a sawmill along the riverbank. His sawed lumber cut from the native trees growing along the river was much cheaper than pine lumber imported from Florida. These additional enterprises of Ruckman were to provide the brick and lumber used in building most of the stores, homes, cabins, and fences of early Helena.

Thomas also enlarged his store as the scattered farmers and ranchers in the area became regular customers. In addition to founding the town and becoming a leading merchant and banker, he also served as the Helena postmaster from 1854 until 1857, was both the principal and a teacher of the Helena Academy, and found time to write some poetry and fiction. He and Jeanie had only one child, Eudora, who married William Cathey Butler in 1882, and had five lovely daughters. Ruckman's love for the county he created is revealed in a handwritten manuscript dated June 1890 and titled "The Census Taker: A Complete Description of the County of Karnes in Southwest Texas." Rather than dryly reciting a litany of facts and figures, he utilized his census assignment to promote the county; in fact, the document has a Chamber of Commerce flavor.

Among the highlights of his life was a nostalgic homecoming trip back to Pennsylvania in 1901. Ruckman maintained a lifelong correspondence with his alma mater, and Princeton compiled a large file concerning his accomplishments. After Thomas Ruckman died at Helena on December 2, 1914, and was buried in the town's Masonic Cemetery, his obituary appeared in the *Princeton Alumni Weekly*.

When he first settled at Helena, Ruckman invited his younger brother, John, and his three sisters — Lizzie, Rachel, and Rebecca — to come from Pennsylvania and live with him. John Ruckman arrived in Karnes County in 1857, and quickly achieved a position of prominence as a Confederate lieutenant, postmaster, banker, store merchant, farmer, and rancher. In 1867, John married Eliza Dickson, whose family had moved to Helena from Arkansas. They would have eight children, with the youngest three being born in a showplace three-story, six-bedroom mansion John built in 1878. The house was constructed of Florida cypress shipped by schooner to Indianola, then transported to Helena by wagon and team. This family residence was the town's social center; circuit preachers always stayed there, and the largest room in the Ruckman house, the family dining room, was usually full of out-of-town guests and ranch hands. After John Ruckman's death in January 1913, home ownership was transferred to his four unmarried children.[4]

The calm of Helena was shattered in 1857 by the Cart War, a series of attacks by Texas cart drivers on Mexican teamsters along the Ox-Cart Road. After San Antonio merchants tired of paying Texas drivers three dollars per hundred pounds to haul freight from Indianola, contractor George Thomas Howard imported hundreds of Mexican drivers and carts who would haul freight cheaper and work for lower wages than the Americans. As a consequence, Mexican teamsters were monopolizing the Ox-Cart Road by 1857. Texas cattlemen also became

---

4. Hester and Margaret Ruckman lived in the mansion until 1958. In 1967, the two deeded the house and eight surrounding acres of land to the Old Helena Foundation, since merged with the Karnes County Historical Society, the home's present owner. The Ruckman House was restored in 1984 by the Society and has been listed on the National Register of Historic Places.

aroused when the Mexican drivers obtained a free beef supply by stealing and butchering their grazing herds along the road. Yet another point of contention was the suspicion that the Mexicans were helping runaway slaves to escape to Mexico.

The Cart War began when jobless Texas freighters sneaked into the Mexican camps at night and cut the spokes of the cart wheels, causing the wheels to collapse at the first turn the next morning. However, such pranks quickly escalated into guerrilla warfare near Helena and Goliad. A series of six attacks were made on Mexican cartmen. In 1857, seventy-five Mexican drivers were said to be killed by a masked secret organization. The decisive battle occurred on Cibolo Creek in Karnes County, when the Texan and Mexican drivers formed two great hollow circles and shot it out. As the bloodshed increased, San Antonio merchants began to demand that Maj. Gen. D. E. Twiggs, in charge of the Department of Texas, provide federal military escorts for the Mexican convoys. In mid-November 1857, Governor E. M. Pease sent an emergency company of Texas Rangers to protect the freight wagons and drivers.

This violent labor dispute took a new turn when prominent and influential men at Goliad began to hang Texas badmen who were raiding Texas carts driven by Texas drivers. The vigilantes' "Hanging Tree," where up to five bodies at a time were left dangling, stands today on the courthouse lawn at Goliad. Finally, on December 4, 1857, a public meeting at Helena passed eight resolutions. In Number Six, the citizens of Karnes County resolved that the continued presence of "peon Mexican teamsters" on the Ox-Cart Road was an "intolerable nuisance" and requested that the citizens of San Antonio withdraw them and substitute other drivers. By this time, however, the Mexican drivers had returned to Mexico, Texas teamsters were back on the road, and the war was over.

Just prior to the Civil War, the population of Karnes County was 2,171; Helena was its largest town, with possibly 600 residents. The tax rolls listed only 255 slaves in the county. When the Secession Convention met at Austin on January 28, 1861, Karnes County was represented by John Littleton, a stockman who owned two slaves and voted for the ordinance of secession. The county was to provide six volunteer companies for Confederate service, including the "Helena Guards." This company of fifty-seven men was organized on May 4, 1861, with Charles A. Russell elected as captain, John Ruckman as first sergeant, and each man providing his own arms and equipment.

The Helena Guards was among the units that participated in the Rio Grande campaign.

During the war years, Helena was called upon to provide several thousand bushels of corn for Confederate troops stationed along the Rio Grande. The town also had a Confederate post office, with David W. Dailey serving as postmaster from 1861 until 1863. Helena was one of only seven Texas towns to issue its own privately printed stamps during the war; this gold-colored, ten-cent stamp could be cut in half for five-cent postage (currently it is valued at $3,000 by philatelists). The town was on the lifeline road used to transport contraband goods to and from the neutral port of Matamoros, Mexico. Much of the Confederate cotton bound for Mexican ports was routed through Helena, and it also served as a receiving station for smuggled food, clothing, medicines, arms, and ammunition.

In the postwar years, Karnes County developed a reputation as a "Bad Man's Paradise," a refuge and hideout for rustlers, outlaws, and gunfighters from other states, while Helena became the self-proclaimed "Toughest Town on Earth." Since the county was in the center of the "Cattle Kingdom," it attracted more than its share of rowdy drovers gathering herds of Longhorns to trail to Abilene and Dodge City, Kansas. Rustling cattle and looting the great freight wagons carrying goods from Indianola to San Antonio were everyday occurrences. Horse-stealing was also a regular line of business, as outlaws found a ready market across the border. Cart drivers would stop at Helena to rest, carouse, and dissipate at one of the four saloons, where whiskey could be bought by the keg. The drinking problem became so acute that 105 of the permanent, law-abiding residents, including twenty women, sent a petition to the state legislature requesting legislation to prohibit the sale of intoxicating liquors within five miles of Helena.

The first jail in town was a wooden structure in the northwest corner of the courthouse square.[5] It apparently lacked bars and cells; locals recalled that the sheriff would take his prisoner to a blacksmith shop, fit him with shackles, then chain the jailbird to some immovable object within the building. Justice was often summary in Helena. Late one evening, five suspected horse thieves were put in jail; the next morning they were found hanging from the limbs of two nearby live oak trees. The lawlessness and bloodshed associated with the town gave rise to the infamous "Helena Duel" in which two duelists would be

---

5. It was later replaced with a rock building which was eventually torn down and moved to Karnes City, rebuilt, then used as Jauer's Store for many years.

stripped and have their left wrists lashed together with buckskin. Each was then armed with a razor-sharp knife having a three-inch blade, a weapon too short to reach a vital organ or cause a single fatal stab. After the combatants were whirled around a few times, they slashed away at each other until one bled to death from the accumulation of cuts and stabs. Crowds of blood-thirsty spectators viewed this gory, gruesome spectacle and even bet on the outcome.

Helena was a rowdy but prosperous town with over 300 residents by the late 1870s. Townspeople could boast of two civilizing influences — a church and an academy. The Helena Union Church, built in 1866, was used by Methodists, Presbyterians, and Baptists, who alternated holding services there.[6] In 1867, Charles Russell, A. J. Trueman, and John Ruckman organized a joint stock company for the purpose of creating a coeducational college, the Helena Academy, by private subscription. Fifty-five citizens contributed twenty-five dollars each or donated livestock rather than cash. The two-story rock structure housing this "male and female institution of the highest order" was completed in 1872 and soon enrolled thirty-five girls and even more young men. Males and females were taught on separate floors. The college operated until the mid-1890s, then the old rock structure was used to store corn for a few years before burning down.[7]

W. K. Hallum started publishing *The Helena Record* in 1879 with a motto of "Don't Tread On Me." By this time, the town had six gen-

---

6. The old church was blown down by a hurricane in 1973, was then carefully dismantled, and the pieces were stored for future restoration.

7. Some of the original rock from the academy building is still on display behind the old stone courthouse. In November 1937, an article titled "Reminiscences of Helena Academy" appeared in the 50th Anniversary Edition of the *Karnes County News*. The article was based on an interview with Mrs. Eudora Ruckman Butler, the only child of Thomas Ruckman, who recalled the following funny experience related by classmate Callie Mayfield:

One day a very jealous and strict sort of old father came to the Academy to see how well his daughter was doing in school.

Her teacher called up the Latin Class and asked this girl to conjugate the verb "Amos." "Amo, amas, amat, amamms, amatis, amaant," the apt pupil glibly called out.

"All right, now translate the forms," the teacher said, very proud of her pupil. "Amo, I love," the girl began to translate. "Amos, you love; amat, he loves; amamms, we love; amatis, you love; amant — ." But this was too much for the very careful father, and he began to rave, "Love, love, I love, you love, he loves. Love, love. All you teach here is love. I sent my girl here so she wouldn't fall in love so soon. I want to educate her, not make a lovesick fool of her. Come on. You are going home!" And he took the bright pupil at once.

eral stores, four saloons, two hotels (the American Hotel and the Butler House), a drug store, blacksmith shop, boot shop, saddle and har-
ness shop, livery stable, and a hanging tree in the plaza. The stores
were located directly across the street from the courthouse on the old
Ox-Cart Road from Indianola (now FM 81). The September 5, 1879,
issue of the *Record* advertised the services of four lawyers — T. S.
Archer, L. S. Lawhon, L. H. Brown, and John Bailey — and of a physician and surgeon, Dr. J. W. Harmon. Proprietors Hoff and Meyer of
the Pearl Saloon ran the following ad that day: "Keeps constantly best
kind of liquors and segars (*sic*). With polite and attentive barkeepers,
Recherche Liquors and Cigars that are *Bon,* we cannot but please the
taste of the *ton.*" General store owner Max Cohn boasted of a new addition, a furniture store, which had "long been wanted in Helena."
The little city was also a chief stop on the stagecoach route connecting
San Antonio, Goliad, and the Gulf Coast with four-horse stages passing through town daily.

On Friday, December 26, 1884, a killing took place that was to
spell the doom of Helena. At 4:00 that afternoon, a gang of drunks
shot up a saloon, and one of their stray bullets killed a man on the
street. The hapless victim was Emmett Butler, the twenty-year-old son
of Col. William G. Butler, the county's richest rancher with large
landholdings south and west of town. Colonel Butler buried his boy on
Sunday, then rode into Helena the next day with twenty-five armed
ranch hands. Riding up and down the nearly deserted main street, he
shouted to the store owners to produce the killers. By then most of the
rowdies had left town, so the colonel's shrill demands echoed on the si-
lent street. Finally, the anguished, frustrated father shouted as he rode
away, "All right! Then I'll kill the town that killed my son!"

His revenge was not long in coming. When the San Antonio and
Aransas Pass Railroad started building through Karnes County in
1885, the citizens of Helena summarily rejected paying a $35,000
bonus and refused to donate the right-of-way for a rail connection.
Colonel Butler, however, seized the opportunity and contacted the
traffic manager, Benjamin Franklin Yoakum, a pioneer railroad
builder. Butler was quick to offer Yoakum a free right-of-way through
his range land, subject to one condition: the rails had to be laid far to
the west of the San Antonio River and Helena. By then Judge Ruckman had frantically raised $32,000, but to no avail. Yoakum had ac-
cepted Colonel Butler's offer. Within a year the line was built on the
other side of the river, seven miles southwest of Helena. After the rail-

road came through the county in 1886, the Ox-Cart Road was abandoned, and two new towns, Kenedy and Karnes City, soon sprang up on the line. In 1887, Kenedy became a roundup station for cattle grazing on the open range. It was first located four miles from its present site and named for Mifflin Kenedy, a financier of the railroad. In 1892, Karnes City became a railway shipping point on the new line and was the largest town in the county within a year.

Colonel Butler's curse of Helena became a reality as stores, businesses, and homes began to move to Karnes City and its rail connection. On December 21, 1893, a countywide election was held to choose a county seat. Karnes City received 862 votes, while only 120 people wanted the county seat to remain at Helena. On January 2, 1894, the Commissioners' Court ordered the county records moved from Helena to Karnes City.

Losing the election was a bitter blow to the angry residents of Helena, who refused to turn over the records. A group of Karnes City men decided that the safest way to carry out the mandate of the court was to literally steal the county seat under cover of darkness. They thus brought twenty horse-drawn wagons into Helena one night and made off with all the county records and files. As a face-saving gesture, a solitary guard from the now-ghost town resigned himself to riding "shotgun" on one of the wagons.

The new county seat had a population of 600 by 1900. Helena, however, eventually was left with only an empty rock courthouse back in the mesquite, a deserted church, and a main street once ridden by Colonel Butler but reclaimed by scrub and cactus. Today there are only five lonely reminders of the boisterous, busy town that once was Helena. The old courthouse and post office, the Ruckman House, the Carver-Mayfield store, and the adjacent old Masonic Lodge are all owned by the Karnes County Historical Society. The unsuspecting tourist who stops at the Helena service station at the intersection of FM 81 and SH 80 is in for a treat if he bothers to read the nearby state historical marker. What awaits is a tour of an historic ghost town with a fascinating past.

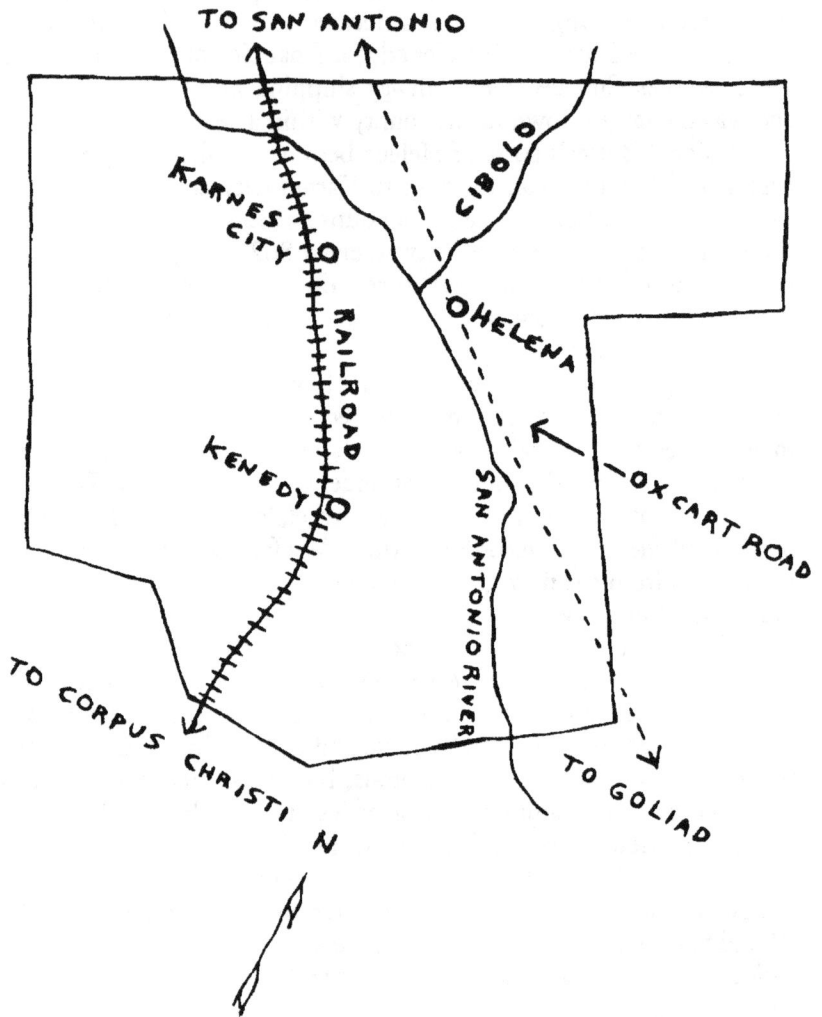

Map of Helena and Karnes County.

— By Joe Tom Davis

Thomas Ruckman, founder of Old Helena.
— Courtesy Karnes County Museum, Helena, Texas

Home built by Thomas Ruckman in 1857.
— Courtesy Karnes County Museum, Helena, Texas

John R. Ruckman
— Courtesy Karnes County Museum, Helena, Texas

John R. Ruckman House, 1880s.
— Courtesy Karnes County Museum, Helena, Texas

A street scene in Old Helena, from Sykes McClane Historic Photo Collection.
— Courtesy Karnes County Museum, Helena, Texas

Helena Union Church
— Courtesy Karnes County Museum, Helena, Texas

John R. Ruckman House during restoration, 1984.
— Photo by J. C. Hoke, Wharton, Texas

Karnes County Courthouse, built in 1873, Helena, Texas.
— Photo by J. C. Hoke, Wharton, Texas

Old Helena Post Office.
— Photo by J. C. Hoke, Wharton, Texas

Carver-Mayfield Store and Masonic Lodge building in Helena, Texas.
— Photo by J. C. Hoke, Wharton, Texas

Bibliography

I   East and West Columbia

Adriance, John. Papers. University of Texas Archives, Austin, Texas.

Barker, Eugene C., ed. *The Austin Papers.* 3 vols. Washington, D.C.: American Historical Association, 1922.

————. *The Life of Stephen F. Austin.* Austin: Texas State Historical Association, 1949.

Beals, Carleton. *Stephen F. Austin: Father of Texas.* New York: McGraw-Hill, 1953.

Bernhard, Virginia. *Ima Hogg: The Governor's Daughter.* Austin: Texas Monthly Press, 1984.

Brazoria County Historical Museum and Brazoria County Historical Commission. *A Window To The Past: A Pictorial History of Brazoria County, Texas.* Privately printed, 1986.

Bugbee, Lester G. "The Old Three Hundred." *The Quarterly of the Texas State Historical Association,* I (October 1897): 108–117.

Coleman, Ann Rainey. *Victorian Lady on the Texas Frontier.* Norman: University of Oklahoma Press, 1971.

Cotner, Robert C. *James Stephen Hogg: A Biography.* Austin: University of Texas Press, 1959.

Creighton, James A. *A Narrative History of Brazoria County.* Waco: Texian Press, 1975.

Day, James M., comp. *The Texas Almanac, 1857–1873: A Compendium of Texas History.* Waco: Texian Press, 1967.

Dixon, Samuel Houston, and Louis W. Kemp. *The Heroes of San Jacinto.* Houston: Anson Jones Press, 1932.

Durham, Ken, Jr. Steely, Skipper, ed. *Santa Anna: Prisoner of War in Texas.* Paris, Texas: The Wright Press, 1986.

First Capitol Historical Foundation. *Ammon Underwood House.* West Columbia, Texas. Undated pamphlet.

First Capitol Replica Board, comp. *Historical Scrapbook of West Columbia, Texas.* West Columbia, Texas, 1980.

Foster, Catherine Munson. *Ghosts Along the Brazos*. Waco: Texian Press, 1977.

Gambrell, Herbert. *Anson Jones: The Last President of Texas*. Austin: University of Texas Press, 1964.

Greer, James F., ed. "Journal of Ammon Underwood, 1835–1838." *Southwestern Historical Quarterly*, 32 (October 1928): 132–146.

Hogan, William Ransom. *The Texas Republic: A Social and Economic History*. Norman: University of Oklahoma Press, 1946.

Holley, Mary Austin. *The Texas Diary, 1835–1838*. Austin: University of Texas Press, 1965.

Johnson, William R. *A Short History of the Sugar Industry in Texas*. Texas Gulf Coast Historical Association Publications V, No. 1 (April 1961).

Jones, Marie Beth. *Peach Point Plantation: The First 150 Years*. Waco: Texian Press, 1982.

Kelley, Dayton, et. al. *Capitols of Texas*. Waco: Texian Press, 1970.

Kuykendall, J. M. "Reminiscences of Early Texas." *Southwestern Historical Quarterly*, 6 (April 1903): 236–253; 7 (October 1903): 29–64.

McCormick, Andrew P. *The Scotch-Irish in Ireland and America . . .* Privately printed, 1897.

Moody, Mary Sue. "Martin Varner, the First White Settler of Wood County." *Junior Historian*, 6 (September 1946): 19–22.

Plumb, Mrs. Alto P. "Early Life of Wood County's First Settler Revealed." *Wood County Democrat* (Quitman), August 5, 1954.

Puryear, Pamela Ashworth, and Nath Winfield, Jr. *Sandbars and Sternwheelers: Steam Navigation on the Brazos*. College Station: Texas A&M University Press, 1976.

Rister, Carl Coke. *Oil! Titan of the Southwest*. Norman: University of Oklahoma Press, 1949.

Rundell, Walter, Jr. *Early Texas Oil: A Photographic History, 1866–1936*. College Station: Texas A&M University Press, 1977.

Shipman, Daniel. *Frontier Life: 58 Years in Texas*. 1879. Reprint. Pasadena, Texas: Abbotsford Publishing Co., 1965.

Siegel, Stanley. *A Political History of the Texas Republic, 1836–1845*. Austin: University of Texas Press, 1956.

Smith, Katherine, and Katherine Grier. *Historical Narrative: Varner, Patton, Hogg Plantation*. West Columbia, Texas. Privately printed, 1979.

Smith, Travis L., Jr. *Steamboats on the Brazos*. Houston: Privately printed, 1958.

Smithwick, Noah. *The Evolution of a State: Or, Recollections of Old Texas Days*. Reprint. Austin: The Steck Company, 1935.

Stroebel, Abner. *The Old Plantations and Their Owners of Brazoria County*. Houston: Union National Bank, 1926.

Taylor, Robert Lewis. *Vessel of Wrath: The Life and Times of Carry Nation*. New York: New American Library, 1966.

Toth, Sharon. "East Columbia." *Texas: Houston Chronicle Magazine.* September 6, 1987.

Van Tassel, David D. "The Legend Maker" (Mason Locke Weems). *American Heritage,* 8, no. 2 (February 1962): 59, 89–94.

Webb, Walter Prescott, et. al., eds. *The Handbook of Texas.* 2 vols. Austin: Texas State Historical Association, 1952.

Wiggins, Gary. *Dance & Brothers: Texas Gunmakers of the Confederacy.* Orange, Virginia: Moss Publications, 1986.

II   Egypt

Bate, W. N. *General Sidney Sherman: Texas Soldier, Statesman and Builder.* Waco: Texian Press, 1974.

Clay, Comer. "The Colorado River Raft." *Texas State Historical Quarterly,* 52:410–426.

Colorado County Historical Commission, comp. *Colorado County Chronicles: From the Beginning to 1923.* Austin: Nortex Press, 1986.

Day, James M., comp. *The Texas Almanac, 1857–1873: A Compendium of Texas History.* Waco: Texian Press, 1967.

Dietrich, Wilfred. *The Blazing Story of Washington County.* Rev. ed. Quanah, Texas: Nortex Publications, 1973.

Duncan, Ginny. "Egypt, Land of Plenty." San Antonio: Unpublished manuscript, May 1974.

Eli Mercer File. Northington-Heard Museum, Egypt, Texas.

Frantz, Joe B. *Gail Borden: Dairyman to a Nation.* Norman: University of Oklahoma Press, 1951.

Heard, F. L. *Texas Is Their Reward.* Rosenberg, Texas: Privately printed manuscript, n.d.

Hudgins, Edgar H. *Hudgins: Virginia to Texas.* Houston: Larksdale Printing, 1983.

Lee, Nantie. "Family Records from Bible of Laura Frances Bowie White." *Oak Leaves,* Matagorda County Genealogical Society, Bay City, Texas, 7 (August 1988): 145–147.

Murray, Lois Smith. *Baylor at Independence.* Waco: Baylor University Press, 1972.

Thrall, Homer S. *Pictorial History of Texas.* St. Louis: N. D. Thompson & Co., 1879.

Tolbert, Frank X. *The Day of San Jacinto.* New York: McGraw Hill, 1959.

Wharton County Abstract Company. *Statement of the John C. Clark Estate.* Files of William A. Cline, Sr., attorney-at-law, Wharton, Texas.

Wharton County Historical Commission. *Post West Bernard.* Wharton, Texas: Privately printed pamphlet, n.d.

William Jones Elliott Heard File. Northington-Heard Museum, Egypt,
    Texas.
William Menefee File. Northington-Heard Museum, Egypt, Texas.
Williams, Annie Lee. *The History of Wharton County, 1846–1961*. Austin:
    Von Boeckmann-Jones Co., 1964.

III   Matagorda

Allen, Arda Talbot. *Miss Ella of the Deep South of Texas*. San Antonio: Naylor
    Co., 1951.
———. *Twenty-One Sons of Texas*. San Antonio: Naylor Co., 1959.
Baty, Ruby, comp. *Christ Church, Matagorda, Texas, 1838*. Wharton, Texas:
    Privately printed, 1988.
Braman, D. E. E. *Information About Texas*. Philadelphia: J. B. Lippincott &
    Co., 1857.
Brannon, Jack. *Mr. Robbins, I Miss You*. Austin: Nortex Press, 1985.
Brown, Lawrence L. *The Episcopal Church in Texas, 1838–1874*. The Church
    Historical Society. Austin: Von Boeckmann-Jones, 1963.
Cazneau, Jane McManus Storins. *Papers, 1834–1878*. The University of
    Texas Archives, Barker Texas History Center, Austin, Texas.
Clay, Comer. "The Colorado River Raft." *Southwestern Historical Quarterly*, 52
    (1949): 410–426.
Dixon, Malcolm R. "A Brief History of the Family of Richard Royster Royall
    and Ann Underwood Royall." *Oak Leaves*, Matagorda County Geneal-
    ogical Society, Bay City, Texas, 4 (November 1984): 15–39.
Donohoe, Ural Lee. "The Horse Marines." *Oak Leaves*, 4 (August 1984):
    136–137.
Douglas, C. L. *Thunder on the Gulf: Story of the Texas Navy*. Rev. ed. Austin-
    Dallas: Graphic Ideas, 1972.
Ellenberger, Matthew. "Notes on Albert Clinton Horton." *Southwestern His-
    torical Quarterly*, 87 (1985): 363–386.
Fischer, Ernest G. *Robert Potter: Founder of the Texas Navy*. Gretna, Louisiana:
    Pelican Publishing Co., 1976.
Fisher, Samuel Rhoads. *Papers, 1830–1845*. The University of Texas Ar-
    chives, Austin, Texas.
Harris, Annie P. *Reminiscences, 1823–1852*. The University of Texas Ar-
    chives, Austin, Texas.
Helm, Mary S. *Scraps of Early Texas History*. Austin: B. R. Wainer & Co.,
    1884.
Holland, Evelyn. "1850 Census of Matagorda County, Texas." *Oak Leaves*, 5
    (August 1986): 122–154.
Holley, Mary Austin. *Texas*. Fac. Austin: The Steck Co., 1935.
Hollon, W. Eugene, and Ruth Lapham Butler, eds. *William Bollaert's Texas*.

Norman: University of Oklahoma Press, 1956.

Hopkins, James G. "Early Days in Texas: Reminiscences of Mrs. Fannie Newsom." *Oak Leaves,* 5 (May 1986): 83–85.

Horton, Albert Clinton. A. C. Horton Files. Wharton County Historical Museum, Wharton, Texas.

Ingram, Ira. *Papers, 1830–1835.* The University of Texas Archives, Austin, Texas.

Ingram, Mary B. "The Selkirk Ledger, 1855–1858." *Oak Leaves,* 7 (November 1987): 14–17.

Jecmenek, Jessie. "The Wightmans: Two Great Men of Matagorda, Texas." *Texas Historian,* 44: 13.

Kuykendall, J. H. "Reminiscences of Early Texans." *Texas Historical Association Quarterly,* 6 (1903): 236–253.

Marr, John Columbus. "The History of Matagorda County, Texas." Master's thesis, The University of Texas, 1928.

Matagorda County Historical Commission. Mary B. Ingram, comp. *Historic Matagorda County.* 3 vols. Houston: D. Armstrong Co., 1986.

Matagorda County Historical Society. *Historical Markers, Matagorda County.* Bay City: Privately printed, 1969.

Matagorda County Junior Historian Chapter No. 310. *Matagorda Cemetery, Matagorda, Texas.* Bay City: Privately printed, 1973.

Matagorda Day Historical Celebration. Matagorda: Privately printed, 1973.

McAllister Junior Historian Chapter No. 241. *Research Papers on Historic Matagorda, Texas (founded in 1829).* Bay City: Privately printed, 1973.

Murray, Lois Smith. *Baylor at Independence.* Waco: Baylor University Press, 1972.

O'Connor, Kathryn Stoner. *The Presidio La Bahia del Espiritu Santo de Zuniga, 1721 to 1846.* Austin: Von Boeckmann-Jones, 1966.

Ryman, Mrs. Carroll. "Matagorda Methodist Church." *Oak Leaves,* 7 (May 1988): 106–111.

Siringo, Charles. *A Texas Cowboy.* Fac. New York: William Sloane Association, 1950.

Stieghorst, Junann J. *Bay City and Matagorda County: A History.* Austin: Pemberton Press, 1965.

Williams, Annie Lee. *A History of Wharton County, 1846–1961.* Austin: Von Boeckmann-Jones Co., 1964.

IV   Houston

Bartholomew, Ed. *The Houston Story, 1836–1865.* Houston: Frontier Press of Texas, 1951.

Baughman, James P. *Charles Morgan and the Development of Southern Transportation.* Nashville: Vanderbilt University Press, 1968.

Bernhard, Virginia. *Ima Hogg: The Governor's Daughter*. Austin: Texas Monthly Press, 1984.

"Big Time in Houston: Opening of the Shamrock Hotel." *Fortune*, May 1949, 80–82.

Buchanan, James E., comp. *Houston: A Chronological and Documentary History, 1519–1970*. Dobbs Ferry, New York: Oceana Publications, 1975.

Dittman, Ralph E. *Allen's Landing: The Authentic Story of the Founding of Houston*. Houston: A. C. and J. K. Allen Publishing, 1986.

Fuermann, George. *Houston: Land of the Big Rich*. Garden City, New Jersey: Doubleday, 1951.

Hogan, William Ransom. "Pamelia Mann, Texas Frontierswoman." *Southwest Review*, 20 (Summer 1935): 360–370.

Hollon, W. Eugene, and Ruth Lapham Butler, eds. *William Bollaert's Texas*. Norman: University of Oklahoma Press, 1956.

Kilman, Ed, and Theom Wright. *Hugh Roy Cullen: A Story of American Opportunity*. New York: Prentice-Hall, Inc., 1954.

King, John O. *Joseph Stephen Cullinan: A Story of Leadership in the Texas Petroleum Industry, 1897–1937*. Nashville: Vanderbilt University Press, 1970.

Lasswell, Mary. *John Henry Kirby, Prince of the Pines*. Austin: Encino Press, 1967.

Lewis, Pamela, and Susan Chadwick. "Market Square Renovation Under Way." *The Houston Post*, November 5, 1989, Sec. J, 1–4.

Lubbock, Francis R. *Six Decades in Texas*. C. W. Rains, ed. Austin: Ben C. Jones & Co., 1900.

Macon, N. Don. *Mr. John D. Freeman and Friends: A Story of the Texas Medical Center and How It Began*. Houston: Texas Medical Center, 1973.

Maxwell, Robert S. *Whistle in the Piney Woods: Paul Bremond and the Houston East and West Texas Railway*. Houston: Texas Gulf Coast Historical Association, 1963.

McComb, David G. *Houston: A History*. Rev. ed. Austin: University of Texas Press, 1981.

Milburn, Douglas. "Houston: Designed for the 21st Century." *Texas Highways*, June 1990, 2–9.

Miller, Ray. *Ray Miller's Houston*. Houston: Cordovan Press, 1982.

Morris, Sylvia S. "William Marsh Rice and His Institute; a Biographical Study." *Rice University Studies*, 58 (Spring 1972): 1–112.

Muir, Andrew Forest. "The Destiny of Buffalo Bayou." *Southwestern Historical Quarterly*, 47 (October 1943): 91–106.

———. "Railroads Come to Houston, 1857–1861." *Southwestern Historical Quarterly*, 64 (July 1960): 42–63.

———. "William Marsh Rice, Houstonian." *East Texas Historical Journal* 2 (February 1964): 32–39.

Patton, Phil. "Philip Johnson: The Man Who Changed Houston's Skyline."

Houston City Magazine, 4 (January 1980), 36–47.

Peacock, Howard. "A Healing Place." *Texas Highways,* July 1990, 18–25.

Sibley, Marilyn McAdams. *The Port of Houston: A History.* Austin: University of Texas Press, 1968.

Timmons, Bascom N. *Jesse H. Jones: The Man and the Statesman.* New York: Henry Holt and Co., 1956.

Tolbert, Frank X. *Dick Dowling at Sabine Pass.* New York: McGraw-Hill, 1962.

Urban, Jerry. "A Kinship with History." *Texas Magazine,* Houston Chronicle, October 8, 1989, 8–13.

Wallis, Jonnie Lockhart, and Laurance L. Hill. *Sixty Years on the Brazos: The Life and Letters of Dr. John Washington Lockhart.* Los Angeles: Dunn Bros., 1930.

Writers' Program, Work Projects Administration. *Houston: A History and Guide.* Houston: Anson Jones Press, 1942.

Young, Dr. S. O. *A Thumb-Nail History of the City of Houston, Texas; From Its Founding in 1836 to the Year 1912.* Houston: Rein & Sons Co., 1912.

V   Texana

Brown, John Henry. *History of Texas; From 1685 to 1892.* 2 vols. Fac. Austin: Jenkins Publishing Co., 1970.

Crosby, H. Anthony. *Architecture of Texana, 1831–1883. Jackson County, Texas.* Palmetto Bend Reservoir Series, Vol 2. Austin: Texas Archaeological Survey, University of Texas at Austin, 1974.

Grimes, Roy, ed. *300 Years in Victoria County.* Victoria: Victoria Advocate Publishing Co., 1968.

Heard, F. L. "Texas Is Their Reward." Rosenberg, Texas: Privately printed manuscript, n.d.

Jackson, Marsha F. *Texana: Excavations at a Nineteenth-Century Inland Coastal Town. Jackson County, Texas.* Palmetto Bend Reservoir Series, Vol. 1. Austin: Texas Archaeological Survey, University of Texas at Austin, 1974.

Kilman, Ed. "James Bowie, Man of Mystery." *The Houston Post,* February 16, 1936.

Rayburn, John C. "Count Joseph Telfener and the New York, Texas, and Mexican Railway." *Southwestern Historical Quarterly,* 68 (July 1964): 29–42.

Roland, Charles. *Albert Sidney Johnston, Soldier of Three Republics.* Austin: University of Texas Press, 1964.

Sibley, Marilyn McAdams. *George W. Brackenridge: Maverick Philanthropist.* Austin: University of Texas Press, 1973.

Syers, William. *Off the Beaten Trail.* Waco: Texian Press, 1972.

Taylor, I. T. *The Cavalcade of Jackson County.* San Antonio: Naylor, 1938.

Texana Foundation, Inc., Twin Centennial Committee. *Twin Centennial Commemorative History: Edna-Ganado, 1882–1982.* Edna, Texas, 1982.

"Virginia City, Nevada: America's Richest Town." *Colonial Homes,* February 1989, 96–117, 142.

VI   Helena

"Boy's Death Spelled End of a Town." *Corpus Christi Caller,* November 17, 1966.

Didear, Hedwig. *A History of Karnes County and Old Helena.* Austin: San Felipe Press, 1969.

Old Helena Foundation, Inc. *The Life and Times of Thomas Ruckman.* Karnes City, Texas, 1968.

———. *Ox Cart Days in Old Helena.* Karnes City, Texas, 1968.

Syers, William. *Off the Beaten Trail.* Waco: Texian Press, 1972.

Thonhoff, Robert H. *A History of Karnes County.* Fashing, Texas, 1963.

Index

247